The How and Why of Third World Missions

An Asian Case Study

Marlin L. Nelson

William Carey Library

533 HERMOSA STREET • SOUTH PASADENA, CALIF. 91030

In accord with some of the most recent thinking in the academic press, the William Carey Library is pleased to present
this scholarly book which has been prepared from an author-
edited and author-prepared camera-ready manuscript.

Library of Congress Cataloging in Publication Data

Nelson, Marlin L   1931-
    The how and why of third world missions.

    Bibliography: p.
    Includes index.
    1. Missions--Asia. I. Title.
BV3151.N44   266'.023'095   76-47658
ISBN 0-87808-318-9

A companion volume to this book by the same
author and publisher is Readings in Third
World Missions: A Collection of Essential
Documents.

Published by the William Carey Library
533 Hermosa Street
South Pasadena, Calif. 91030
Telephone 213-682-2047

PRINTED IN THE UNITED STATES OF AMERICA

Contents

PART FOUR: EVALUATION, REVIEW AND
FUTURE OF MISSIONS IN ASIA

Foreword

Asian Protestant Christians are beginning to realize their strength.   Seven million in India, four million in Korea, a million in Japan/Taiwan, five million each in the Philippines and Indonesia, plus smaller numbers in Burma, Ceylon, Hong Kong, Malaysia, and the Near East add up to a total of 25 million. The figure is conservative. The actual will be larger and is increasing rapidly.

Granted that many Asian Christians are poor by Eurican standards, nevertheless their ability to send missionaries who live on Asian standards is the ability of *25 million Christians*. They have substantial strength.

The end of the era of European empires and the rise of sovereign Asian nations means that the Churches in these lands are beginning to hear the call of the Lord to send missionaries of their own to aid in the tremendous task of world evangelization. The Friends Missionary Prayer Bands of South India, entirely on Indian resources, have recruited and sent (across several language barriers) more than 60 missionaries to the Hindi and Urdu-speaking missions in North India. A hundred and fifty Koreans are missionaries in Germany. Asians are beginning to flex their muscles and taste the sweetness of obeying the Great Commission.

The great merit of Dr. Nelson's book is that he gives us a factual account of the missionary awakening in Asian Denominations. We see its glories and its weaknesses. We hear its leaders agreeing - and on occasion disagreeing - as to policy. We become part of the debate as to whether it is better to send one lone missionary to each of ten different lands, there to work as part of a largely European team of missionaries, or to send a team of ten Asian missionaries all from the same cluster of congregations in Japan, Korea, the Philippines or some other land to multiply churches in *one* receptive population in *one* city or *one* district.

Missionary-minded Euricans will find this book fascinating. Asians leading the missionary awakening in Asia will read it to great profit. There is no need for Asian missionary societies to repeat the mistakes of their Eurican opposite numbers. There is no need for them to revel in the false comfort that, because they are Asian, they will automatically do what is missionarily effective, and need no missiological training. Japanese missionaries feel just as foreign in Pakistan, let us say, as Norwegians would. They suffer just as much from ethnocentrism. They find the language just as hard to learn...and possibly receive less sympathy for their mistakes in speaking it.

The missionary awakening in Asia needs exactly the kind of light which Dr. Nelson throws on the varied and immensely encouraging picture.

While three billion have yet to hear and obey the Gospel, it is foolish to imagine that the younger Churches all by themselves will take over the task of world evangelization. Increased numbers of missionaries are needed. The awakening of Asian Christians to their strength and to Christ's call to mission will provide some of the missionaries needed. Christians in the other five continents will provide the rest. The task is enormous and urgent. The day of harvest is upon us.

I commend this book. It will cheer and enlighten many and lead to more missions and more effective missions. Devout Christians of every land will fare forth to those multitudes in other lands who have never heard of the Saviour. There they will proclaim Jesus Christ as God and Saviour, and there persuade men and women to become His disciples and responsible members of His Church.

July 1st, 1976   Donald McGavran, School of Missions
                                  Fuller Seminary, Pasadena, California

Preface

The How and Why of Third World Missions: An Asian Case Study is
written from the perspective of having lived several years in
the Orient. Beyond doubt, Asian mission agencies are being
raised up of God to help provide workers to bring in the ripen-
ing harvest. People are turning to Christ in unprecedented numbers in non-Western countries.

We hear calls for a moratorium on Western missionaries. However, with the world's population now exceeding four billion,
with an estimated 2.7 billion (6/-1/2%) unreached (1975), a moratorium seems inappropriate. Western missions need to make changes
in attitudes, structures, and priorities. A new strategy must
be prepared. But the goal of world evangelization remains the
same. This cannot be achieved by either Western or non-Western
missions alone. This task requires active involvement of all
who are members of the Body of Christ. All Christians must
learn to work together as partners in obedience to Jesus, our Lord.

Research data was obtained from personal interviews, questionnaires, correspondence, reports, archival research, and years
of personal observation in Korea. The McAlister Library at the
Fuller Theological Seminary and the library and files at World
Vision International have been valuable sources of information.

My research has revealed the scarcity of current, factual data
on this new subject. Perhaps my study will be more helpful in stimulating questions than in providing new policies and practices. I

have only begun to learn about a few missions in Asia, representing one area of the Third World.

Many new missionaries will soon join the more than 3,000 who have already gone out from Third World countries. There is not time for them to repeat unnecessarily the earlier mistakes of Western missions. The task is too urgent. Lives are too precious Advanced missiological insights now provide improved cross-cultural communication.

One group of Asians plans to send out 10,000 missionaries by 2000 A.D. This goal can and must be achieved. But careful strategy must be prepared. I hope this research will help to clear up some of the "fog" of idealistic thinking about Third World Missions and raise the vital issues that need clarification so we can *plan together* realistically.

I am indebted to World Vision International for giving me a sabbatical leave for study. The faculty at the School of World Mission has all been most cooperative and stimulating on this comparatively new subject for research. I express sincere gratitude to my mentor, Dr. C. Peter Wagner, who provided encouragement and help in many ways. Dean Arthur Glasser and Dr. Ralph D. Winter have also given invaluable counsel and guidance as committee members. I am also thankful for the artist work by Betty Lankford, and for the typing by Elizabeth McNee and Vera Crouch.

My wife Kay, and the children, have all provided much emotional support and understanding for this year of research and study. Above all, I am thankful to God for daily strength and blessing as friends in many countries have faithfully prayed for me. I present this dissertation as a love offering to my Lord, with the prayer that God will use this to honor and encourage the unrecognized but faithful Asian missionaries.

Marlin L. Nelson
Glendale, California
April 8, 1976

Part One
Introduction

1
A New Dimension of Missions in Asia

"Christ Seeks Asia" was the theme of the Asia-South Pacific Congress on Evangelism at Singapore in 1968 (Mooneyham 1969:9). "Winning Asia to Christ by Asians" reflects increasing nationalism in some countries (Tingston 1966:449). Themes and slogans have a purpose, but seldom contain a complete truth. "God so loved the *world* that He gave His only begotten Son..." (John 3:16). "I have been given all authority in heaven and earth. Therefore go and make disciples in *all the nations*...(Matthew 28:18,19 Living Letters). "Go ye into *all the world*, and preach the gospel to every creature" (Mark 16:15). These teachings provide the Biblical basis for world evangelization.

Missions can no longer be described as missionaries going from the Western world to other nations. "The missionary movement now involves Christians in all six continents and in all lands. It must be the common witness of the whole Church, bringing the whole Gospel to the whole world" (Orchard 1964:175). A new emphasis has appeared in missions. The organization of scores of new mission agencies in the Third World has become a dynamic new resource for world evangelization. In *Missions From The Third World: a world survey of non-Western missions in Asia, Africa and Latin America* by Wong, Larson and Pentecost, they identified 211

missionary-sending agencies from 46 countries in the Third
World with 2,994 missionaries (Wong, Larson, Pentecost 1973:
107). This book lists sending agencies in each country
and the number of missionaries to the different countries.
Though some Third World Mission Agencies were organized
in the late 1800's, many more have been organized since
World War II.

    During the last decade we have seen a new movement of
the Spirit of God for evangelism and mission. The 1966
World Congress on Evangelism in Berlin brought together
more than 1,200 delegates from 100 countries. Three years
of prayer and planning made possible ten significant days.
Stanley Mooneyham, a special assistant to Evangelist Billy
Graham was coordinating director. The Congress was a tenth
anniversary project of *Christianity Today*, founded by
Carl F.H. Henry, chairman of the Congress. The Congress
was the vision of Billy Graham who said in his opening
greetings:

> Today, thousands of Christians on every
> continent are praying that from Berlin
> the sparks of revival, evangelism, and
> missions will fly--that will touch the
> entire world. The elements of spiritual
> fire are here and could make this Congress
> as significant in the history of the Church
> as the World Missionary Conference which
> was held in Edinburgh in June, 1910. We
> need a greater comprehension of the world
> in which we labor. We need a greater
> unity among the laborers. We need a
> greater dynamic. We need no new organ-
> izations and movements. We need no new
> message. But we do need a fresh and
> larger bestowal of supernatural power
> for the accomplishment of our stupendous
> task of evangelizing our generation. We
> need a greater enthusiasm. Today, if the
> Christian Church could be aflame with en-
> thusiasm for the Gospel of Christ, with
> the spirit of burning devotion to the
> Person of Christ, and with an overwhelm-
> ing passion for the multitudes still out-
> side of Christ, we could change our world
> (1966:10).

The theme of the Congress was "One Race, One Gospel,
One Task" (Henry & Mooneyham 1967). The closing statement
was that "Our goal is nothing short of the evangelization
of the human race in this generation, by every means God
has given to the mind and will of men" (1966:5). Did the
Congress fulfill Graham's vision and give guidelines to
meet this goal?

About 60% of the speakers were from the Western world
and many of the addresses emphasized the theology, methods
and obstacles to evangelism. The lack of attention given
to cross-cultural evangelism made this a contrast to Edinburgh 1910. This was probably because the planners were
primarily evangelists and theologians, rather than missionaries. A missionary emphasis did come from some Asian
speakers such as Akira Hatori who confessed the weakness
of the Japanese church but recognized the growth of a new
concern for evangelism. "The national church has caught the
vision of foreign missions, evidenced by the fact that it
has sent out 80 missionaries from its own ranks" (1966:194).

Though the World Congress on Evangelism in Berlin was
neither a second Pentecost nor an Edinburgh II, it was a
new thing to bring together over 1,200 evangelical leaders
from 100 countries. Friendships were made as various barriers were removed. God did a significant new thing in the
lives of many.

The Asia-South Pacific Congress on Evangelism in
Singapore, November 5-13, 1968 was also the vision of Billy
Graham and sponsored by his association. W. Stanley Mooneyham was again the coordinating director as he had been in
Berlin. The Congress purpose was *to discover* ways of
implementing the proposals of the 1966 World Congress on
Evangelism in our area challenged by an exploding population
and social upheaval; *to expound* the relevance of the Christian evangel...*to study* the obstacles to evangelism inherent
in the diverse cultures of Asia...*to share* in discussion the
tools and techniques of evangelism which we may successfully employ to cope with our unique problems and opportunities in Asia today...*to evaluate* existing evangelistic
programs and policies...*to summon* the Church corporately
and its members individually to recognize and accept
the priority of evangelism; *to challenge* the churches
and Christian organizations to a bold cooperative programs
of evangelism and missionary outreach (1968:8).

Singapore was a contrast to Berlin in many ways. Over
1,100 delegates came from 25 countries stretching from Afghanistan to Fiji, from Japan to New Zealand. Approximately

half were laymen, a few women, a handful of western observers and one Roman Catholic priest who came as an
observer from Ceylon (Mooneyham 1968:7). Only history would
reveal whether this gathering would revive and renew the
churches and become "a blessing which would inevitably be
followed by a new evangelistic thrust into the majority
non-Christian cultures" (Mooneyham 1968:7).

"The Asian Congress was primarily an evangelistic
enterprise, and gauged by this objective it was highly
successful" (Henry 1968:12). Asians burdened for evangelism were encouraged by meeting other Asians with a common
concern. The new unity for the cause of evangelism in Asia
and the vision gained in Singapore was one of the by-products
of the 1966 World Congress in Berlin. Invitations for evangelism were given to nationals from other Asian countries and
Asian missionaries became increasingly concerned to reach
Asian groups elsewhere in the world, as the Chinese have done
in parts of the United States.

Evangelistic vitalities existing in Asia were acceler-
ated with new unity and concern in the Singapore gathering.
In each of the 25 countries represented at the Congress,
a follow-up Congress was planned. Specific results from
the Congress included:

> projection of a clearing-house to coordi-
> nate the availability and itinerary of
> Asian witness teams and Bible ministries
> crossing national lines; encouragement
> of an evangelical theological commission
> with national sections devoted to a study
> of the expanding edge of the Church, the
> theology of evangelism, the status of non-
> Christian religions in view of Christian
> evangelization, and of the social impli-
> cations of evangelism; preparation of a
> master list of evangelical literature
> available in Asian lands and of required
> reading, and a survey of present publish-
> ing resources and the prospect of low-
> cost cooperative publication of paperbacks
> (Henry 1968:13).

In addition to this, World Vision was invited to
have pastors' conferences in New Guinea and the South Pacific
Islands. Evangelism In Depth was invited to New Zealand,
World Evangelical Fellowship projected theological conferences, Australian institutions offered aid to theological
students returning to Asia to minister and a Chinese

Evangelical Fellowship was newly organized, with fervent prayers for mainland China, where almost half of the Asian population lives.

In contrast to the Berlin Congress, most of the speakers were Asians. G.D. James reminded his co-laborers that the church is on the threshold of an altogether new era in its history, so far as its mission is concerned. While we are looking for more money, means and new methods, God is looking for new men. Evangelization of Asia is not an option, but an obligation; it is not giving charity, but discharging our debt. Unless we evangelize, Asia will perish (1968:156). Hatori asserted, "I believe Christ is seeking men who will willingly work together to evangelize Asia and *the world*" (1968:266). What spiritual insight to these servants of God! World evangelization was being emphasized not by Western missionaries but by respected Asian leaders.

A new concern for evangelism and missions was spreading across Asia. In September 1971, the Second Annual Asian Foreign Missions Seminar was held in Osaka, Japan (*Asia Pulse* 1972). In 1972 the Japanese Overseas Missionary Association was formed (*Asia Pulse* 1972). During the same year the First Pan-Malaysian Christian Missions Conference was organized. "The Overseas Missionary Fellowship considers the growing interest in missionary outreach among Asian Christians as one of the most significant and exciting trends in the church today" (*Asia Pulse* 1972). With the increasing interest in evangelism and in missions, Asian leaders were preparing for a new historic meeting to occur in Seoul, Korea in 1973.

Following the Asia-South Pacific Congress on Evangelism, the Coordination Office for Asian Evangelism (COFAE) was established with Chandu Ray as Executive Director with offices in Singapore. Through his travels, speaking and monthly Newsletter, the new concern for evangelism and missions was promoted.

During the First Strategy Conference of the Korea International Mission (KIM) held in Hong Kong, August 26-30, 1970, the urgent necessity of a consultation among Asian mission leaders was discussed, emphasized and re-emphasized. Finally a proposition to promote and start the framework of an All-Asia Mission Consultation in 1973 was approved (Chun 1973:38).

In a banquet honoring Chandu Ray in Seoul, attended by thirty-three Christian leaders, the necessity of this

consultation was reiterated. Chandu Ray later reported in
his Newsletter:

> The question arose as to whether the mission
> boards and societies and Asian churches will
> take up this challenge and merge their own
> identity for the sake of the mission of
> Christ...Perhaps we should pray that we may
> be shown ways of establishing an All-Asia
> School for Missionary Orientation in Korea,
> where I understand facilities already exist
> (1971:2).

While David J. Cho, Billy Kim and Samuel Kim were attending the Evangelical Mission Executive Study Conference held
at Green Lake, Wisconsin, in September of 1971 sponsored
by the Interdenominational Foreign Mission Association (IFMA)
and the Evangelical Foreign Missions Association (EFMA) they
made known the plan of an All-Asia Mission Consultation.
There was keen interest among missiologists present and staff
of the National Liberty Foundation (Chun 1973:39). David
J. Cho and Myung Soo Hahn made an extensive trip from July 17
through August 19, 1972 in order to have personal contact with
key leaders of missions in various countries of Asia to survey
the basic issues to raise and discuss at the Consultation.
Further plans were made during January 10-12, 1973 by Kyung
Chik Han, Akira Hatori, Chandu Ray, Andrew Furuyama and
David J. Cho.

The First All-Asia Mission Consultation was held in
Seoul, Korea, August 27 through September 1, 1973. Sometimes referred to as "Seoul '73" this historic meeting included 25 Asian delegates from 14 countries--(4 from Hong
Kong; 1 from India; 2 from Indonesia; 2 from Japan; 1 from
Khmer Republic; 5 from Korea; 1 from Malaysia; 1 from Pakistan; 3 from Philippines; 2 from Republic of China; 1 from
Singapore; 1 from Thailand and 1 from Vietnam (Chun 1973:
373-379). Western missiologists were invited to present
papers and to attend some meetings, but not during the first
three days. Did this represent an anti-Western missionary
attitude? Not especially. Rather, the Asian leaders wanted
time to recognize their own responsibility as Christians
to fulfill the Great Commission (Chun 1973:42).

In the opening address, Kyung Chik Han reminded the
delegates that though many of them represent younger
churches, they still have the responsibility to preach
the gospel both to their own people and also to those in
other countries. He encouraged them to pray, think and plan
together on the following items:

1. How can we help our churches in Asia to catch a
   world vision of missions and awaken missionary
   zeal among Christians?

2. What are the best mission strategies for Asia
   today?

3. How can we be more effective in training missionary personnel for service in Asia today?

4. How can we promote better mission cooperation
   among churches in both sending and receiving
   countries?

5. How can we achieve closer and more effective
   cooperation with Mission Agencies from Europe
   and America (1973:36-37)?

What were some of the results of this historic meeting?
In the concluding statement on August 30, 1973 they said:

> We appeal to the Christian churches in Asia
> to be involved in the preaching of the Gos-
> pel, specially through sending and receiving
> Asian missionaries to strengthen the witness
> to the saving power of Christ.
>
> We are compelled by the Holy Spirit to de-
> clare that we shall work towards the plac-
> ing of at least two hundred new Asian mis-
> sionaries by the end of 1974.
>
> These missionaries will be involved primarily
> in evangelism in the power of the Holy Spirit
> in order that men and women may come to be-
> lieve God's work of grace through Jesus
> Christ and in turn be agents of evangelism
> in the fellowship of His Church, the body
> of Christ. These missionaries will also be
> sent to plant evangelistic churches where
> they do not already exist (Chun 1973:349).

Donald McGavran, founder of the Church Growth Institute,
correctly noticed the contrast between "Seoul '73" and the
"Salvation Today" meeting in Bangkok. The Asians meeting
in Seoul had no time to discuss a moratorium on missions.
Rather their goal was to send at least 200 new Asian missionaries by the end of 1974 (Chun 1973:347).

"Seoul '73" was followed by the "First Summer Institute
of Mission" organized by David Cho. This two week institute
was attended by 64 Koreans and delegates from six other Asian
countries. Though much of the teaching was done by Western
missiologists through interpreters, it was a significant
beginning of another new aspect for training Asian missionaries (Chun 1973:395-398).

One of the Asian delegates at "Seoul '73" was Isabelo
Magalit from the Philippines, General Secretary of the International Fellowship of Evangelical Students and planner of
the "First Asian Student Missionary Convention" held in Baguio
(near Manila), Philippines, December 1973. The motto was
"One Lord, One People, One Task" (*Asian Outreach* 1974). Though
following "Seoul '73" there was no organizational relationship as between the Congresses in Berlin and Singapore. This
is an encouraging fact as we have reason to believe the
Spirit of God is doing a new thing among many Asians.

> The First Asian Student Missionary Con-
> vention began as a spark of suggestion.
> The International Fellowship of Evangelic-
> al Students (IFES) to East Asia was in a
> meeting at a regional conference in
> Malaysia in May 1972 when a Filipino dele-
> gate suggested the possibility of expand-
> ing the Philippine triennial missionary
> convention slated for December 1973 to
> become an Asian convention, in fact, the
> first Asian student convention. The re-
> sponse was enthusiastic. It was to be
> a partnership between the I.V.C.F.
> Philippines and the I.F.E.S. in East
> Asia. We aimed for 400 people to come
> mostly from all countries in Asia where
> an I.F.E.S.-related movement was at work
> (*Asian Outreach* 1974).

There were 788 people registered from 25 countries
representing all continents. Though about 600 were from the
Philippines, the convention was clearly Asian, yet truly
international with the presence of Africans, Latin Americans,
Europeans and North Americans. About 65% were students, but
the majority of the rest were young graduates concerned
about finding God's will for their lives. Of this group
seventy-seven offered themselves for overseas missionary
work (Chun 1973:11).

In July 1974, the Church was blessed by the International Congress on World Evangelization (ICOWE) in Lausanne, Switzerland, which had fourteen years in planning. Billy Graham said:

> It was here in Montreux, Switzerland,
> fourteen years ago that a small group
> of us met for several days of prayer and
> discussion about the task of world evange-
> lization. Partly as a result of that meet-
> ing the Berlin Congress was held in 1966...
> Since Berlin a number of regional congresses
> have been held--at Singapore, Bogota, Min-
> neapolis, Amsterdam, and other places. Al-
> most all of the major countries of the world
> have had a congress on evangelism in the
> last eight years. Three years of intense
> prayer and careful planning have brought
> us to this moment and in the providence
> of God I believe that this could be one of
> the most significant gatherings, not only
> in this century, but in the history of the
> Christian Church. During the last few years
> we have heard many voices. We have heard
> the voice of the philosopher who often
> raises more doubts than certainties, who
> would rather seek than find, who doubts
> life's meaning. We are gathered in
> Lausanne to let the earth hear His voice
> (1974:16).

The I.C.O.W.E. brought together pastors, missionaries and laymen from both the younger and older churches. Careful preparation went into the selection of speakers and topics. Strategy papers were prepared in advance and mailed to the participants in advance to secure their responses. During the Congress the speaker then addressed himself to these responses rather than reading his original paper. This procedure increased the efficiency and effectiveness of the Congress, and also made possible the early publication of all reports (Douglas 1975). Though some felt the theme of evangelism lacked sufficient emphasis on missions (Communicating the gospel across geographical, language, cultural, social and economic barriers) about 50 percent of the speakers were from the Third World, a significant contrast to Berlin.

The climax of the Conference was the reading and signing of the "Lausanne Covenant." The Covenant emphasized the fact that world evangelization requires the whole church

to take the gospel to the whole world. The section, "Churches
in Evangelistic Partnership" stated, "We rejoice that a new
missionary era has dawned...God is raising up from the younger
churches a great new resource for world evangelization..."
(ICOWE 1974:6). During the Lausanne Conference, Asian Christians as well as those from other continents, realized anew
their responsibility for world evangelization.

The Lausanne Conference was followed by "Explo '74" in
Seoul, Korea sponsored by Campus Crusade For Christ. A
vision of an "Explo" in Asia was given to Joon Gon Kim and
the Korea C.C.C. staff during prayer on the mountain and was
announced by Kim at the close of the Explo '72 in Dallas,
Texas without any advance word to Bill Bright. One could
hardly imagine a gathering in Seoul larger than in Texas.
Yet the C.C.C. staff prayed, planned and worked faithfully
to prepare. God overcame insurmountable obstacles even during the last days, making possible this cross-cultural witness in Seoul, August 14-19, 1974.

In addition to the 300,000 Korean students, laymen and
pastors who came from all parts of Korea for training, 3,000
students and Christian leaders also came from 80 nations,
representing every continent in the world. During "Explo"
the nation mourned the death of Madame Park, killed by an
assassin's bullet intended for President Chung Hee Park.
The church and populace united in a new way, praying for
their nation and for their president who had been provident-
ially spared. Though the heat and rain would probably have
caused the meetings to be cancelled in most Western countries
(or at least be poorly attended), the Asians endured much
suffering with thousands praying through the night. Some
of the evening rallies had a million present and many made
commitments to God for salvation and for missions to their
own people and to those in other cultures. Many Christians
around the world experienced changed lives because of what
they saw God doing in the lives of Korean Christians.

During these international meetings, Asian church and
mission leaders continued to meet and to share their vision
for Asian missions by Asians. This led to another historic
meeting in Seoul in 1975, with the organization of the "Asia
Missions Association." Asians from the Republic of China,
Hong Kong, Philippines, Indonesia, Brunei, Singapore,
Thailand, Bangladesh, India and Pakistan joined with Korean
leaders to issue "The Seoul Declaration on Christian Mission"
on August 31, 1975. They examined the past work of the
church with an attitude of repentance for their failures.
They criticized and reflected upon the present attitude

and actions of some church and mission leaders, and as they
recognized the vastness of the unfinished task, pledged the
development of a new mission force with the cooperation of
Christians in the East and West. They concluded by saying,
"We therefore declare that we are obligated to carry out
that commission in the Pauline spirit, proclaiming nothing
but the Gospel of the Cross, and trusting in the Word of
our Lord Who said, 'and lo, I am with you always, even unto
the end of the world'"(Matthew 28:20) (*Asia Missions Association* 1975: Sect. V).

Western missiologists from the United States, West
Germany, Netherlands, United Kingdom and Hong Kong recognized
that the Spirit of God was moving in a wonderful new way in
lives of Asian Christians. Though representatives came from
distant countries, representatives of some large Christian
groups in Korea did not attend. Likewise, there was no re-
presentation from Japan. Chandu Ray who helped David Cho
plan "Seoul '73" was absent. Every effort must be made to
enlarge the base of cooperation for the sake of missions
and those who still have had no opportunity to hear the
gospel with understanding.

Even before the "All-Asia Mission Consultation" in
Seoul in 1973, young missiologists became interested in
learning more about the extent of non-Western missions.
Three research associates at the School of World Mission of
Fuller Theological Seminary, Pasadena, California did a world
survey of non-Western missions in Asia, Africa and Latin
America. The team consisted of Peter A. Larson (Latin
American data and coordinator), James Wong (Asian data),
Edward Pentecost (African data) with C. Peter Wagner (faculty
advisor) and William Needham (Missions Advanced Research and
Communication Center--MARC) consultant. They prepared and
mailed letters and questionnaires to 697 people and received
244 replies, representing 35% response. Though there were
many limitations in completing this large survey in less
than one year, their preliminary findings revealed data that
brought a new movement into perspective. With the rapid
increase of new mission agencies sending additional missionaries annually, even a perfect and complete compilation of
data in 1972 would be outdated in 1976. Nevertheless, their
findings brought worldwide attention to Third World Missions
and the results of this survey were published in *Missions
From the Third World*, by Wong, Larson and Pentecost. They
identified 211 missionary-sending agencies from 46 countries
in the Third World with 2,994 missionaries (1973:107). This
1973 publication is now out of print.

The appendix of this book's companion volume has an annotated
bibliography on Third World Missions with emphasis on Asia
consisting of more than 300 entries.* Because Third World Missions has become a significant new movement for world evangelization, I chose to study its policies and practices for this
dissertation. In the near future, the number of Asian missionaries will double. During the next decade, the number of
Korean missionaries can and should increase by 500%. How will
these missionaries be selected and trained? Will they be
sent with money from Korean Christians, with money from Western
Christians, or some from both? Will they be sent by church
denominational mission societies, by individual churches, by
church denominations, by interdenominational mission agencies,
by groups of individuals or in other ways? Will they repeat
mistakes experienced by Western missionaries? These and other
questions need careful thought in order to avoid wasting time
and money while missionaries are frustrated with ineffective
service and responsive groups of people remain unreached.
As a result of interviews, questionnaires, and studies at
the School of World Mission, I want to identify some key
issues that need study in order for Third World missionaries to become most effective.

The Kinds of "THIRD WORLD" Missionaries

First of all, what is the meaning of the "Third World"
and what kinds of people live there? The response to this
question by several top authorities was printed in the *U.S.
News and World Report*, March 31, 1975. The "Third World" is
not a formal organization. It doesn't even have a membership
roll. Rather, it consists of "have not" nations, still un-
developed, whose interests differ from those of developed
nations in the other two "worlds," the Communist and non-
Communist "worlds."

Recently the "Third World" has shown unexpected economic and political power because of their possession of large
supplies of oil and because of their majority vote in the
United Nations. Some "Third World" nations, as Saudi
Arabia, are no longer poor, yet their people have a highly
emotional conviction that throughout history, they have been
cheated by richer nations. Some want revenge for wrongs of
the past. The main targets are the United States, Western
Europe and Japan.

Others generalize by saying the "Third World" is the
southern half of the Earth pitted against the richer northern
half. Some may detect a racial connection--the darker-
skinned peoples getting together to demand "economic justice"
from the lighter-skinned populations. Though the world is

*See *Readings in Third World Missions*, edited by Marlin L.
Nelson, William Carey Library (1976).

getting smaller in a sense because of satellite communication
and jet travel, this has also created a new problem. The
peoples of the "have not" nations are far more aware of
just how little they actually have, compared with the two
other "worlds." Previously they were fairly ignorant of
that fact.

Wagner says the Third World refers generally to Asia,
Africa and Latin America. But this needs some clarification.
The United States, Russia, and Germany are clearly not Third
World. But Korea, Indonesia and Bangladesh clearly are.
What is the criterion? (1974:106).

It cannot be strictly *economic*. We cannot say that only
the underdeveloped or non-industrialized countries are Third
World. That would exclude countries as Japan. It cannot
be strictly *cultural*. If only non-Western countries are
Third World, most of the nations in Latin America would be
excluded as they consider themselves Western nations.

It cannot be considered strictly *political*. If we
identify Third World Nations as those separated from the
Communist or capitalist nations, we would then omit countries as China. It cannot be strictly *geographical*. There
are Third World peoples on all continents. There are Spanish-
Americans and Orientals in the United States and Chinese and
Japanese in Korea.

Wagner considers the best definition of "Third World"
as *psychological*. The mentality of a people classifies
them as Third World. They feel themselves independent to
some significant degree of the two great Western power blocks.
Though the world is changing continually, those in Korea,
Indonesia, Bangladesh, India and Latin America share many
things in common (1974:107).

Now let us see how we can classify different kinds of
missionaries and clarify our thinking. Ralph Winter has
made a significant contribution by introducing categories
based on the cultural distance (or difference) at which a
missionary is working. It first appeared in print in 1970.

Missions is not just a matter of geography. The crucial
question is not *where* you work, but *at what cultural
distance*. In the diagram, M-1 means mission to people
in your own cultural sphere, using your mother tongue,
whether in the U.S. or in an American community in a
foreign city. M-2 means mission to people at a slight
cultural distance, like, say, a U.S. Anglo dealing with

people who are essentially European, such as the Spanish-
speaking people of Los Angeles, Mexico, or Argentina.
M-3 means mission to people who are totally other: Navajo,
Chinese, Zulu, etc.

Very simply, it is not that M-3
mission is *holier*. It is *harder*.
The culture shock is greater.
Not everyone can be effective
in an M-3 task...A good course
in cultural anthropology will
help a great deal, but cross-
cultural empathy is not merely
a matter of training. Some
people have it, some don't.
(1970b:22).

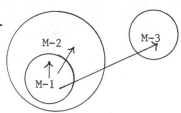

Diagram 1:1.
Cultural Distance

Later, the same scheme, accommodated to the phraseology
at the International Congress on World Evangelization, employed E for Evangelism instead of M for Mission. In this
new dress it first appeared in an article in *Christianity
Today* and later in the Lausanne *compendium*.

The Evangelism-One (E-1) sphere is where we can reach
people of our own language and culture and realistically
expect to bring them into our own churches.
The Evangelism-Two (E-2) sphere includes all those people
with whom we have some common ground culturally...but are
far enough away so as not to be candidates for membership
in our own local church. E-2 people for me are those whose
mother tongue is Spanish...or the American blacks, whom
I understand only partially, or new immigrants from Europe,
whether from England or the Continent.
The Evangelism-Three (E-3) sphere includes all those
people beyond any significant common ground of language
and culture, that is, people totally strange to us. For
me, E-3 people include most of the Navajo Indians, the
newly arrived refugees from Hong Kong, many of the Koreans
among us and so on (1973:11).

Though this use of the word *distance* has been helpful,
it has also caused confusion in the minds of many seeking to
understand these distinctions. I suggest referring to the
cultural *difference* instead of the cultural *distance*. A
person in the E-3 category may live next door or half way
around the world. His language and culture is radically
different.

C. Peter Wagner explains that the Fuller Seminary research team used the original M system to produce an additional refinement, using M and G symbols. M stands for missions and is divided into the same three subcategories as follows:

1. Mission-one (M-1). These are missionaries who go to plant churches in their same culture, like "Jerusalem and Judea" of Acts 1:8.
2. Missions-two (M-2). These missionaries go to *another culture,* but the difference between the two is not a radical difference. In Acts 1:8, "Samaria" would be an example.
3. Missions-three (M-3). These missionaries go to a *radically different* culture or to the "uttermost parts of the earth" as in Acts 1:8 (1974:108).

How *far* these people go is the other important dimension. Those who leave their own country encounter unique problems that they would not experience if they stayed home. Using the symbol G for geography, we can make two subcategories:

1. Geography-one (G-1). The worker ministers in his *own* homeland. This is called "home missions."
2. Geography-two (G-2). The worker leaves his own country and ministers in *another* country. This is called "foreign missions" (1974:109).

Instead of using G-1 for "home missions," I prefer to use "HM." In place of G-2 for "foreign missions," the letters "FM" are easy to understand and to remember.

An additional dimension was later developed, using not only E for *evangelism,* but N for *nurture* and S for *service.* The result is a grid that can be attributed to Winter and Wagner as well as my own modifications, and will be used throughout this book.

	Location		Primary Activity			
	HM	FM	E	N	S	Total
M-1						
M-2						
M-3						
Total						

(left axis label: Cultural Difference)

Diagram 1:2. Cultural difference and Primary activity

A Korean missionary pastoring a Korean church in Hong Kong would be FM-1-N. A Christian worker from southern India working among people with a different language and different culture in northern India would be HM-2-E. A Japanese doctor working in Nepal would be FM-3-S. These distinctions provide new tools for missiological studies.

The Meaning of "MISSION"

If that is what is meant by "Third World" what then do we mean by "Mission?" Alan Tippett in "Clear Thinking on Mission(s)" distinguishes missions from mission. Missions are the human organizations and mission is the mandate from our risen Lord (1973:347-349).

John R.W. Stott believes "mission" is a comprehensive word, embracing everything which God sends His people into the world to do. It includes evangelism and social responsibility since both are authentic expressions of the love which longs to serve man in his need (1975:35).

Some say that mission is everything the church does. If mission is all kinds of activity, then it can go on without any propagation of the gospel at all, i.e. it results in no growth of the church.

McGavran believes that "a chief and irreplaceable purpose of Christian mission is to proclaim Christ *and to persuade men to become His disciples and responsible members of His Church*" (1970:82). Church growth must be a *chief* end--not more or less the center, but a chief goal. And it must always be there, i.e. must be *irreplaceable.*

The statement concerning "The Church and Evangelism" in the Lausanne Covenant asserts:

> In the church's mission of sacrificial
> service evangelism is primary. World
> evangelization requires the whole church
> to take the whole Gospel to the whole
> world. The church is at the very center
> of God's cosmic purpose and is His appoint-
> ed means of spreading the Gospel (1974:5).

In "Continuity and Change in Christian Mission" Jack F. Shepherd says:

Let witness, evangelism and mission be seen as three concentric circles with mission in the middle. Though you cannot have mission without evangelism and witness, not all evangelism and witness properly fits the category of mission. I know what I am saying is in contrast to Stott's suggestion that mission is "wider than evangelism." In my view it is narrower and more specialized (1973:86).

Diagram 1:3.
Shepherd's View of Mission

I regard witness as most general and all inclusive, including all we do and say. Every believer is a witness. Evangelism is winning people to a personal faith in Jesus Christ and incorporating them into a local church. Evangelism is measured by our *intention* to make disciples. Only God can cause the church to grow. Mission is concerned with the establishment of churches. Churches are the products of mission and become centers for direct evangelism. The members are witnesses as they become involved in spiritual and secular responsibilities in society.

The opening paragraph of the Lausanne Covenant states that "We believe the Gospel is God's good news for the whole world, and we are determined by His grace to obey Christ's commission to proclaim it to all mankind and to make disciples of every nation" (1974:3).

In Asia, there remain 98% who are not yet Christians. Even in Korea where the indigenous church is strong and growing, 85% are still not Christians. Is the goal of missions simply to plant an indigenous church in each country? If so, missionaries in many countries should hurry home.

Rather, our goal is to preach the gospel to every person. Wagner has recently coined the phrase "Fourth World" to describe all people who have not yet committed themselves to Jesus Christ as Saviour. There are fourth world people in Russia, England, the United States, Africa, Korea, India and in every other tribe, tongue and nation (1972:213-216).

Some have used the "Fourth World" to describe the American Indians (Tippett 1975:250). More recently the "Fourth World" has been used to describe the 42 nations still essentially trapped by poverty (Low and Howe 1975:35-44). It seems proper

to use this term for those who are experiencing physical suffering and need assistance from the more affluent nations.
Recognizing the importance of food for life, we cannot neglect
their spiritual need for eternal life. Jesus said, "And whoso-
ever shall give to drink unto one of these little ones a cup of
cold water only in the name of a disciple, verily I say unto
you, he shall in no way lose his reward" (Matthew 10:42). And
again Jesus said, "I am come that they might have life and that
they might have it more abundantly" (John 10:10).

How then can we define "Third World Mission Agencies?"
*These are organizations based in a Third World country, founded,
administered and financed by Third World Christians, sending
their people as missionaries, across linguistic, racial, cultural
and geographical barriers to preach the Gospel and multiply Christian churches.* Sometimes they receive finances from non-Third
World Christians, but they are relatively free of Western support
and control.

We are entering an exciting new phase of world evangelization with the organization of scores of new mission agencies.
What will be the relationship between the Eastern and Western
mission societies? Will Western Christians tend to become mere
spectators or can we become partners in obeying the Great Commission? As various members of the one body of Christ, how well
will we cooperate in helping those in the "Fourth World" who have
physical and spiritual wounds? Will we honor Jesus Christ as the
head of the church, obeying the Word of God, being led, inspired
and empowered by the Holy Spirit? Some of these questions will
be answered in my research entitled *The How and Why of Third
World Missions: An Asian Case Study.*

Part Two

Evaluation of Mission Trends in Asia

2
Western Missions in Perspectiive

 A History of the Expansion of Christianity by the late
Kenneth Scott Latourette will undoubtedly remain the classic
on this subject for many years. Ralph Winter has continued
the description of this movement in *The 25 Unbelievable Years
1945-1969*. In the preface Winter writes:

> One of the unusual elements in Latourette's
> perspective was his desire to go beyond mere
> Church history and to describe what may be
> called the *infra-structure* of the Christian
> movement--that is, to describe Christianity
> as a movement which is more than an account
> of the rise and development of the various
> churchly structures (1970a:10).

 A British visitor in the U.S. recently observed that
Americans have been overtaken by a fit of compulsive pessimism. Everything is assumed to be going wrong on both the foreign
and domestic fronts. Winter writes to offer hope and insight to
students, laymen, pastors and even missionaries. There is nothing honorable about a pessimism that is unwarranted.

 The reader of missiological journals and articles may
easily get the impression that the day of the Western missionary is past. Articles such as "Missionary, Go Home" (Gatu 1974:
70-72), "The Ugly Missionary" (Nida 1960:74-78), "Mission But
Not Missionaries" (Nacpil 1974:78) cause many to think that the

past 150 years of missionary work have been insignificant. In
discussion on moratorium, some critics imply that Western missionaries have hindered rather than helped the people. The
political, social and psychological mood of the present day
seems to be riddance of the past in order to try anything new.

While criticism is necessary and can be constructive,
we must remember our goals and objectives in order to make a
correct evaluation. Who is criticizing and why? What are their
credentials of experience and effectiveness in mission today?
What modifications are under consideration for change? Is there
any indication that this change will bring an improvement? How
valid is the opinion that all the work of Western missions was
a failure and God is now replacing them by raising up a new movement for evangelization of Asia by Asians only? We need a correct perspective of both Western and Asian missions in order to
correctly evaluate some of these assumptions.

Early Contributions of Western Missions

China

Let us review some of the contributions of Western missions
during the past 150 years. Western missionaries brought the gospel to many countries where the people were resistant to any religious change, especially to what many considered a western religion. Arthur Glasser, writing about his experiences in China,
said:

> When missionaries first arrived, they found
> nothing but unrelieved darkness insofar as
> the knowledge of Jesus Christ was concerned
> ...They achieved relatively few break-throughs,
> and only saw massive Christ-ward people move-
> ments among its tribal peoples. They suffer-
> ed, labored and died. Outside the walled cities
> of inland China I've often come upon their
> graves, and the graves of their children. The
> Christianity these missionaries brought always
> remained a minority faith, a Western religion
> that was almost universally regarded as inimi-
> cal to the best interests of the Chinese people.
> Even so, by 1949, when the Communist regime
> began to "encourage" missions to leave, one
> could draw a line across China in any direc-
> tion and on an average of 20-30 miles come
> upon an evangelical, Christ-exalting, Bible-
> believing Christian congregation. Baptized Pro-
> testants numbered about one million. Catholics
> were almost three times that number (1973:256).

Korea

But the experience of Christianity entering neighboring
Korea was quite different, though the resistance to the gospel
and persecution of believers was similar. I am indebted to
Edward J. Farren for many of these ideas concerning the church
in Korea.

> Korea did not follow the usual pattern of
> missionaries coming and then, after slow and
> agonizing beginnings, the people accepting
> the faith from the foreigner or from the mis-
> sionaries from abroad. The pattern was reversed
> and it seems to be one of the few such cases, if
> not the only such case in the history of the mod-
> ern Catholic Church. It was not the mission-
> aries who brought the truth to the Korean people,
> but it was the Korean people who went seeking
> for the truth. When they found some books from
> China about Christianity, a few of their scholars
> came to believe that this is the truth and they
> established what is perhaps the only Church set
> up by laymen without the help of a priest or mis-
> sionary. It was only years later, when the Church
> numbered at least 4,000 people, that they final-
> ly welcomed a priest. It is this fact of the
> origin on the Church in Korea that all speak of
> with pride (1970:20-27).

Matthieu Ricci, an Italian of noble birth and a Jesuit missionary, took up residence in Peking in 1601. His profound
scholarship in Western science, especially in mathematics and
astronomy, made a great impression on the court and the people
of the ancient capital. It was then customary for the king of
Korea to send an annual envoy to Peking to present compliments
and gifts to the Emperor of China. In 1631, Chung Du Won, a
member of the annual embassy contacted Ricci and brought back
books on science, a pair of pistols, a telescope and other
Western products, including Ricci's book on the "True Doctrine
of the Lord of Heaven."

Hangul, the language of Korea, had been invented and
introduced in 1446 under King Se Jong. But most of the scholars
rejected the "new" language and knew well the Chinese writing.
It was due to this happy circumstance that they could understand
the books Ricci and others wrote in Chinese.

In 1783, Yi Seung Hoon went to Peking with the annual
embassy, was converted, baptized and given the name Peter. It
was hoped that he would be the first stone of the Korean Church.
Peter Yi returned to Korea and baptized his friend Yi Duk Cho and

both began to preach earnestly winning converts in Seoul and the provinces. Suspicion and persecution broke out and the Christians were ordered to give up their faith or die. Thomas Kim became the first Christian martyr in Korea, dying of injuries caused by the torture. Though many died for their faith, there were also those who denied their faith, including the first two converts (1929:28).

One of the most inspiring facts of the history of the church is the fact that Korea was clearly known as the mission of the Martyrs, and that to be sent to Korea was like being assigned to martyrdom. And yet the Paris Mission Fathers kept sending missionaries whenever it was possible to get men in.

In 1866, the greatest persecution of all was begun. Many priests and Bishops were put to death. In the month of September over 2,000 Koreans died for the faith. A monument was erected in Pyongyang to testify to the fact that at last the Catholic faith had been completely destroyed in Korea. But the seed had been well planted and was well watered with the blood of martyrs. In September 1970, there are more than 779,200 Catholics while the number of Protestants is reported as 3,192,621, according to statistics of the Ministry of Culture and Public Information for February 1970. Christianity was spreading in Asian countries, but at the cost of lives of both missionaries and national believers.

The Korean Church and the Nevius principle are synonymous in the minds of many Christians. In June 1890 Dr. and Mrs. John L. Nevius visited Korea and reported their experiences in China. It is significant that this "consultation" was in Korea, and not in the mission headquarters in the United States, England or Australia. After serious thought and prayer, a deliberate decision was made by seven missionaries to adopt the "Nevius method." The four cardinal points are:

> *First,* to let each man 'abide in the calling wherein he was found,' teaching that each was to be an individual worker for Christ and to live Christ in his own neighborhood, supporting himself by his trade.
> *Second,* to develop church methods and machinery only so far as the native church was able to take care of and manage the same.
> *Third,* as far as the church itself was able to provide the men and means, to set aside those who seemed the better qualified to do evangelistic work among their neighbors.
> *Fourth,* to let the natives provide their own church buildings, which were to be native in architecture, and of such style as the local church could afford to put up (1908: 109,110).

Though the Korean church is often used to illustrate the
success of these indigenous principles, we must recognize that
these methods alone do not bring church growth. Roy E.
Shearer in *Wildfire: Church Growth In Korea* proves by careful research
that the church did not have equal growth all over Korea (1966:
216).

This does not fault the Nevius method, but indicates the
presence of other factors that can help or hinder the growth of
the church. I am convinced that there would not be over 12,000
churches in Korea today if the principles introduced by Nevius
had not been followed.

The Korean church has grown and expanded its influence
around the world. It has been the site for recent international
Christian conferences. Christians are developing not only a
social consciousness but also an awareness of their responsibility for world evangelization. There are presently 18 missionary-sending agencies in Korea and this number should double during this decade. Missionaries are still welcomed and have opportunities to preach and to teach the Christian faith in several
segments of society.

Burma

Burma provides another good example of the contributions of
early missionaries. In an article, "Burma: Mission Without Missionaries" Addison J. Eastman said, "The real test of Christian
missions has always been what happens after the missionaries leave.
For this reason what is taking place in Burma today is of special
interest to Christians in other parts of the world" (1967:9).

The major Protestant missions in Burma were the American
Baptists, two Anglican societies, the American and British Methodists and the Seventh Day Adventists. The Baptist work, which is
both the oldest and largest, dates back 154 years to Adoniram Judson, America's first overseas missionary. Long before the missionaries were forced to leave (1965) the major responsibility for
the life and witness of the church rested firmly in the hands of
the Burmese. Missionaries were occupied mainly in the Bible
Schools, seminaries and other programs aimed at training new
leaders. It is estimated that today there are at least 3,000
nationals serving full time as pastors, evangelists and Bible
workers in the Protestant churches of Burma. According to Eastman, the number of young people in training for the ministry is
up nearly 15 percent over two years ago.

The government nationalized all Christian schools and hospitals in 1965 and some thought that the church had suffered
a critical blow. Today most Christian leaders think differently.

As a former school principal said recently, "We Christians should be glad that our government is taking full responsibility for the education of all of its citizens. Furthermore, our Christian teachers who are now scattered all over the country are in a much better position to witness in the world."

Christians of Burma have long been noted for their love of the Bible and the hymnal. But scripture distribution has increased 20 percent. There are numerous reports of laymen organizing Bible study groups in their homes. The Burmese churches also have a long tradition of supporting pioneer work in unevangelized regions of their own country. Eastman says:

> The large Karen Baptist Convention is supporting its own missionaries in many different parts of the country. It has ten evangelists in the Naga hills alone in a project shared with the Kachin churches. One of these men reports that he has baptized 102 persons in the past four months—this is one of the most remote sections of Burma where only 13 years ago the Nagas were still sacrificing human beings and collecting their heads as a part of their spirit worship. Organized missionary work is also being carried on among the Lahus, the Was, the Padaungs and the Chins. In addition, it is not unusual for laymen to give weekends to evangelistic work. Student and youth groups spend most of their vacations travelling to "the districts" in "gospel teams." As a result, many are turning to Christ and new congregations are being established (1967:11).

The Christians of Burma face an uncertain future but with great courage and optimism. The pastors are now doing the work of former missionaries. They consider the challenge and opportunities for mission work are bright and the sky is the limit. Truly they caught the spirit of Adoniram Judson who once said, "The future is as bright as the promises of God."

The early missionaries not only preached and taught the Bible but were also involved in social concerns, establishing schools, hospitals, orphanages, preparing dictionaries, teaching people to read plus scores of other good things. In those days most mission societies were involved in *both* evangelism and social work. Winter says:

This tension between evangelism and social
action was wrongly reduced by some to a
simple choice between "words" versus "deeds,"
when actually it was a question of words plus
different kinds of deeds at different levels.
Missionaries had always emphasized good deeds.
William Carey initiated a movement that eventually resulted in the outlawing of widow-
burning in India. Robert Morrison and a host
of other missionaries up until World War II
opposed the custom of foot-binding in China
(1970:60).

Today we speak of mission on six continents. Latourette
says, "Those who laid the foundation of the future Protestant
churches did so usually with heroism and often at the sacrifice
of comfort, health, and even life...and...in the face of frequent
unfriendliness and hostility of the populace and officials (1929:
407). "Erst wägen, dann wagen" meaning "look before you leap,"
describes how difficulties were faced.

Today we have improved transportation, added anthropological
knowledge of cultures and cross-cultural communications plus
gains in missiological theory and church growth. With our added
knowledge and tools for world evangelization, we dare not lightly
dismiss the courage and devotion of many early missionaries who
did their best.

Criticism of Western Missions

Few words have had the impact worldwide as the address by
John Gatu from Africa, entitled "Missionary, Go Home," delivered
at the Mission Festival '71, a gathering of the Reformed Church
in America in Milwaukee, Wisconsin (1974:70-72). Instead of
reviewing the good effects of the missionary movement which are
already well documented and found in our libraries, Gatu chose
to point out the incoherencies and conflicts involved:

In this address I am going to argue that
the time has come for the withdrawal of
foreign missionaries from many parts of
the Third World, that the churches of the
Third World must be allowed to find their
own identity, and that the continuation of
the present missionary movement is a hindrance to this selfhood of the church (1974:70).

About the same time a similar remark was made by an
American concerning Latin American work and he included both
money and personnel. Father Daniel Berrigan said, "I suggest

we stop sending anyone or anything for three years, and dig in
and face our mistakes and find out how not to canonize them (1974:
70). Gatu was pleased that this statement was made by an American
and included money also.

The British Empire was built by travelers, missionaries
and traders, followed by seekers of trade, commerce and settle-
ments. These then developed into protectorates followed by
annexation of the territories, thereby completing the cycle of
slavery both at home and abroad. It is therefore very clear what
kind of Christianity came to Africa, for side by side with the
natural aggressiveness and a lust for power and wealth which are
so evident in European history, there were also new spiritual
forces driving Western man toward the new destiny.

Let mission be the mission of God in the world, but *not of
the West to the Third World!* Gatu concludes by saying:

> ...it is my view that by discontinuance
> of missionaries and money in the churches
> of the Third World we shall have provided
> for a definite transformation, not only
> of a new relationship but of new images
> of the church that we have today by
> accepting the necessity for change. The
> Gospel will then have a deeper and a more
> far-reaching effect than our mission Chris-
> tianity has provided so far (1974:72).

Unfortunately it is true that in some "mission fields"
the mission institutions and personnel are still far too
paternalistic and foreign, but it is debatable if a sudden
withdrawal of all funds and personnel would solve this.
We need to recognize the places where a moratorim would be
useful, set the period of time and not limit the moratorium
to money and personnel. Alan Tippett says:

> I would hate to think of our limiting our
> thoughts on this subject to personnel and
> funds. The *ultimate mark* of an indigenous
> church, though related, is not to be measured
> in terms of personnel and funds, but whether
> or not the community sees itself as the Body
> of Christ in that place, ministering the mind,
> love, mission and ministry of Christ. For any
> Church ultimately, this alone is *selfhood* or
> *entity*. Anything less than this is still a
> foreign ministry (1973a:277).

Tippett then adds a word of caution as this policy would also apply to missionaries from younger churches in The Third World.

> ...these problems of missionary thrust and
> withdrawal are not only those of the white
> or Western missionary, but of all cross-
> cultural missionaries, including those of
> the Third World Churches which are (as they
> all should be) sending agencies. I speak as
> much of the Fijian among the Australian abo-
> rigines, the Korean in Thailand, the American
> Caucasian among Mexican Americans as of the
> Englishman, Frenchman or German in Africa.
> Missiological guide-lines and formulations
> for our day and generation have to allow for
> a wide diversity of cross-cultural evangelism,
> because a Christian mission from Japan or
> South India or Nigeria can be just as foreign
> as one from America or Australia...there is
> a time for missionary thrust and a time for
> withdrawal, but every situation must be judged
> on its own merits. The Christian mission must
> go on. Situational problems must be researched,
> but the moratorium must not become a cliche
> for the notion that the day of mission is
> dead (1973:278).

C. Peter Wagner considers the moratorium as a very prag-matic issue. "To the degree that a moratorium on missionaries facilitates the fulfillment of the Great Commission of our Lord, it should be supported by Bible-believing Christians. It hardly needs to be mentioned that the reverse equally holds: if a mor-atorium on missionaries *hinders* the progress of world evangeli-zation, it should be opposed" (1975:165-176).

Wagner continues by suggesting the necessity of a mor-atorium in four areas: 1) missionaries who extend Western cul-tural chauvinism, including economics, politics, technology or methods of communication; 2) missionaries who indulge in theo-logical and ethical imperialism; 3) missionaries who are dedi-cated to paternalistic interchurch aid, the syndrome of church development and 4) missionaries who are involved in counter-productive activities as described in the first three points. These four areas, the cultural, the theological, the ecclesiasti-cal and the missiological dimensions cry out for moratorium. However, we need simultaneously, a new movement in each of these new areas in which the Spirit of God can work out His purpose through us. A major shift in this movement will be an explosion of Third World Missions. God will raise up in the Third World

hundreds of mission agencies that will send forth tens of thousand
of black, brown, red and yellow missionaries to join (not replace
the continuing Western missionary enterprise. A properly applied
moratorium will help assure a culturally relevant and evangelistically efficient movement under the leadership of the Spirit of
God.

Many of the criticisms of Western missionaries are included
in a paper presented at a consultation of Methodist missionaries
and churches in Asia at Kuala Lumpur, Malaysia, February, 1971
by Emerito P. Nacpil, Dean of the Union Theological Seminary in
Manila, Philippines. His paper "Mission But Not Missionaries"
centers around two questions: a) Whom does the missionary serve
b) What does he do? (1974:78-81).

The answer to the question--whom does the missionary serve,
largely determines his answer to what does he do. The answers to
these basic questions is no longer clear and unequivocal. Nacpil
says that *theologically* he serves the denomination or mission
society which sends and supports him. *Functionally* he serves the
people who benefit directly or indirectly from his mission activi
Vocationally insofar as he works in his chosen calling, he serves
himself despite any pretension to self-sacrifice. And *inciden-
tally*, as a foreigner, he serves his own country and culture by
being a representative.

Formerly the various dimensions of his service and loyalty
were held together integrally. The mission of God in Christ was
understood essentially in terms of converting unbelievers and establishing churches. These were to multiply and were inevitably
shaped after their own historical patterns of life, thought and
worship. The missionary's job was to evangelize people, organize
churches, pastor congregations, build service agencies (schools,
hospitals, hostels, etc.) and manage the new denomination or
church. This work required a life-time commitment. His financia
support from the West was further undergirded by the "superiority
of the missionary's culture and by the imperialistic ethos of a
colonial or non-colonial era. In those days the missionary's
understanding of his loyalty, the nature of his work and the char
acter of the times he lived in mutually supported each other. He
had no doubts. He had few misgivings.

Nacpil also says:

> Because the churches it has founded have
> grown and now desire to be independent and
> to develop their own life according to their
> own best lights under the demands of the ecumen-
> ical imperative, the clamor for human liberation,
> the requirements of nation-building and develop-
> ment, and the need for ecclesial selfhood and
> identity, those of us involved in missions

are no longer certain that the mission of
God in Christ can be understood adequately
in terms of church growth and church ex-
tension (1974:79).

The missionary's leadership role has been replaced by
national church leaders. The new leaders have a different
agenda for priorities of action. The missionary becomes a
form of interchurch aid. Instead of career missionaries, there
is more need for a short-termer and an expert in specialized
fields. This change often involves an identity crisis for his
own vocation and faith.

The missionary can still depend on the security of his
mission board structure and his right to live the standards of
a developed and superior culture in a developing world in whose
desire for liberation he wants to help! The modern missionary
system and its affluent and efficient standards and personnel
stand alongside the younger churches struggling for identity
and selfhood. Whom does the missionary serve and what does he
do? Is it God or man? Is it the struggling receiving church or
the affluent sending church? Is it the developing society or
his own developed society and superior culture? Some would argue
for partnership--partners in obedience. But is this possible
under the present condition? It would be a partnership between
the weak and the strong which involves continued dependence of
the weak upon the strong and the continued dominance of the strong
over the weak. Nacpil then states:

> I might point out that the younger generation
> today does not have fond and cherished memories
> of the good old lovable missionaries. I have
> asked many young people what they see when they
> see a missionary. They tell me that when they
> see a missionary, they see green--the color
> of the mighty dollar. They see white, the
> color of Western imperialism and racism. They
> see an expert, the symbol of Western tech-
> nology and gadgetry. They see the face of a
> master, the mirror of their servitude. They
> do not see the face of a suffering Christ but
> a benevolent monster which must be tamed be-
> cause it can become useful for their own con-
> venience. In some instances, they do not even
> see a man but a C.I.A. agent which must be
> crushed. The young people in my own country
> have a name for missionaries and ecclesiastics.
> They call them "clerico-fascists" (1974:80).

Such a missionary image cannot symbolize the authenticity of the gospel and the universality of the church. The present structure of missions is dead and should be buried, though such an action would be painful and expensive. The former missionary structure performed magnificently the role of a successful mid-wife giving birth to the Christian community in the lands of the Third World. But now the child is grown-up and is ready to enjoy his freedom as a son and to assume his rights and duties as an heir. The day of his independence and maturity has arrived All guardians and trustees must now withdraw. Nacpil says:

> The most *missionary* service a missionary
> under the present system can do today in
> Asia is to go home! And the most free and
> vital and daring act the younger churches
> can do today is to stop asking for mission-
> aries under the present system...the death
> of the present missionary system does not,
> however, mean the end of mission (1974:80).

David J. Cho, a Korean and promoter of Third World Missions, is sometimes critical of both the Western and Asian Missionary Societies. During the First All-Asia Mission Consultation in Seoul, Korea in 1973 he said:

> Western mission history for the past 150
> years has left to us endless missionary reports
> and thousands of missionary volumes. Begin-
> ning with the initial meeting at Edinburgh in
> 1910, followed by the Jerusalem Conference in
> 1928 and the Madras Conference of 1938, along
> with the growth of Hockingism, and finally in
> the Salvation Today Conference in Bangkok in
> 1973, major Western missions have had to face
> formidable obstacles in their struggle to sur-
> vive. While we must never forget that the plan-
> ters of the Asian churches were Western mission-
> aries, our purpose here is not to debate the
> merits and demerits of our predecessors; but
> rather, to turn from preoccupation with unin-
> tentional failures, gloomy pictures, and un-
> pleasant memories gathered over a long period
> of time (1973:105).

Cho continues the emphasis that we are in an acute situ-
ation and must evaluate and analyze the realistic situation of the Asian society which has "come of age." He then item-
izes seven aspects for consideration.

1. The secularized interest of our church
    leaders in vast mission properties built
    by Western missionaries over the past
    150 years.
2. The halfway thinking that still causes
    some to place missionary responsibilities
    upon Western organizations.
3. The credibility and practicality of those
    striving to stand on their own feet, in-
    dependent of Western financial support.
4. The subsiding zeal for foreign missions
    of many Western churches.
5. The continuing decrease in Christian
    population proportionate to the world
    population.
6. The remaining virgin territories of the
    earth yet to be evangelized.
7. And, the countless areas where the evan-
    gelistic mission is still publicly pro-
    hibited (1973:105).

These are the very critical reasons which never allow us
to stand still or to be hesitant to assume the responsibilities
of world mission, averting our misconception that we are im-
mature and ill-prepared. Cho is not only critical of Western
missions but also of Asian missions. "Shall we overlook the
prevailing missionary "commercialism" which exhibits exaggerated
missionary reports and statistics?...Let us not hesitate to criticize ourselves openly before God and before our brethren"
(1973:108).

Referring to our attitude toward the Western Missions
Cho says:

> We should be frankly critical of the rest-
> lessness, confusion, and degeneration of
> the major Western missions during the last
> five years, at the same time admiring con-
> tributions made by early Western missionary
> fathers. We would, however, like to see
> Western missions humbly accept the severe
> biblical judgment and frank critique of them-
> selves, openly admitting they have somehow
> lost their fundamental missionary views and
> direction. We would like to see their will-
> ingness to expose themselves to God's sur-
> gical operation in order that they may be
> cured and revitalized. Only under these
> conditions can we of the Third World mission

cooperate with our Western counterparts
on an equal basis (1973:109).

Western missions have excessively emphasized
denominationalism and have contented themselves with nominal converts whose ulterior
motives make them poor advisors for their
white fathers. Vast sums of money have been
poured into non-evangelical building projects
such as hospitals and schools. Then, too,
the unnecessarily dissimilar living standards
have become barriers between the missionaries
and the people they wish to serve (1973:110).

During the discussion period some of the other Asian
delegates considered David Cho's paper as too critical of Western missions. Cho replied that linguistic differences and the
difficulty of adequately expressing his thought in English must
have given such an impression. His intention was to distinguish
between the evangelical and ultraliberal views on mission, and
to evaluate and analyse the situation, not to merely be critical
(1973:73).

With this clarification, we can further appreciate the conclusion of this address:

We must decide how to keep a position of
prestige as a united task force not in opposition to, but in cooperation with, the
Western Missions. We must give up ineffective methods and competitive feelings if together we are to achieve our goal of reaching all of Asia (1973:110).

For several years missionary statesmen have been proclaiming the necessity of indigenous principles in overseas mission
efforts. Yet Chua Wee Hian of Malaysia says that we still
desperately need dramatic changes in missionary policies and
practices in his article "Missionaries Must Change" (1968:20).
Chua states that nationalism is booming in Asia and old
religions are being reformed and revived. Some, like the
Buddhist sect of Soka Gakkai of Japan, take aggressive roles
in politics and their hatred for anything "foreign" is alarming. The missionary zeal of Islam and the training and financing of Muslim missionaries to Africa and Asia is alarming.
Ancient religions are awake and on the move.

How genuine is this revival of ancient religions? It
seems that old religions are being politicized. Externally,
they convey the impression of reformation and revival, but
internally, they **represent** drastic attempts to adapt to the
contemporary political and social upheavals of the day.

Why is Christianity still weak after 100 years? Why
are most churches still not self-supporting and sadly lack
missionary vision? Chua observes that before World War II,
theological liberalism emphasized social reform rather than
conversion. Institutions had priority over the indigenous church.
Secondly, the missionaries ran everything and the Asian Christians
were mere spectators. The strange thing was that they did not
rebel against such a passive role! Rather, they rejoiced to have
"professional men" to care for their soul and doctors care for
their health. The missionaries were like priests and monks of
other religions. Chua then states:

> By failing to train local believers to
> positions of spiritual leadership and to
> pass on our Lord's missionary mandate to
> them, they made the Asian Church feel that
> it must regard itself as the *receiving* church
> and not the *sending* church. Where there is
> no evangelistic thrust and missionary commit-
> ments there is no growth. No wonder the
> Asian Church is not virile and strong! (1968:
> 20).

After World War II, there was a new restlessness among people
in Third World countries. They wanted political independence.
Many missionaries promised "nationalization" but realized lack
of capable leadership. Recognizing the impossibility of "go-
it-alone" policy, "partnership" became the watchword. The missionary role must change from that of a performer to a trainer.

Another necessary role change is from a patron to a servant.
Gradually missions are becoming integrated into denominational
churches. Chua states that they "always have room for those who
voluntarily assume the roles of servants. Further, such humility
and selfless giving do not pass unnoticed. Aid without strings
attached is something radical to us Asians!"

Chua's third recommended role change for today's missionary
is from a director to a catalyst. "Hallmark of the modern
missionary is the ability to say, "God has called me to this task
and in obedience to His commission I am here serving among you.
But the Lord gives the same commission to His disciples everywhere. Come, let us serve the Lord together by going to town
or village X." Such changes should no way be considered a "loss"
to western missions, but a significant "gain" in world evangelization.

Some may be oversensitive to these criticisms from leaders
in the Third World. Each would probably realize the dangers of
over-generalization. Certain groups in various countries have

probably said and done things that would not characterize the
entire missionary program during the last 150 years. Even so,
we can identify with Arthur Glasser when he says, "We are pain-
fully aware that our Western Churches and missions do not have a
very good record in Asia. Would that we had served Asia's peoples
more biblically and more faithfully" (1973:255). Missiologist
Glasser analyses mission work in China and reports lessons considered relevant to new missionary agencies being established in the
Third World in his address at the First All-Asian Mission consultation in Seoul '73 (1973:255-279).

Under the topic of "Missionary Preparation" Glasser notes
that even Latourette who commended the devout evangelical commitment of the early missionaries realized how poorly prepared
they were for their task. "Many of them remained ignorant of the
wider reaches of Chinese institutions, literature and thought,
and looked upon the culture around them with critical and unap-
preciative eyes..." (1929:409). Their ignorance made them vul-
nerable to the delusion of Western moral superiority. Their
insensitivity to local customs and their proneness to pass moral
judgments estranged them from the gentry and ruling class. Their
readiness to identify China's endemic dirt, suffering, and disease
with moral corruption alienated them from the common people. They
aggressively proclaimed the superiority of Western values but were
tragically unaware of the deep social and political implications
of abruptly substituting them for Chinese standards. Because of
their failure to understand the nature and implication of ancestor
worship, they unwittingly gave the impression the West condemned
all forms of filial respect.

Because Western missionaries regarded the Chinese as
individuals to be won to faith in Christ, one by one, their meth-
odology had serious flaws. They tended to ignore the corporate
dimensions of Chinese social structure, especially at the village level. Only late in the 20th Century does one find in
their manuals any references to the complex web of relationships
in which the Chinese lived, which had a bearing on individual
decision-making. They found out very late that the Chinese
village was anything but a collection of individuals.

The missionaries tended to investigate very inadequately
the manner in which the Chinese lived. Many basic questions
remained unasked as how the land was cultivated and managed,
how village patterns of family division, popular religion,
urban immigration, feasts and festivals influenced an individual's
reaction to Western missionary penetration and how the power
structure functioned at the village level and related to the
decision-making of individual villagers.

When it came time to establish a village church they regarded all their problems as "spiritual." They were not able to discern the sociological dimensions. By ignoring such phenomena as class mobility, class status and interclan rivalry, they often failed to see why some churches did not grow. When churches did grow, success was often attibuted to the wrong reasons.

Glasser describes the above in some detail, not to fix blame but to alert ourselves to the complexity of the missionary preparation. Fortunately we now have new insights from sociology and anthropology and know much more about the animistic subcultures of the religion of the common people of Buddhist, Hindu, Islamic, Confucian and Shinto lands. Fortunately, we can prepare missionaries far better today than China missionaries were prepared yesterday.

The real flaw in the missionary movement, Glasser points out, was its inadequate use of the Word of God. It took seriously only part of the Bible. Godfrey E. Phillips made a study of the use of the Old Testament in China and discovered that the "real Christian canon" was the New Testament and Psalms. He found the viewpoint of a pastor in North China to be representative of the perspective of Christians throughout the country. He advised:

> Intending missionaries or evangelists waste
> their time if they spend a lot of it studying
> the Old Testament...The Old Testament teaching
> given in theological colleges in China is, in
> the experience of most students, devoid of in-
> terest or value for their work. Reading the
> Old Testament is like eating a large crab; it
> turns out to be mostly shell, with very little
> meat in it...We don't need to start with Moses
> and Elijah. It is enough to teach men about
> God as Jesus taught or revealed him (1942:23).

The Bible not only contains the Evangelistic Mandate of the New Testament. It also contains God's call to the cultural task--a stream of obligation that courses throughout both Old and New Testaments. Whereas the New Testament largely focuses on the individual before God, the Old Testament stresses his corporate relationships (family, community, nation.) These two mandates embrace our total Christian responsibility. Unfortunately, Western evangelical missionaries were relatively unconcerned about social issues. They accepted without question the simplistic thesis that evangelistic and church planting work would somehow eventually bring about the social regeneration of China. Most missionaries tried to convince the Chinese that their problems were all spiritual. Since its theology did not include the Cultural Mandate its leadership did not reflect the social concerns of the Hebrew prophets!

> Analysts of the Western missionary pene-
> tration of China commonly attribute its
> "apparent" failure to six basic factors:
> 1) Their undue reliance on the power and
> prestige of the West; 2) Their presentation
> of a Western form Christianity alien to
> the Chinese heritage; 3) Their unwilling-
> ness to appreciate and utilize Confucian
> culture as a vehicle for communicating the
> Christian faith; 4) Their organizational
> and theological disunity; 5) Their inability
> to relate the social and religious dimen-
> sions of their message; 6) Their failure to
> utilize trained Chinese in the vanguard of
> all evangelistic advance (1973:273).

Though criticism is frequently considered only in a negative sense, I want this analysis of Western missions to be constructive. Many international conferences and seminars research
a problem and pass a resolution, but then nothing happens. There
is not enough time left for us to repeat these mistakes in strategy, action and attitude.

Westerners have tended to emphasize the differences between
the people in different countries and cultures. It was not a
theologian, but anthropologist Goldschmidt who noted that "people
are more alike than cultures" (1966:134). Relativity, though
applying to cultures, does not apply to basic man. Goldschmidt
points out that cross-cultural studies of human cultures suggests
a series of generalizations concerning human commonality that dare
not be as lightly dismissed as has been customary among anthropol-
ogists.

Many of our mistakes resulted from an attitude of our natural
superiority to all other people. This may relate to influences
of biological superiority stemming from Darwin's theory of
biological evolution, or it may simply be another evidence of
the self-centered nature of mankind.

With increasing nationalism, some say the missionary must
become the servant of the church. I disagree. Rather, we are
to be servants of Jesus Christ and faithful members of the
church. We are not to work *over* or *under* the national Christian,
but *with* him. The diagram of the triangle represents the proper
missionary attitude. David said,
"O magnify the Lord *with* me and
let *us* exalt his name *together*"
(Psalm 34:3).

Diagram 2:1.
Proper attitudes and relationships

A missionary must use his spiritual gifts if he is to have a fruitful and satisfying ministry. A missionary evangelist in Korea "laid aside" his spiritual gift and became a servant of the church, providing transportation for the district superintendent visiting rural churches. The frustrated missionary soon returned to America where he was free to minister effectively.

Others criticize the missionary's lack of identification. Many think only of the external and physical aspects rather than the attitudes which are so prominent in relationships with people of other cultures. We are not citizens of our "adopted country" and few nationals would expect us to change our national allegiance. However they can expect our *respect*. No one is perfect, but everyone can show this attitude in cross-cultural relationships. Koreans have told me that they don't want a new car, increased salary or a larger house, but they want *respect*. This we can and must give generously. This is important not only for Western missionaries, but also for Asians who go to minister in other countries.

Contemporary Modifications and Projections

Much of the pain of history results from the clash of the new and the old. In "Missions Under Divine Scrutiny," Wilbert R. Shenk says, "Change is threatening and often costly because it abolishes as well as imperiously installs" (1971:7). Many respond to the pressures of our times by a defense of the status quo. This reflects a misplaced confidence and a flawed perspective. A missionary church should be prepared to live with the tensions inherent in an ambiguous situation.

Shenk seeks to bring clarification by noting the ease with which one can "replace mission with methods." There is also a danger of substituting "Christianity for the gospel." We are inclined to call the West "Christian" and the rest of the world "non-Christian." Another mistake is confusing "Christian activity for the essence of the church." Elaborate facilities of the church cannot replace the experience of fellowship with Christ. Missions need continual evaluation and clarification of objectives if the goal of world evangelization is to be accomplished.

One effort to achieve this goal was "Green Lake '71"--the joint retreat and study conference co-sponsored in September 1971 by the Evangelical Foreign Missions Association (EFMA) and the International Foreign Mission Association (IFMA) in Green Lake, Wisconsin. The theme was "Missions in Creative Tension." The conference was attended by 406 invited delegates and observers from 104 member missions and organizations present, including 24 pastors, 34 college and seminary educators, 10 student observers and 15 overseas nationals.

The general theme of the conference was church/missions/
church relationships, discussing the "sending" church, various
church planting and service missions and the "receiving" church.
Ted W. Engstrom reported:

> Delegates were urged often by the con-
> ference leadership to "listen" to the voices
> from overseas, but, unfortunately, the few
> men representing national church leadership
> were a minority and the "listening" process
> was pretty much one of mission leader "lis-
> tening" to fellow-mission-leader. What
> "voices" were heard from the overseas national
> was a plea to hear the cry for "change" from
> abroad and to have an openness to the "new
> thing" which the Holy Spirit is doing in His
> Church in the world today (1971:28).

Hector Espinoza from Mexico, was one of the fifteen national "consultants." He was disappointed that so much time was
taken for discussion of organizational structures and so little
time was given to viable solutions. Espinoza states:

> By the end of the conference it was easy
> to discover at least one of the causes of
> tension: out of fifteen national "Consult-
> ants," only six received the opportunity of
> addressing the conference in a general ses-
> sion, and then strictly only three minutes
> each. By then, it was obvious to some mis-
> sion executives and nationals, that unfor-
> tunately there still widely prevails the old
> mentality of having the missionary do all
> the talking and let the national do all the
> hearing (1972:206).

It was a consensus that initiative and leadership have
not been shared with receiving church leaders soon enough.
There was a frequent call for "repentance" for past and present
errors in judgment and tactics in these missions/national church
relationships. But despite the call--there was little action
taken! Engstrom concludes his report saying, "The shape of modern missions could well have been altered for the good because
of the four days at Green Lake '71. But will it? One wonders"
(1971:29).

Many believe that the major challenge confronting the Christian church is to break through the structures inherited from the
past. Today the church's worldwide strategy is being reap-
praised. Evangelical Christians see the necessity of rethinking
the whole programs of missions. A biblical view of the Holy

Spirit in relation to the church, which is the body of Christ,
will not allow us to imagine that the external shape of the
Christian community is inflexible. What then will characterize the future shape of missions?

In an effort to lead Evangelicals in the West from a pre-
colonial to a post-colonial understanding of mission, Dennis
Clark in his book *The Third World and Mission* proposes a number
of major policy changes for a new and creative partnership between "sending" churches, missionary societies and the growing
churches of the Third World. He envisions the transfer of all
major policy-making for Third World ministries from Western bases
to the nation and region concerned. He also advocates the mul-
tiplication of leadership training centers, communications con-
sortiums and evangelistic teams--in all of which nationals would
lead and direct the program with a minority of Western colleagues.

Further proposals recommend the dismantling of all foreign
mission compounds and the breaking up of concentrations of foreign
mission personnel (with the possible exception of pioneer base
camps in primitive areas.) For "sending" churches who still think
"West is best" the author pleads for an embargo on exporting Western ecclesiastical disputes and cultural taboos to the new churches
of the Third World. Having talked with Christian leaders in some
fifty nations, he notes the heavy-handed influence of home boards
and churches which often try to control field policies from a distance without firsthand knowledge of the situation.

Ted W. Engstrom writes "Some Positive Thinking on Missions"
stating that "many missiologists believe that we stand at the
threshold of the greatest ingathering the Christian church has
ever known" (1972:8). Many point to the changing status and shape
of contemporary missions and say a new dawn of nationalism is emerging that will end Christian missions. The recent decrease in
the number of missionaries on various fields are proof. However,
Robert Coleman of Asbury Seminary has said, "The world stands on
the verge of the greatest spiritual awakening since Pentecost."
The late church historian, Kenneth Scott Latourette of Yale University has written, "The church has never been so widely planted or
so deeply rooted as it is today." Missionary leader Don Hillis
says, "This is missions' greatest hour! Greatest in its conflicts and conquests...greatest in its use of the media...greatest
in the response of nations to the carrying on of foreign missions...
greatest in its invitation to (us) to get involved." But this isn't
true of the 19th century mission structure or missionary mentality.

The Great Commission is to go and make disciples of all peoples.
The new "band of disciples" doing cross-cultural evangelism however, will be teams international in personnel, policy, financing
and attitudes. "Serving the Lord with all humility of mind" (Acts
20:19) could well become the motto for the closing years of this

20th century. New organizations are being formed with new structures. Old structures are taking on new attitudes. There remains
hope for partnership in this worldwide challenge of evangelism.

   Qualifications of "The New International Missionary" are
discussed in an interview of Michael C. Griffiths by Robert
Larson (1975:14). Larson asks what is the future role of the
Western missionary, either as a professional missionary or as
a teacher? Griffiths replies:

> While I come from the West myself, I don't
> think any longer in terms of the Western
> missionary. We in O.M.F. (Overseas Mission-
> ary Fellowship) today are not only internation-
> al, but interracial, so that "missionary" is no
> longer synonymous with "Westerner." We have
> Chinese missionaries from Hong Kong, Singapore
> and Malaysia. We have Japanese, Filipino,
> Maori and Fijian missionaries, although still
> far too few in number, compared with Caucasian
> ones. We find that national churches do not
> distinguish, when they ask for missionary
> help...
>
> Larson: What about the receiving countries?
> Is there less prejudice, then, toward receiv-
> ing a non-Caucasian...?
>
> Griffiths: I think it depends entirely upon
> the character and the contribution of the
> individual. There is a kind of missionary
> who is acceptable irrespective of his race.
> It's much more a matter of character. I
> don't deny that there is a certain amount of
> anti-Western feeling, some of which is entirely
> deserved. Some missionaries never get close
> to the culture of the people they're serving.
> They scarcely identify. They live in mission-
> ary ghettos. On the other hand, I am glad to
> say, there are Western missionaries who are
> thoroughly acceptable because they *do* identify.
> They come in alongside, not to work *on* the people,
> but to work *with* them as brothers in the Lord.
> There are some countries, undeniably, where
> the non-Western missionary, particularly the
> Asian missionary, is more acceptable. I am
> thinking of countries resistant to the gospel,
> like Turkey for example, where the fact that a
> fellow Asian brings the good news causes great
> acceptance. But sometimes there is racial pre-

> prejudice between different Asian nations.
> Our efforts to get a very well-qualified
> Korean missionary into Japan were refused;
> the Japanese regarded it as inappropriate.
> I am glad to say, however, that they did
> not refuse a visa to a Filipino missionary
> couple. Until very recently we regarded
> Japanese as unacceptable in the Philip-
> pines because of their wartime experience.
> Now I think that day has gone, and Japanese
> missionaries would be acceptable there also.
> I still remember being up in the Himalayas
> in Katmandu, with people saying to me, "Can't
> you get us more Japanese missionaries in Ne-
> pal like Dr. So-and-so?" (1975:15).

While the Overseas Missionary Fellowship is to be commended, we recognize that changes in leadership come slowly.
Until non-Westerners are given administrative responsibility
with authority, the O.M.F. will remain a Western organization
employing staff from various countries.

Not only do interdenominational organizations see the need
for changing, but also large denominations as the Presbyterian
Church In the United States. G. Thompson Brown, Director of the
Division of International Mission explains their Board's new
program called "The Internationalization of Missionary Personnel."

> This is an endeavor to support and to encour-
> age more missionaries being sent of the churches
> of the Third World. There has been some re-
> sponse but not as much as we had hoped. We
> now have joint sponsorship with the United
> Church of Christ in Japan in their sending a
> missionary to India. Also, a partnership
> agreement with the Presbyterian Church of
> Korea in sending a missionary to Indonesia.
> One more appointment of a similar nature
> which was approved by our Board was a Mexican
> serving an ecumenical agency for Latin America
> called CELADEC (Christian Literature) (Brown
> 1975).

Various boards and agencies have taken steps in the direction of internationalization and the ecumenical sharing of
personnel. The East Asia Christian Council has a fund to aid
Asian Churches to send missionaries and the Board of World
Mission has contributed. The World Council of Churches now
has before it a report of the CICARWS/CWME Joint Committee on
Ecumenical Sharing of Personnel which recommends the setting
up of a structure for facilitating personnel exchange through

the W.C.C. It was voted "that beginning in 1973, the B.W.M.
designate up to 5% of its Personnel Budget annually for the
partial support of non-U.S. missionaries, ordinarily from the
third world, in countries other than their own" (Board of
World Missions 7-4-504).

Contemporary modifications and projections affect not only
the life style of the missionary, the organization of the send-
ing-agency as the Overseas Missionary Fellowship, the relationship of denominations with Third World Mission personnel, but
also new structures of supporting-agencies are being created.
The United Presbyterian Order For World Evangelization is taking
a new hard look at the three major functions of mission: the
man who sends, the man who is sent and those who support the
administrators of this task. (Newsletter 1975).

An historical example of this "supporting" dimension of
foreign missions came into existence around the close of the
15th century during the Pietist revival in Germany. Led by
Count Zinzendorf, a small community called Herrnhut began an
extensive campaign dedicated to the evangelization of unreached
people. Kenneth Scott Latourette describes this community in
his volume *The History of the Expansion of Christianity:*

> Here was a new phenomenon in the ex-
> pansion of Christianity, an entire com-
> munity, of families as well as of the un-
> married, devoted to the propagation of the
> faith. In its singleness of aim it resem-
> bled some of the monastic orders of earlier
> centuries, but these were made up of celi-
> bates. Here was a fellowship of Christians,
> of...families...(1939:48).

It is the dynamics of this community of believers that
illustrate the value of coordination around a common effort in
initiating missionary activity in the world. It was the breadth
of commitment, the desire to set aside culture and create a possible vehicle for functionally reaching others with the gospel,
that caused relationships and meaningful interaction among
God's people.

The United Presbyterian Order For World Evangelization
was designed to give Presbyterians in the pew a more meaningful involvement in world evanglization. The Newsletter states:

> Our first concern is specified in the name
> of the organization by the words "World evan-
> gelization." While we are the members of
> the UPOWE fully recognize the validity of
> church to church relationships, shared min-
> istry and inter-church aid, we also seek to

respond to what we conceive to be specific
call to share the gospel among people to
whom no credible witness of the redemptive work of Jesus Christ is offered. Our
second concern is suggested in the name of
the organization by the word "order." We
confess our conscious and unconscious acqui-
escence to the consumer-oriented values of
our society which have not left us free to
act as responsible stewards of the bounty
entrusted to us (1975:2).

The United Presbyterian Order For World Evangelization
as a community concept does not gather its constituency into
one geographical location as the Moravians did. Rather, it
consists of a network of *individuals* worldwide who each have
a common commitment to world evangelization. Some of the
guidelines are: 1) To minimize expense and rules and to maxi-
mize outreach and flexibility always mindful of human needs
of each member; 2) To establish a living standard within the
United States similar to that of missionaries in the foreign
field; 3) To give direction to level of consumption and how to
use resources for world evangelization, not control what members earn or where they live or how they support themselves;
4) To give phased encouragement and training them to avoid unnecessary expense of time, money and health; 5) To *not* give away
funds necessary for the basic securities of life, health, auto-
mobile, home and "termina" insurance; 6) To seek a significant
intellectual mastery of the overall task of world evangelization
and will seek to employ them in this task: 7) To consciously
join after a screening process and be subject to dismissal also
by the decision of the order; 8) To avoid involuntary socializa-
tion of members' children. The U.P.O.W.E. is an order designed
for committed *individuals* not for families; 9) To work along
denominational lines while also encouraging fellowship and community with others having the same purpose and life style;
10) To prevent its activities from conflicting with a member's
relationship and responsibilities to local congregations.

"The basic service rendered by the U.P.O.W.E. to its constituency would be two-fold: a sense of fellowship and identification with those of common concern, and the education of its
constituency as to the dynamics of World Christianity" (1975:5).
Anticipating the development of a similar fellowship in other
traditions, a liaison structure has been established called simply O.W.E. (1605 E. Elizabeth St., Pasadena, CA 91104). This type
of fellowship provides a new innovative effort to make personal
the responsibility and opportunity for individual Christians in
obeying our Lord's Great Commission.

The Mission Handbook: North American Protestant Ministries Overseas contains valuable research significant to those interested in Third World Missions. In "Changes and Trends in Missions Today," Edward R. Dayton and William L. Needham summarize information used to assess the present situation in North American missions as follows:

> *Milieu in North America:* 1) Greater recognition of the need for Christian proclamation on the part of conciliar denominations; 2) Growing dissatisfaction with apparent overseas political involvement of their mission on the part of constituencies at local church level.
>
> *Milieu Overseas:* Increasing nationalism.
>
> *Mission Organization:* 1) Increase in the number of specialized ministries such as research, training and technical support. Greater use of specialists in cooperative efforts between missions and national churches; 2) New organization patterns and relationships between missions and national churches forcing a considerable shift in the role of "sending agencies."
>
> *Personnel:* Trend toward overseas assignments patterned after American corporation practice: frequent return to North America, home assignments during children's high school --perhaps coincident with missionary continuing education programs, frequent reassignment to different tasks on fields and/or different fields.
>
> *Operation:* More emphasis on the part of older agencies to design programs and train personnel to reach a specific cultural group.
>
> *Revenue:* 1) Shift of income distribution to more support of lay (vs. "professional") missionaries; 2) New patterns of giving as increasing number of local denominational **churches** shift support to new forms of missions; 3) Growing concern for evangelism in many local churches channels more funds to independent missionaries.

> *Philosophy:* Trend to incorporate local
> cultures in Christian worship and life
> styles, while holding biblical positions.
> (1973:77-79).

These are but a few examples of contemporary modifications and projections. Changes in structures, attitudes and personnel are occurring, though undoubtedly slower than some Third World leaders desire. The foundation of many missions was laid over one hundred years ago, involving the sacrifice of lives and mission resources. While appreciating the work of "pioneer missionaries," critics zealously urge us to appraise the rapid changes at the close of this 20th century. This new voice from Asia is being heard as it comes from maturing church leaders in the Third World. Because God's Spirit is also working in their midst, they too sense the awesome responsibility of increased involvement in world evangelization. A new resource has been added with the development of Asian Missionary Societies. Let us see this new movement in perspective also, observing their history, some of their present problems with the potential they represent.

3
Asian Missions in Perspective

Missions From the Third World by Wong, Larson and Pentecost is a valuable book as it gives reasons for mission-minded Christians to be encouraged. This survey of non-Western missions in Asia, Africa and Latin America reports 2,994 missionaries being sent out by 211 mission agencies in the Third World. This book does not report how many are doing E-1, E-2 or E-3 evangelism in home missions (HM) or in foreign missions (FM). There is a need for someone to supplement this survey with additional facts giving the geographical area and describing the type of ministry by each agency.

Some criticize this book saying it gives the impression that Third World Missions is a new movement. However, chapter four "Historical Perspectives," summarizes the activities of Third World missionaries in the nineteenth and early twentieth centuries and I have used many of these ideas in this section. Though the questionnaire mailed asked the date when the mission was founded, this information was not included in the report edited by James Wong. According to 43 questionnaires from Asia used for research in 1976 by School of World Mission associates, I compiled the following data concerning the periods when these Third World Missions were organized. There were no agencies organized *before* 1900, 8 agencies *between* 1900 and 1950 and 35 new agencies between 1950 and 1976. A graph showing the development by *decades* in the 1900's is as follows:

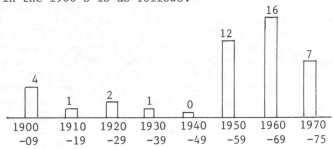

Diagram 3:1.

Oceania Missionaries:

I added Oceania to this section of my research to give proper depth and perspective to this movement. Oceania presents many challenges and lessons from the powerful movement of the Holy Spirit through which great church growth and people movements have occurred. Latourette calls the nineteenth century record of the spread of Christianity among the Pacific Islanders "one of the most spectacular in the history of that or of any other faith" (1943:263).

Though the European missionaries experienced hardship and suffering, so also did the missionaries from the Islands. Quali-ties of bravery, devotion and enthusiasm were evident among Third World missionaries. Martyrdom was the price paid by Pacific Is-landers as well as Western missionaries as they spread the gospel across the Pacific. Charles Forman states that the College Chapel of the Pacific Theological College in Fiji has been dedicated to those who have gone out as missionaries. Forman reports that this memorial represents over 1,000 national missionaries, not includ-ing their wives. The principal sending churches being Fiji (Meth-odist) with 269, Samoa (Congregational) with 209, the Cook Islands with 197 and the Solomon Islands with 139 (1970:215).

Alan Tippett informs us that frequently the Island mission-aries preceded those from the West. In 1829 a Tongan teacher was sent to "spy out the land." Tongans traveled long distances by canoe and organized devotionals rather than continue their acts of plunder. Quoting Thomas Williams, Tippett says, "No better pioneers could be found" (1962:16). Tippett says the advantages of these men for pioneer missionary activity were: 1) They knew the Pacific and the Island people: 2) They under-stood the Tongan language; 3) They knew how other island people had become Christians; 4) Through this apprenticeship system, the able men were selected; 5) Inspiration and dedication was

felt as a team; 6) Confirmation of God's call in being sent was
also experienced as a team (1962:34).

It is necessary for us to understand the organization and
function of the Melanesian Brotherhood described by Tippett as a
"thoroughly indigenous mechanism" (1967:45). Tippett attributes
its importance to the fact that it was a Melanesian concept for
Melanesian action, in which the national island people were able
to take the movement into their hearts and give it to the support
it needed. This support was primarily through the establishment
of a Company of Companions who would pray daily for the missionary brothers and their work (1967:51).

The Melanesian Brotherhood, called the "Retatasiu," which
means the "Company of Brothers," began during the 1920s by Ini
Kopuria, a pupil of Bishop Steward who later gave guidance in the
structural forms of this new movement. The Brotherhood was initiated with six who promised absolute obedience to Bishop Steward
The rules were simple with missionary evangelism taking precedence

Batak Missionaries:

Another of the younger churches with a missionary vision
and zeal is the Lutheran Batak Church of Indonesia. In 1899 the
Kongsi Batak (Home Missionary Society) was founded primarily to
do evangelism among their own people and to continue the philan-
thropic work previously done by the Rhenish Mission. This missionary work met with many difficulties as they tried to evangelize other Batak groups. There was a strong desire for local
autonomy and a decentralized organizational structure. However,
the dedication and enthusiasm of the Toba Batak members were
significant factors in the spread of Christianity through Batak-
land (Beyerhaus and Lefever 1964:82). The Kongsi Batak did not
flourish until after 1921 when it was reorganized and integrated
into the church by Johannes Warneck and re-named, Zendig Batak,
Batak Mission. After the change it proved extremely successful.

The Bataks had a missionary vision to reach their own
people scattered on various islands. Often large groups of Christians would migrate to other areas of Indonesia and secure po-
sitions of authority such as teachers. They continued not only
as faithful Christians but also evangelistic, sharing their faith
with others. Money for sending evangelists was collected at the
annual mission festival that followed the harvest. This harvest
festival was popular in pre-Christian Batak society as one of the
ceremonies of the traditional religion and was taken over by the
church as an opportunity for the Bataks to show their gratitude
to God and to share with others the blessings that He had given
in the harvest.

The Karens of Burma:

The account of the beginning of the Baptist Church in Burma
by Adoniram Judson is well known. Much of this early church growth
is attributed to the receptivity of the Karen people who were pre-
dominantly animistic in their religion. Under the ministry of
George Boardman, Ko Tha Bya became the first Karen won to Christ.
He became a flaming evangelist to his own people (Latourette 1944:
231). This became the foundation for an effective cross-cultural
ministry.

Herman Tegenfeldt, an American Baptist Missionary to Burma
from 1941-1960 has done important research on the early missionary activities of the Karens of Burma (Tegenfeldt 1972) I am indebted to him for much of the following material.

As early as 1833 Mission Societies were formed by the Karens
with considerable American missionary involvement. In 1850 the
Bassein Home Mission Society was established among the Karens
primarily to support evangelists among their own people. This
indigenous movement required the crossing of political and geographical barriers into Thailand. The Karens also crossed cultural barriers in taking the gospel to other ethnic groups. These
included the Asho Chins, Zomi Chins, Lahus, Was, Akhas, Shans and
the Nagas. Rev. Cope gave tribute to the work among the Chins
with the following description:

> We owe everything to the Karens...for a
> long time they were the only evangelists
> here. They went out to strange villages
> where no preparations had been made for them
> and where they were threatened direly...The
> Chin preachers were put under these Karens
> and some of our finest workers were trained
> by them. They learned the language, learned
> the ways of the people, and won their con-
> fidence. In the first literary work I did,
> it was the Karens who helped me. (Shwe Wa
> and Sowards, quoted by Tegenfeldt 1972:20).

Though Burma is now closed to foreign missionaries, the national church is still growing. We recognize the importance of
the early missionaries not only in winning converts and establishing a national church but also in giving a vision, encouragement
and guidance for establishing a Karen Missionary society.

Wong, Larson and Pentecost summarize Tegenfeldt's conclusions
as follows:

1. A missionary vision and passion has been part of the Karen church growth story.
2. Early concern was primarily for groups with whom they sensed common bonds of relationship such as the Kachins and Chins.
3. Karen missionaries received support from National Christians through the Bassein Home Missionary Society, from the American mission, from institutes in which they served and from the people to whom they ministered.
4. The Karen missionaries endeavored to learn the local languages and were instrumental in Bible translation among the Asho Chin and the Lisu.
5. Their outstanding musical ability was a great contribution to the congregational singing and choirs among the people to whom they had gone.
6. The missionary example of the very early Karen converts seemed to have set the tone for Karen outreach.
7. Missionary outreach to the Burmese Buddhist was not to the same degree of scale nor intensity as to the other tribal groups (1973:87).

Chinese Missionaries:

Thousands of Western missionaries have worked in China with the result of some four million Protestant and Catholic Christians by 1949 (Glasser 1973:256). Christian churches were established in many areas among Chinese of the various dialects and communities. One of their early experiences as cross-cultural missionaries was coming to Korea.

Archdeacon J.R. Wolfe of the Church Missionary Society living in Foochow, China, visited Korea in 1884 and felt their great need of a religion. He reported this need and opportunity for missionary work at the annual meeting of the Provincial Council of the South China Mission. One Chinese pastor and three Chinese lay evangelists volunteered to go and begin a mission. Wolfe wrote the Church Missionary Society three times for a grant or for permission to personally raise funds to support these Chinese missionaries in Korea. The Board rejected Wolfe's request as they were not ready to establish a regular mission of the society in Korea nor to accept the responsibility of a purely native mission (Paik 1929:79).

Unwilling to betray his new missionary vision, he collected money from those at Foochow and from friends in Australia. After a year, the dream became a realization when the "First Protestant Mission to Korea" left Foochow, November, 1885 and sailed to Fusan (Paik 1929:79). Archdeacon Wolfe and two Chinese evangelists established a Third World Mission Society and were probably unaware

of the significance of this strategy. It is true that Horace
Allen, a medical doctor, arrived in Korea, September 20, 1884
to become the *first* Protestant missionary to Korea. We also
realize that Horace Underwood and Henry Appenzeller arrived on
Easter morning, April 5, 1885 to become the first *ordained* Protestant missionaries to live in Korea (Paik 1929:104). But the
Chinese were clearly the first *Asian* Protestant missionaries to
live in Korea. Though arriving after the Americans, their early
preparation began in 1884.

It is interesting to note that when the Korean church sent
its first missionary, they received an offering on Thanksgiving
day, "the Wednesday following the third Sunday in November...
the significance attached to it was 'the date of the arrival in
Korea of the first missionary.' However, we do not know who that
first missionary was" (Paik 1929:378). I think they were celebrating the arrival of the first *Asian* missionary from China.

We have no record of the progress of this Chinese missionary band until Wolfe visited in the fall of 1887 with Bishop
Bickersteth of Japan and Bishop Scott of North China. These
churchmen were cordially welcomed and met no opposition when
preaching. The Chinese missionaries had contacted a small group
of literary men, but none had accepted the faith. In 1888 Rev. J.
Martin of the Church Missionary Society resident in China, visited
Fusan and found 50 or 60 friendly, ready to embrace the religion
if the king withdrew the prohibition of Christianity.

The Chinese evangelists could not engage in public preaching
but met a few from the literary class who could enjoy the Chinese
classics with them. The mission from China withdrew in 1890 when
the Church of England mission entered Korea.

As far as we know, the Chinese evangelists won no converts.
However, Wolfe appealed to Australia for funds and missionaries
and Henry Davies became the first Australian missionary to Korea.
Wolfe was also indirectly responsible for introducing an English
missionary society to Korea, with Bishop Corfe arriving in 1890.

In addition to Oceania, Indonesia, Burma, China and Korea,
there are many other Asian countries where scores of national
Christians have crossed language, cultural and geographical
barriers to proclaim the gospel. The West has never had a mono-
poly on God's message for the world. What we now witness is a
rapid increase of Third World missionaries in contrast to a rapid
decrease of Western missionaries from the traditional denominational societies.

Problems Experienced:

While recognizing the significant fact of the emergence of scores of new Third World Missionary Societies with a new potential, there are many problems that need a realistic solution. Kyung-Chik Han, in an evaluation of the All-Asia Mission Consultation Seoul '73 said:

> It seems to me that the chief problem is our lack of *quality personnel* for missionary service. We Asians do not yet have built into our church life the tradition of the missionary vocation. I think that it will take a few years before we are able to develop the pattern of having our finest young people volunteer for missionary service and take steps to secure the training they will need to qualify for mission membership (1973: 378).

Recognizing the prestige given to Third World people whenever they travel abroad, there is the danger that some volunteers for missionary service may be seeking a new status for themselves. The fact that several Korean missionaries immigrated to the United States supports my opinion. Though we noted many criticisms of Western missionaries, it is still true that many would prefer the comfort and security of living in their own culture, rather than in a foreign land. This contrasting view of living abroad must be one of the facts considered in the selection of Asian missionaries. The Korea National Strategy Group Report at Lausanne said, "it is regrettably true that among those (missionaries) who have gone, there have been a considerable number who have stayed only a year or two and then have gone on to other places to live and work" (Hunt 1974:1,399).

Many of those who have experienced living overseas as Korean missionaries say the biggest problem is *finances;* how to secure adequate funds and then how to legally transfer them to other countries. The Christian and Missionary Alliance Church of the Philippines (CAMACOP) provides full support for their missionaries in Indonesia. They have arranged for the transfer of funds throug their mission in other countries. Variations of this pattern are used by many Asian churches that still have contact with Western missions.

I interviewed a missionary who had returned to Korea after three years of service, and asked if he thought more Korean missionaries would soon go to other countries. He shocked me with

his negative response. He said that few will go because of inadequate financial support. He had to use personal funds to
supplement his salary and to provide transportation. While on
the field he was separated from some of his children because of
finances and inadequate schools. His sending mission was either
unaware of the actual cost of living overseas or unwilling to
provide even the minimum amount necessary.

I personally know another young man who had successfully
pastored a Korean church and was asked by his denominational
leaders to go overseas as a missionary. He resigned his pastorate,
began deputation, studied English and even learned how to drive.
But did the large church send him as expected? Misunderstanding
concerning finances kept this laborer home from the harvest field.
He requested not only a minimum salary for living but also a "work-
budget." He refused to go to another country merely to live. He
desired funds to enable him to have a fruitful ministry. The decision not to send this family as a missionary was discouraging
to them, to the church and also to other potential missionary
candidates. Realistic problems as this need practical solutions.

Another serious problem is having the proper *sending agency*.
Money for missionary work comes primarily from Christians, and in
Asia, most Christians are members of local churches. How do these
Christians become informed about missions and motivated to give?
What structure or structures are most effective in Asia? Is giving most effective from a local church, several local churches, a
denomination, a group within the church or denomination, an institution as a school or hospital, a group of individuals or is
there some other Asian pattern? It is urgent to learn what plan
or plans are most effective in Asian countries. Four patterns
being used for the support of Asian missionaries are included in
Chapter Eleven. Western missiologists must tenaciously avoid a
paternalistic attitude toward Third World Mission structures.

Though some countries closed to Western missionaries are
open to Asian missionaries, they often experience more *government restrictions* than Westerners in securing passports and
visas. Three young missionaries from Ewha Womans University
in Seoul, Korea had their passports and plane tickets but were
unable to secure visas to go to Pakistan. Several Asian countries do not have diplomatic relations with each other. Others
do not want Asians because of prejudice. Michael Griffiths reported that Japan refused a visa to a well qualified Korean missionary but did accept a Filipino missionary couple (Larson and
Griffiths 1975:15).

Lack of *adequate training* is another serious problem.
The Korean National Strategy Group Report at Lausanne stated
the "need for a stronger program of training academically, practically and spiritually for cross-cultural evangelization"
(Hunt 1974:1,399). Several of the seminaries in Korea have

subjects on missions but lack a mission curriculum. There are
few courses on anthropology, linguistics, church planting, personal evangelism, mission strategy, cross-cultural evangelism,
traditional religions, church growth case studies and other necessary subjects. Fortunately, Asian leaders are recognizing
this lack in training for missionary candidates. "The Seoul
Declaration on Christian Mission" states:

> There are significant potential mission
> forces emerging from various countries of
> Asia, Africa and Latin America. We realize
> the urgency to mobilize and train these forces.
> This is the purpose that has called into being
> the Asia Missions Association, and that has in-
> spired the foundation of the East-West Center
> for Missionary Research and Development (Asia
> Mission Association 1975:Sect.IV).

However, as I study the building plans and organizational
structure of the proposed East-West Center, it seems that it
might be as much Western as Asian. Is this the plan needed for
soliciting funds from Western organizations or is it the most
effective plan for training Asian missionaries? Chandu Ray,
one of the organizers of the All-Asia Mission Consultation Seoul
'73 hesitates to comment on the East-West Center for this reason:

> I feel that until national associations
> have been formed, and it is they who decide
> what sort of training must be given, the
> East and West Center could very easily get
> bogged down with the Western way of think-
> ing. I believe that has happened. Now, my
> vision and the vision of many of us, was
> that the new center should be much more
> Asian in thinking, in order to present the
> Gospel to the Asians taking it to the people
> of the major communities, relating it to
> their customs and culture and to their an-
> thropological thinking. Various forms and
> modes of the Gospel need to be rethought
> and training given to the missionaries to
> go and present the Gospel in these terms.
> But this is not being done. This is where
> I feel that Brother Cho and I differed. He
> has depended on the Western bodies to fill
> the role, while I do not see Westerners
> filling this role (1973:375).

Another difficulty is *communication* on many different
levels. Asian missionaries who become a part of an international team or work in an interdenominational institution as
a school or hospital usually need to adapt to the Western culture for their private living and social life, to continue their
own national culture for self identity and their children's
education, and to adjust to the national culture of their host
country for an effective ministry.

Asian missionaries can easily become trapped in a "mis-
sion-compound-mentality" unless their goals are clearly defined.
Becoming a member of the "western community" requires a knowledge of spoken English plus a Western living style to avoid a
feeling of inferiority. However, if Asian missionaries depend
only on their own people for their support, this style of living
is impossible just as it would be if they were doing evangelism
in their own country.

There is a communication problem also with the people
of one's "adopted country." Because there are some similarities
among Asian languages, some missionaries are not provided either
the time or the finances for six months to one year of language
study. Because of the similarities of Asians, the nationals of
the host country may be doubly surprised and offended that the
Asian missionaries cannot speak their language well. While it
is recognized that few Western missionaries have learned the
language fluently, the nationals may accept this difference as
there are so many other differences too between the cultures.
This is not to excuse the Western missionary for not learning
to communicate well in another language or dialect, but simply
to note that the nationals of the host country have different
attitudes toward the Western and Asian missionary's fluency
in their "heart" language.

Another aspect of the communication problem is with the
sending agency or denomination. Samuel Kim, speaking of "Problems of Third World Missionaries" at the All-Asia Mission Consultation Seoul '73 states:

> Communication between countries in the
> Third World must be carried out in English.
> A majority of mission administrators in
> Korea are unable to use any foreign language
> and therefore must depend upon interpreters
> or translators in order to communicate with
> receiving churches as well as with other in-
> ternational agencies. While this problem is
> not as great among the English-speaking coun-
> tries of Asia (Philippines, Malaysia, Singa-
> pore, India, etc.) official letters from

                    mission secretaries of other Third World
                    nations can be very confusing (1973:116).

Asian missionaries also experience difficulties in coming
from churches that have *limited resources*. Often the Western
missionary provides everything from used clothing to a new
school or hospital. If a national pastor's son need tuition
for school or a letter of recommendation to get a passport or
visa, many Western missionaries will offer assistance. If funds
to repair the roof or build an educational building are not available through the church-mission finance committee, the missionary
may write directly to some friends for a "designated gift."
However, few Asian missionaries have contacts who can provide
these additional funds. If the criterion for success is the
missionary's ability to establish institutions or provide financial assistance to those in need, he feels inferior to the
Westerner and may even be despised in the eyes of some fellow
Asians.

Though the above problems are real enough to those involved, they are actually a symptom of a more serious problem--
the problem of *secondary objectives*. Missionaries do many good
things from teaching literacy to managing an orphanage. Asian
missionaries can easily become employees in an institution or
fraternal workers in the established church. It is much more
difficult to do cross-cultural evangelism with the goal of establishing new churches. The "Statement of the All-Asia Mission
Consultation Seoul '73" clearly defines the goal of the two hundred new Asian missionaries by the end of 1974 to do church
planting.

                    These missionaries will be involved pri-
                    marily in evangelism in the power of the
                    Holy Spirit in order that men and women may
                    come to believe God's work of grace through
                    Jesus Christ and in turn be agents of evan-
                    gelism in the fellowship of His Church,
                    the body of Christ. These missionaries
                    will also be sent to plant evangelistic
                    churches where they do not already exist
                    (1973:349).

The committee is to be commended for clearly defining
their goal. The committee now needs to measure their progress
and evaluate the results. How many missionaries were actually
sent by December, 1974? What were the sending and receiving
countries? How many sending agencies were involved? How
many are doing M-1, M-2 or M-3 evangelism? How many are
active in home missions (HM) and how many are involved in
foreign missions (FM)?

In January, 1977 the committee should receive a report
of the *total* number of new churches established by these *new*
missionaries. Did these churches become members of an existing denomination in the receiving country, become a part of
the denomination in the sending country or become independent
churches? Who are the pastors of these newly established churches?
To what degree are they indigenous? Such careful planning and
evaluation by Asian Missionary Societies would reveal maturity
that excels the practices of the average Western mission.

As few Western missionaries now establish churches, the
Asian missionaries may not know how to do this or fail to realize the importance of this ministry unless they are properly
trained. Hugh Linton is one of the *few* successful church planting missionaries in Korea today who has a systematic, well
thought out plan.

Chua Wee Hian believes the greatest sin of the Chinese
church is *parochialism and chauvinism,* being concerned only
for those of the Chinese race. A Chinese pastor had an evangelistic campaign among Chinese in Laos. When he was asked about
the possibility of preaching to Laotians he remarked, "The
Laotians are useless, backward, lazy and unresponsive to the
Gospel. Let's form a mission to the Chinese in that country"
(1969:11).

I will close this section by noting an obvious problem to
both Asian and Western missionaries, the threat of a *Communist
instigated war.* Missionaries were forced to leave China in 1949,
and in 1953 Korea was divided, resulting in no freedom of religion in the North. Vietnam, Laos and Cambodia are now under
Communist control and the future of the Christian church is unknown. Countries in the Middle East, Africa and Latin America
are also experiencing conflict. Two Koreans in an elevator of
a Hong Kong hotel will usually refuse to greet each other,
fearing the possibility of some Communist implication. The
various types of Communism treat the Christian church with
changing degrees of persecution. There is a need to enter
countries while permission is granted, preach the gospel and
begin training Christians how to live under a Communist regime.

Potential of Asian Missions:

As some Asians consider these problems plus numerous others
involved in sending their missionaries to other countries, they
may wonder if missions are necessary. They may use the analogy
of exporting rice from Korea while many living in Korea suffer
from hunger. Why not *first* evangelize all of Korea before going
to other countries? This would be an easier task, less expensive and very important.

Tsuyoshi Tadenuma, Executive Secretary of the Japanese
Evangelical Overseas Mission, received a lengthy letter from a
Japan foreign missionary berating him for being unbiblical in
his emphasis of persuading Japanese believers to also obey the
Great Commission. The missionary said that the Acts 1:8 outline
of missions priority is like a "four-stage rocket." When the
first stage is burned out (Jerusalem is evangelized) only then ca
Judea (the second stage) be evangelized. And only when Jerusalem
Judea and Samaria (the third stage) are evangelized, can you ig-
nite the fourth stage of the rocket, referring to a witness to
the ends of the earth. The Japanese should not become missionaries until Japan is first evangelized. The gist of Mr. Tadenuma
brief answer was in effect:

> I am sorry you believe us to be unbiblical.
> I have searched my Bible but can find no
> mention of rockets and missiles. However,
> I do find two-wheeled chariots. The evan-
> gelization of the world is like a two-
> wheeled chariot; one wheel is home missions,
> the other is foreign missions. One of the
> reasons you had so few converts in Northern
> Japan may be because your chariot had only
> one wheel--therefore, you went around in a
> circle. If you would put not only the wheel
> of home missions in Japan but also the wheel
> of foreign missions from Japan on your char-
> iot, we believe you will go down the road suc-
> cessfully evangelizing...(Joseph 1961:10).

Timothy Monsma in "The Advantage of Carrying Coals to
Newcastle" relates how the Tiv church in Nigeria has been
strengthened because of their involvement in the Great Commission to other tribes (1975). He emphasizes the fact that
Third World missionaries often have the advantage of entering
countries (as well as the minds of people) often closed to
Westerners. Tiv churches involved in missionary work, became
stronger spiritually. He also observed that church leaders became more understanding and sympathetic with Western missions
when they began experiencing similar problems in sending missionaries.

Though Third World missionaries have great potential,
many agencies are relatively young and inexperienced. Someone
asked how a person gets good experience. "By making good decisions," was the reply. "How do you learn to make good decisions?" "By making bad decisions." Few Third World Missions
have achieved their potential because they are still young and
inexperienced. Their great potential is like a child's "I-Q."
It must be carefully developed in order for a person to become
successful.

Donald McGavran gives insights for developing a high Third World Mission "I.Q." in his article "Basics of Effective Missions Anywhere." Because of the shortness of time and the experiences of Western Societies, it is not necessary to repeat the same mistakes. McGavran cites six basic principles:

First, the missionary society must create bands of Christians who burn with desire to tell others about Jesus.
Second, the missionary society must create a system of support.
Third, most new missionary societies should select reasonably responsive populations...sending a band of missionaries...who will find comradeship and spiritual support from fellow workers who come from the same sending churches.
Fourth, train missionaries before they go out the first time and on their first and second furlough.
Fifth, missionary societies have two tasks. They must keep both the senders and the sent blessed and marching under the Great Commission, honest accounts, capable administration and patient understanding...
Sixth, the missionary society must be flexible...while remaining utterly committed to bring *ta ethne* to the obedience of the faith (Romans 16:25) (1975:430-432).

We do not want to limit the Asian Mission potential by requiring them to follow a Western pattern or organization. For example, many Asian Christians do have a concern for their ethnic group living in other countries and make a concentrated effort to establish a church among them. Though FM-1 evangelism is comparatively easy and should soon become self-supporting if done properly, it is still very important and needs careful research. For example, in what cities and countries does a community of Koreans now live? What plans have been made to establish a Korean church among them? There are now thousands of Korean nurses and miners working in West Germany, a Korean community in Djarkata and recently many Korean truck drivers were employed in Saudi Arabia. With rapid development of technology and industry in Korea, the population is being scattered in many countries other than Japan, Brazil, Argentina, Canada and the United States. These FM-1 diaspora missionaries need qualifications and policies different than a Korean doing evangelism in Taiwan (FM-2) or in Bangladesh (FM-3).

A concern for involvement of Christian laymen in fulfilling the Great Commission is not a new thing. At the International Missionary Council in Willingen, Germany, Max Warren said:

There is a call for an entirely new type of missionary activity to be developed alongside the traditional modes. We need,

for instance, to envisage men and women of
scientific training who will be ready to
give service in development schemes, going
to their work as ordinary salaried officials
and bringing their expert knowledge to bear
on some local situation. But they will go,
not merely as those whose Christian convictions are marginal to their work...Rather,
they will go with a vocation consciously
and deliberately to seek to work out a "disciplined and purified technology" in the light
of Christian insights...I envisage the possibility of such a missionary brotherhood being
pioneered by a number of men who would be banded
together in a dedicated fellowship (Loffler 1964:
297).

According to Edward Dayton, a new trend in American missions is an "increasing number of highly motivated non-professionals who find new avenues of overseas ministry" (1973:78).

Chaeok Chun describes a new type of missionary work in Korea
as follows:

The University Bible Fellowship is an
indigenous student movement currently sending 158 missionaries, student missionaries,
to Europe, North America and Bangladesh. Most
of the missionaries, except for the couple in
Bangladesh, are self-supporting. In fact,
they sometimes support the University Bible
Fellowship of Korea in their evangelism endeavors among students and in their training
of missionary volunteers who spend six months
in concentrated life together training at a
center in Seoul. They are not sent by any
denominational churches in Korea although all
of them are church members (1973:20).

The University Bible Fellowship was organized in 1961 by
Sarah Barry, a Southern Presbyterian missionary with Inter-
Varsity experience, in cooperation with Chung-Woo Lee, the
present director. Lee was discipled by Navigator trained Doug
Cozart and readily gives credit to his teacher. Lee also writes
the Daily Notes for Scripture Union in Korean and is a capable
Bible teacher. Before U.B.F. missionaries are sent out, they
must complete an intensive study of the Bible and learn how to
share their faith with others. Though the U.B.F. seldom provide
financial support they do provide spiritual support by keeping
in touch with their alumni. On special occasions they have

collected funds for typhoon and earthquake victims in other lands.
These laymen are commissioned missionaries, sent to other countries
with the primary purpose of sharing their faith. However, they do
not become involved in starting new churches. This is another example of the great flexibility we can observe in patterns of Third
World Missions (Chua 1969:23).

Asian missionaries also experience a freshness and zeal in
their missionary outreach. The pastors from the Ami Tribe in
Taiwan, sent by the "Burning Bush Mission" to work among the Dyak
Tribe in Sarawak, Indonesia, have experienced the change from can-
nibalism to Christianity in their own generation. What they may
lack in Christian "culture" as second or third generation Christians, is superseded by the experience of God's power in freeing
them from the power of Satan. Both of these organizations will be
studied more in Chapter 10, "Analysis of Selected Organizations."

Chaeok Chun, a Korean missionary to Pakistan, emphasizes the
common experiences shared among Asians that increase their effectiveness as missionaries:

> Asians share a cultural similarity. Asia
> does house all the major world religions,
> but there is a closeness in their cultures.
> Secondly, suffering has been common among
> Asians. Asian missionaries, wherever they
> may be sent, are able to identify with the
> life of the people because they themselves
> have come from the same kind of life...
> Thirdly, Asian countries have all had col-
> onial experiences with only a few exceptions.
> This helps in following the pattern set by
> Jesus who fulfilled his mission by taking a
> servant's role. He said he came to serve and
> to find the lost. His message cannot be more
> relevant to our time (1973:28).

In these first two parts we have seen that a vital and significant new movement is developing. If Western Missions are
described as the tide coming in, surely Third World Missions are
as the tide going out. It cannot and should not be stopped.
Here is a great power for doing good if properly directed. One
cannot generalize by saying that Western Missions are totally
ineffective and that a moratorium should be unconditionally
declared. That would contradict the Great Commission and the
whole direction of God's concern for the world. Neither can
one expect missions from younger churches automatically to excel
in cross-cultural evangelism. The problems suggested will be
discussed in detail in the following sections.

We are all members of the *one* body, the Church, and need
to learn obedience to what the Spirit is saying to us today.
It is imperative that we maintain an attitude of openness,
humility and expectation. Peter Larson, in "A Challenge to
Western Believers" says:

> The scope of God's missionary activity among
> the churches of the Third World challenges
> Christ's followers in the West to respond
> positively to this increasingly relevant
> missionary fact. Let us meet this challenge
> with joy and thanksgiving, rather than dubious,
> grudging acceptance. Though their organiza-
> tions may vary from western models and their
> patterns of sending and support be very dif-
> ferent may we endeavor to push back the hori-
> zons of our present knowledge and be willing
> to learn new lessons our Lord may teach us.
> Finally, let us fervently pray that as evan-
> gelism and church planting take place in the
> fields in which we are called to labor, God
> will also use us to ignite missionary zeal
> among the younger churches that they too
> will send forth laborers into the whitened
> harvest field (1974:15).

Part Three
Necessary Ingredients of a Viable Missionary Movement in Asia

4
Effective Cross—Cultural Workers

When people speak of a missionary movement, some think of the organizational structures needed, the money involved or how to maintain the purity of the gospel being proclaimed. Still others are concerned about establishing clear measurable goals or about how people in another culture will hear and interpret the gospel into their worldview. While realizing the importance of these issues, I believe the selection of the right person is of primary importance. Jesus began a new movement with the prayerful selection of a small group of men and trained them for three years.

During the Asia South Pacific Congress on Evangelism, G.D. James said, "While we are looking for more money, means and new methods for the furtherance of the gospel, God is looking for new men" (1968:154). God used Moses to deliver the people of Israel from Egypt. When Goliath challenged Israel, God had a faithful man, David. When Jesus needed to feed a multitude of over 5,000 there was a young boy who gave Jesus all he had. The Spirit of God uses men and women to proclaim the gospel today.

This same concern was expressed by another Asian in Singapore when Akira Hatori said, "I believe Christ is seeking men who will *willingly work together to evangelize Asia and the world*. He is seeking men to work as partners, as teams to reach

whole areas with the gospel. I believe that Christ wants us
Asians to labor together, to pray, and weep and work together
to bring Christ to this area and to the world" (1968:266).

Kyung Chik Han, reflecting upon the All-Asia Mission Consultation Seoul '73 said, "It seems to me that the chief problem is our lack of quality personnel for missionary service"
(1973c:378). The most important key to the successful accom-
plishment of a task is having the proper person. It is imperative that Christian leaders recognize qualities essential for
cross-cultural workers.

1) *Christian Commitment:* The initial requirement for a missionary is having a personal commitment to Jesus Christ. Whether a
person is a "third generation Christian" or a former head hunter,
he must have *assurance* of his salvation. I ask some Koreans when
they became a Christian and they reply, "I was a Christian from
my mother's womb." While recognizing the advantages of having
Christian parents, I believe our salvation is the result of our
personal commitment to Jesus Christ as our Saviour and Lord.

The disciple Peter confessed Jesus Christ to be the Son of
God (Matthew 16:16) and we speak of establishing the church upon
this historic confession. Yet moments later, Peter tried to hinder Jesus from doing the will of His Father, and Jesus sharply
rebuked Peter saying, "Get thee behind me, Satan" (Matthew 16:23).
An "experience" years ago must be renewed moment by moment as
missionaries learn to meet new situations with the prayer,"Not
my will but thine be done."

When Archdeacon W.H.A. Butler went to Uganda in 1939 with
the Church Missionary Society, he eagerly looked forward to
meeting the African brethren who had been greatly blessed in
the early days of the East African Revival. After the initial
greetings he was surprised when they asked this newly arrived
missionary, "Are you saved?" Though amazed that they would ask
a missionary that question, he happily replied in the affirmative. A second question followed, "When were you saved, and
how?" The third question overwhelmed him, "And what's happening
now?" Then two years later they asked a fourth question which
led to a new dimension in his spiritual life, "Is your cup running over?" (Butler 1974:7). In this age of changing beliefs,
we dare not assume that every missionary candidate has the same
faith and convictions of earlier Christians.

2) *Disciplined Bible study and a satisfying devotional life:*
As missionaries work among people of a different culture and
different system of values, one often feels insecure, lonely
and frustrated. Many missionaries are unable to attend regular
worship services where they can hear the Word of God proclaimed

in their own language. Few missionaries receive Christian
periodicals or have the opportunity or funds to buy Christian
books available to those who live in their homeland. Unless one
has learned how to study the Bible profitably on his own, there
will be little growth in this vital area of life while living
overseas.

As each person is uniquely different, there is no *one* way
every Christian should "have devotions." Each person should
also have variety in this area of his spiritual life in order to
maintain challenge and blessing. It is important that each missionary learns how to have a *satisfying* devotional life *before*
going to another country. Though a legalistic attitude toward
one's "quiet time" is dangerous, an amount of daily discipline
is required. Paul used the illustration of a soldier enduring
hardness to teach Timothy to avoid giving top priority to secondary values in life. Without proper discipline, every Christian
worker is a potential "drop-out."

The Navigators is one of several organizations that God has
used to teach Christians *how* to study the Bible profitably, *how*
to have a meaningful devotional time, *how* to witness to others
and *how* to disciple a new believer that he might win and train
others also. The "two-two" principle in II Timothy 2:2 is emphasized by this interdenominational organization. Missionary
candidates would be wise to receive this kind of training and
practise using it *before* leaving the physical comfort and emotional security of the homeland.

Often a missionary is assigned to work with a person having a different personality and manner of living. Without renewed inner strength, the witness of loving one another can be
destroyed by anger, pride, envy, selfishness or a score of other
"weights and sins" that hinder the fulfillment of our desired
goals. The one who has learned how to communicate with God has
discovered the source of wisdom, vision, courage, patience,
sincerity and humility. When Jesus saw the people he was "moved
with compassion toward them, because they were as sheep not having a shepherd; and He began to teach them many things" (Mark
6:34). The missionary must be a person who follows this example
of his Lord.

3) *Recognition of the missionary gift:* The word "missionary"
only began to be used in its modern sense in the middle of the
seventeenth century. It is a hybrid word, but its Latin root
simply means someone who is sent, while that upon which he is
sent is a "mission." This is the nearest English and Latin
equivalent of the Greek *apostolos*.

From among His disciples Jesus chose twelve men whom He called "apostles." These men were taught and trained by Him, endowed with apostolic authority and after the Resurrection were sent to make disciples of all nations (Matthew 28:18-20). This group of men undoubtedly had unique privileges and responsibilities. In addition to "The Twelve" others also came to be referred to as "apostles." This second group included Paul, Barnabas, Timothy, Silas, and others.

Some believed the age of the apostles as well as the giving of all spiritual gifts ended when the early church became firmly established in a pagan society. The Reformation set forth convictions which became distinctive features of Protestantism-- justification by faith alone, the priesthood of all believers, the authority of the Word of God as contained in the Scriptures, and the right and duty of each Christian to interpret the Scriptures (Latourette 1953:715).

Ralph D. Winter says that Luther abolished both modalities and sodalities (ecclesiastical and mission structures) but eventually Lutheranism restored a diocesan modal structure. For almost 300 years the Protestant movement had no effective mission sodalites (1971:193-200). The reformers believe the Great Commission had been given to the early apostles and did not apply to the Protestant Christians. The church awaited the coming of the "Great Awakening" in the 1800s when John Wesley declared, "The world is my parish" (Latourette 1953:1026). The modern Protestant missionary movement of 150 years has an embarrassing gap of three centuries when the Catholics ask "Where are your martyrs?"

The pendulum has now swung the other direction and some say that every Christian is a missionary and every unbeliever is a mission field. If the word missionary is synonymous with being a witness, then I agree. Though this emphasis may stimulate local Christians to share their faith, it creates confusion regarding a *cross-cultural* witness.

Others prefer the word "apostolic-gift" when referring to those who are missionaries. C. Peter Wagner emphasizes the *functional* meaning and says the missionary gift should not be confused with the gift of apostlehood or the gift of evangelism.

> The apostle is one who has particular authority in the church at large, and he is sent out in a broad ministry. He is often an evangelist, and he is often a teacher. But in order to be an apostle, he doesn't have to minister in a second culture. Peter is an example of an apostle who was not a missionary. True, he went to Cornelius'

> home, but he went only because of a
> special directive from God, not be-
> cause he had the missionary gift (1974:
> 34).

Paul was an apostle who did have the missionary gift and used his apostolic gift in a second culture. In Ephesians 3 Paul speaks of himself as a prisoner of Jesus Christ for the Gentiles. He was a Hebrew (Acts 22:3; 23:6) and to identify closely with pork-eating Gentiles was not natural for him. Paul says he was made a minister to the Gentiles "according to the gift of the grace of God" (Ephesians 3:7). His ability to preach to the Gentiles was from the "grace given" (Ephesians 3:8) which becomes significant when we realize that the word "grace" is synonymous with "spiritual gift." Wagner continues by saying:

> Paul's spiritual gift enabled him to minister
> in another culture. I call this, in modern
> terminology (since missionary is not a biblical
> word), the missionary gift. The best statement
> of it is in I Corinthians 9:22 where Paul says,
> "I am made all things to all men, that I might
> by all means save some." Not everyone can do
> it. Peter, for example, couldn't. That's why
> Paul says clearly, "the gospel of the uncircum-
> cision (Gentiles) was committed unto me, as
> the gospel of the circumcision (Jews) was un-
> to Peter" (Galatians 2:7). If we adopt the
> hypothesis of the missionary gift, all these
> pieces fall into place. Some missionaries
> are evangelists, some are not. The ones who
> are simply have two gifts, meaning that they
> lead others to Christ (as an evangelist) in
> a second culture (as a missionary). Most
> evangelists use their gifts in their own
> culture because they do not have the gift of
> being a missionary to go along with it (1974:
> 34).

There is then no difference between the missionary "call" and the missionary "gift." God expects every gift to be used faithfully and effectively. There is a difference between spiritual gifts and the role of a Christian. Though every Christian has the role of a witness for Christ (Acts 1:8) every Christian does not have the gift of being an evangelist (Ephesians 4:11) or the gift of being a missionary. Recognition of this important Biblical teaching can help remove a feeling of false pride, a false humility or envy.

How then does one discern whether he has received the
missionary gift? As one prays for a knowledge of God's will for
his life, and especially if this includes a cross-cultural ministry, he needs to ask himself the following question:

1) Have I really made Jesus Christ the Lord of my
   life? A person unwilling to obey the Lord cannot expect to know God's will for his life.
2) How do I feel about serving God in another culture?
   Usually a Christian enjoys developing and using his
   spiritual gift or gifts.
3) How can I experiment using the missionary gift before making a life time commitment? There are increasing opportunities for missionary work during
   school vacation in the summer. A college graduate
   or career person may apply for short-time missionary service. There are increasing opportunities
   for a cross-cultural ministry among international
   students on university campuses. The University
   of Iowa has over 1,000 foreign students (Nelson 1976).
4) Was my "experimental" ministry effective? You
   can evaluate your own feelings about working with
   those of another culture and also the results of
   your ministry. If you really enjoyed being with
   people who are "different" and some of them received new understanding of Jesus Christ as a result of your being with them, it is quite likely
   that God has given you the missionary gift.
5) Do other Christians confirm my "feelings?" Each
   Christian is a member of the body of Christ and
   need not try to work alone. If the fellowship of
   believers share my joy experienced when communicating with people from a different culture,
   there is increased possibility that God wants me
   to do missionary work. Because of unusual opportunities today, one can use new insights to discover whether he has the missionary gift without
   risking the stigma of later becoming a "missionary
   drop-out!"

4) *Academic qualifications:* Most of the mainline church denominations have maintained fairly high academic standards.
Even in the nineteenth century most of their missionaries were
college or seminary graduates. When Hudson Taylor started the
faith missions movement he appealed for those "of little formal education." When Bible schools were established in the last
decades of the nineteenth century they too accepted those of little formal education and gave them enough Bible training to enable them to become effective lay workers in the Christian church
The Bible school graduates who went overseas frequently joined

the faith missions. In recent decades both the Bible schools
and the faith missions have raised their academic standards.

The amount of education needed will depend upon the vocation of the missionary candidate. A doctor or nurse will need
to graduate from medical college and fulfill the required period
of internship. A high school, college or seminary teacher will
also need the appropriate specialized training. A pastor, church
planter or evangelist will also need to graduate from a college,
Bible school or seminary. Various churches and mission agencies
have different requirements. An Asian missionary planning to establish new churches should be ordained. This usually requires
a period of one to three years following graduation from seminary,
when he can gain experience in the ministry and be evaluated by
responsible people in the church and mission.

A missionary candidate needs a thorough knowledge of the
Bible with a carefully thought through theology of missions.
He needs to know what is unique about Christianity, why missionaries are needed, how God communicates to people in different
cultures, how Christianity can become relevant to people of another culture, the meaning of the "unity" of the church and the
reasons for the success or failure of various mission movements
throughout history. A specialized course for training cross-
cultural missionaries needs to be developed. This will be presented in Chapter ten.

Acquiring formal education is no guarantee of success in
the Christian ministry. There are scores of successful pastors
and missionaries who are primarily self-educated. But in order
to cope successfully with the intellectual, social, political
and religious problems that are becoming more complex, additional
education is helpful. This is especially true for the missionary
who plans to work among students and other intellectuals. The
real test of a person's intellectual prowess is whether he keeps
on growing after his formal education has ceased.

5) *Acceptance by the church:* Though this is related to academic
qualifications, the emphasis here is upon *informal* education.
Do the lay missionaries have both professional competence and
Christian commitment? Has the doctor had experience beyond internship? Has this experience been only in a hospital or also
in rural clinics? Has the Christian witness that accompanied the
professional service resulted in any new conversions to Christ?
If this is the goal of the missionary doctor, he should learn
how to get a response from his own people before going to people
with a different language and culture. This same principle applies to a missionary teacher who expects to witness as a Christian in a secular school in another country.

The national Christian leaders should also carefully evaluate the experiences of the seminary graduate. If he worked as an assistant in a larger church, how effective was his ministry? Did he promote unity or division among God's people? Was all of his time concentrated on the nurture of Christians attending the church or did he also become involved in evangelism among those not attending church? What has been his experience in starting a new church? Did he try and fail or not even try? If his goal is to plant churches in another country, cannot the sending church expect him to experience planting a church among his own people first?

This evaluation must be done by the national church *without* the influence of Western missionaries. National Christians are aware of character traits and motivations for travel abroad that a foreigner cannot discern. With an increasing interest in Asia for missions, many young people are volunteering so the church needs to establish policies for acceptance. A missionary candidate who has proven his commitment and ability, should be properly recognized by his sending church. This implies a mutual responsibility of prayer, finances and correspondence, which will be developed in a later section.

6) *Physical and emotional qualifications:* High schools, colleges, and the military all require a physical examination before accpeting the applicant. The reasons for this are obvious. Mission societies have additional reasons to be careful about the health of their applicants. Life on the mission field is usually more strenuous than life at home. Some countries have a humid climate, poor food and contagious diseases. Some families may live a long distance from medical facilities.

Missions are especially concerned about signs of high blood pressure, impaired sight or hearing, nervous disorders, allergies etc. Physical deformities usually disqualify the applicant. The applicant doesn't need to have a near-perfect physique, but he must have a good, consistent, all-round health record. If the applicant is married, his family also needs a physical examination.

Physical health is easier to examine than emotional health. Unfortunately some physically strong missionaries are unprepared to cope with unexpected emotional pressures. This became identified as "culture shock" and in extreme situations resulted in a nervous breakdown. Fortunately, we now have the benefit of added research in this vital area of our life.

I am indebted to Wayne T. Dye for many of the following ideas from his article "Stress-Producing Factors in Cultural Adjustment" (1974:61-77). The term "culture shock" implies something severe but brief. Dye calls this "culture confusion"

as this feeling of total helplessness experienced in a new
culture is soon over. However "culture stress" results from
change to a new way of living and lasts many years.

Stress is *increased* by the following factors:

1) Involvement: the emphasis is upon psychological
   presence in a cross-cultural situation with experiences as learning another language or working
   with nationals.
2) Value difference; not problems with central Christian values, but cultural values as cleanliness,
   sense of responsibility, use of time, etc.
3) Frustration: problems that arise from dealing with
   people of a new culture that hinder the work. This
   frustration builds negative attitudes toward the
   new culture and increases inner resistance to acculturation.
4) Temperament differences; individual differences in
   temperament and personality cause each individual
   to be affected differently by the same cross-
   cultural situation.

Dye continues by giving factors that *decrease* stress as
follows:

1) Acceptance; recognition of the host culture as a valid
   way of life for them.
2) Communication; interaction with those with whom we
   can relax reduces loneliness and a sense of isolation
   from one's own kind.
3) Emotional security; acculturation involves a change
   in one's personality with added stress on those with
   inferiority feelings.
4) Inner spiritual resources; the power of Christ and
   His Spirit are available but don't really help until
   experienced by the individual.

An individual can easily cope with a certain amount of
stress. Some psychologists say a man needs a moderate amount of
tension to work productively (Spradley and Phillips 1972:
520). But as stress increases, more and more creative energy
must be used to handle it. An overload can cause a breakdown.
It is important to learn how to decrease stress *before* going
to another country. Significant factors are: 1) recognize that
stress is inevitable and comes to everybody; 2) learn ways to
escape temporarily by relaxation with reading, music, sports,
rest days and vacations; 3) decrease frustration by establishing realistic goals that can be achieved; 4) build acceptance

and appreciation of cultural values which are valid to others;
5) improve communication by learning the language even though
this discipline will temporarily add stress; and 6) strengthen
emotional security by self-acceptance, acceptance of God's
forgiveness and promises, and acceptance of encouragement from
one's colleagues. The popularity of *I'm O.K. You're O.K.*
(Harris 1967) indicates how this relates to a felt need. Though
it is not a Christian book, it can be helpful to many Christians
who feel a need for emotional growth.

As acculturation is faced in these ways, one can become a
versatile person able to live happily in a cross-cultural situation. Instead of fear of becoming less, such a person is becoming a kind of world citizen, a more capable human being.
Recognition of factors affecting emotional health have a direct
relationship to the life and ministry of a Christian worker.
These need to be studied and practised *before* going to another
country.

7) *The family unit:* Another aspect of effective cross-cultural
workers is the selection of families and/or single adults. In
the missionary body the women outnumber the men three to two
(Kane 1974:60). Single men or women have both advantages and
disadvantages. The necessary financial support for a single
person has the advantage of increased mobility. The single
people often have unusual ability and dedication, overcoming
social and family pressures in order to get to the foreign field.
Disadvantages include a degree of loneliness, depending upon
their assignment and their personality. In some cultures a certain stigma is associated with those not married. However, single
people have made significant contributions to the missionary movement.

A married man may choose the missionary vocation as a career
making possible an accumulation of years of experience. The
"womens-lib" movement has not yet made an impact in Asia, so
the men continue to carry much authority and responsibility. The
nationals are interested in the "family witness" which can reduce
various barriers to communication. The family provides necessary
social life and fellowship, reducing feelings of loneliness. Disadvantages are the increased expense for travel and living in
another country, less mobility to "reap responsive fields," and
difficulties in acquiring proper schooling for the children.

The history of missions contains records of great accom-
plishments by individuals not "qualified" according to policies
and regulations of certain mission boards. While one cannot
limit the power of God, faithful stewardship requires certain
standards for missionary candidates. However the most capable
missionary can be unfruitful if there is some unconfessed sin
in his life.

Conclusion:

I have stated the importance of effective cross-cultural workers as a necessary ingredient of a viable missionary movement in Asia. It is possible for missiologists to think that Third World missionaries provide a quick and and easy way for world evangelization. I have referred to the encouraging information collected by Wong, Larson and Pentecost, reporting 2,994 missionaries sent by 211 agencies in 47 different countries (1973:107). However, this report does not state the number doing evangelism in a similar culture in their own country, (HM-2), evangelism in a radically different culture within their own country (HM-3) or evangelism of their own people in other countries (FM-1).

Though many agencies did not respond to the 1972 survey, some of the agencies that reported then no longer have missionaries *on the field* in 1976. Korea reported seven agencies with 33 missionaries in nine countries (West Pakistan, Brunei, Hong Kong, Thailand, Malaysia, Bolivia, Taiwan and Ethiopia). By 1976 missionaries had left West Pakistan, Hong Kong, Malaysia (Sarawak) and Ethiopia and were *not* replaced. In 1974 two new missionary couples were sent to Bangladesh (FM-3) and to Brazil (FM-1). The total number of Korean foreign missionaries *decreased,* especially those doing FM-2 and FM-3 missionary work. For purposes of comparison, I am not including a large number of lay-missionaries sent by the University Bible Fellowship in Seoul as they were not included in the earlier survey by Wong, Larson and Pentecost. Neither do I list Korean pastors working in the United States and Canada as most of them came as immigrants and have become self-supporting.

Though someone may rearrange these statistics in slightly different ways, I know of three large Presbyterian churches in Korea today *ready* to send missionaries if qualified people were available. Among the thousands of Korean Christians, there must be scores of missionary candidates available if the qualifications were carefully explained. Recognizing the increasing responsiveness to the Christian message in Asia, more qualified workers must be recruited to take the gospel across linguistic, racial, geographical and cultural barriers.

5
Effective Sending Churches

Having established the necessity of qualified workers for cross-cultural evangelism, there arises another vital issue. How are these workers to be sent? Are missionaries sent by churches, by para-church mission organizations, or by both? What does the New Testament teach? What can be learned from studying a history of the expansion of Christianity? Are methods effective in the Western world equally effective in the non-Western world? The answers to these questions will affect strategy of Third World Missions for world evangelization.

Who really sent the first missionaries? The usual response is, "The church at Antioch." Harold R. Cook answers this question with a careful exegesis of Acts 13:1-4 and Acts 14:27 (1975:233-239). He warns of the danger of *implying* many ideas not in the text. Acts 13 gives the names of the prophets and teachers ministering in the church at Antioch. While they were worshipping and fasting, the Holy Spirit told them He had called two of their number for a special task. So after the five fasted and prayed, the other three laid hands on Barnabas and Saul and sent them on their mission.

Cook notes that there is no evidence that the church was involved in this action. Neither is there indication that these men were acting on behalf of the church. The laying on of hands seems to indicate giving God's blessing rather than an authoritative appointment by the church.

The phrase "They sent them away" (Acts 13:3) seems to imply
authority but this English translation lacks the clarity of the
original Greek. Cook says:

> There are three basic verbs in Greek that
> are most commonly translated "send" in Eng-
> lish. Two of them are almost synonymous:
> "pempo" and "apostello." The first means
> simply "sent"--any sort of sending. The
> second means "send forth" and is the verb
> from which the noun "apostle" comes. "Apo-
> stello" is used in Acts 13:4, where Luke says
> that they were "sent forth by the Holy Spirit"
> on their first missionary journey.
> But the verb in verse 3 is neither of these.
> It is a different verb, "apoluo," which means
> literally "release" or "dismiss." This verb
> is *never once* used in the sense of an authori-
> tative sending of individuals on a mission,
> or with a task to perform. So it really
> should be translated, "they let them go,"
> or more freely, "they wished them God-speed"
> (1975:236).

But some will insist, "Didn't Paul and Barnabas feel themselves answerable to the church at Antioch, when they made a
report to it about their missionary work?"

This depends upon the meaning implied in "answerable to the
church." It is true that Paul was eager to report what God had
done among the Gentiles. The initiative seems to be upon Paul
as the text says, "they...gathered the church together" (Acts
14:27). This can hardly be understood as a 20th century missionary being called by the church to give an account of his work.

If the church at Antioch was a missionary sending agency,
surely there would be some further evidence of its missionary
activity after this one trip. But such evidence is completely
lacking. This New Testament passage which is often used to support the claim that the organized church is the only scriptural-
ly authorized missionary sending agency offers no support.

Cook concludes this emphasis by saying, "In the first five
centuries of the Christian era I have been unable to find any
instance where the church, as a church, ever officially designated and sent out missionaries" (1975:237). Adolf von Harnack
says something very similar: "During the first centuries there
is no evidence whatever for organized missions by individual
churches; such were not on the horizon" (1904-05:486).

There is also evidence that the church at Antioch was not
equipped to act as a missionary sending agency. It probably was
not an organized body. There is no record that they had a pastor, bishop, elders or other church officials. It probably was
not a single congregation but a fellowship of many small groups
meeting in individual homes.

Cook re-emphasizes his point saying:

> So the idea that the local church is the
> divinely ordained missionary sending agency
> finds absolutely no support in the Scriptures.
> Who, then, does send the missionaries? Acts
> 13:4 leaves us in no doubt: the Holy Spirit
> (1975:238).

It is true that the Holy Spirit sent Philip to the Ethiopian
eunuch (Acts 8:29). He sent Peter to Cornelius (Acts 11:2).
He kept Paul from going into Bithynia (Acts 16:7) but led him
to Macedonia (v.10). Cook thinks it strange that we have so
little confidence in the Holy Spirit. Stranger still is our
failure to see in history how the organized church has hindered rather than stimulated the work. Early missionary work
was not highly organized but many Christians voluntarily shared
their faith with others. Often Christians traveled at their own
expense to spread the gospel.

This provocative article concludes by saying it is *not* wrong
for the church to send out missionaries. Rather, Cook says:

> Our only contention in this article is that
> it is *wrong* to claim that the organized
> church is *the one agency* prescribed in the
> New Testament *for sending of missionaries*.
> On the contrary, the one indispensable is
> the *sending by the Holy Spirit*. If the
> *church* acts in accord with the Holy Spirit,
> well and good. But if not, the Spirit will
> still send forth His missionaries, whether
> *individually,* as in the early centuries, or
> through *independent societies,* as in more
> recent years. These societies are not an
> aberration, as some would have us believe.
> Rather, they are modern attempts (often
> faulty, to be sure) to follow the scriptural
> principle of letting the Spirit do the send-
> ing as in the early days (1975:239, italics
> are mine).

Though this emphasis upon the Holy Spirit sending out missionaries is a necessary corrective to complex human organizations, many questions still remain. Why were so few Protestant missionaries sent out during the 300 years following the Reformation? What are the characteristics of a *church* that "acts in accord with the Holy Spirit?" How *recent* is this "new" movement? How does one describe a society that follows "the scriptural principle of letting the Spirit do the sending as in the early days?"

Cook has a valid point in emphasizing the fact that missionaries are sent by the Spirit. But the church is a body of believers indwelt by the Holy Spirit. Without churches, we could hardly expect the world to be evangelized today.

World evangelization was the command given to the early Christians, not to an organization. They were to be witnesses, "both in Jerusalem, *and* in all Judea, *and* in Samaria, *and* unto the uttermost part of the earth" (Acts 1:8). God's concern for the *world* was clearly given to the early church. Peter was a leader, who preached the gospel to the Jews, and Paul received the missionary gift and preached to the Gentiles.

These Christians crossed *social* and *psychological* barriers of fear as they boldly preached to the Jews who had crucified Jesus. Barriers of *prejudice* were crossed to reach the Samaritans. *Cultural* barriers were overcome as Paul contacted the Gentiles. *Geographical, linguistic* and *political* barriers were crossed as they took the gospel to people in other countries. This mandate was clearly understood and obeyed by the New Testament church.

Paul thanked God continually for the church at Thessalonica. Though little is said about their organization, it was a "missionary church." In the *Living Bible*, Taylor paraphrases I Thes. 1:7-9 where Paul said, "You yourselves became an example to all the other Christians in Greece. And now the Word of the Lord has spread out from you to others everywhere, far beyond your boundaries, for wherever we go we find people telling us about your remarkable faith in God. We don't need to tell them about it, for they keep telling us about the wonderful welcome you gave us, and how you turned away from your idols to God so that now the living and true God only is your Master."

Though the 20th century has vast differences from the first century, our mandate is still the same. Man has basic, universal needs that can be satisfied only with the gospel. This message is still the power of God able to change lives. This gospel message is communicated to others by Christians filled and led by the Holy Spirit.

Do Christians witness only as individuals or as teams
or as groups or in some other way? The New Testament gives
structures for effective missionary work. During the nearly
2,000 years of church history, there are periods of great
missionary movements and periods of apparent indifference to
the Great Commission. This can be partially explained by the
presence or absence of certain *structures*.

The Necessity of Structures:

In *The Warp and the Woof*, Ralph D. Winter shows that "the
human community, and also the Christian movement, are held together by two different *kinds* of structures, which together express both the unity and the diversity of the whole" (1970:3).
He continues this explanation with an analogy of fabric. The
warp of a fabric is the longitudinal threading and the woof is
the lateral threading. One may be more visible than the other
depending upon the weaving technique employed, but *both* are
utterly essential.

Society is held together by two kinds of structures. The
structures of *civil government* are territorially defined, are
erected "vertically" over a given territory, and have a "general
mission" affecting every citizen. The structures of *private enterprise* involve only part of the people and usually conduct a
very specific mission. Their functions cut "horizontally" across
the civil structures even though they are evaluated and monitor-
ed by the civil structures.

Two similar kinds of structures hold the Christian movement
together. In "The Anatomy of the Christian Mission" (1969) Winter
uses the "vertical" to describe the *church* structures and the
"horizontal" to describe organizations, like the women's associations, youth groups, mission societies, etc. which cut
"horizontally" across the "vertical" church structures. Both
of these structures have the potential of helping or hurting
each other. The use and understanding of these two basic structures will affect the strategy of support and the strategy of
overseas operations.

Definition and use of Modality and Sodality:

In "The Warp and the Woof of the Christian Movement" Winter
introduces two technical terms: *modality* and *sodality*.

> The vertical church or civil structures
> are now called *modalities,* and the horizon-
> tal religious or secular enterprises are
> called *sodalities*...planners and design-
> ers in the Christian movement must be alert
> to the need for both kinds of structures;
> that the health of the one depends on the
> health of the other (1970:5).

During the All-Asia Mission Consultation in Seoul in 1973, Winter used the concepts of "Modality" and "Sodality" to refer to "The Two Structures of God's Redemptive Mission" (1974a:121-139). A clear understanding of these two structures gives insight essential at this point and Winter's article will be briefly summarized in what follows.

The New Testament church is basically a Christian synagogue. Paul's missionary work consisted primarily of going to synagogues scattered across the Roman Empire, and making clear to the Jewish believers that the Messiah had come in Jesus Christ. Christ had authority greater than Moses and this made possible the winning of Gentiles without forcing upon them any literal cultural adaptation to the ritual provisions of the Mosaic Law. An outward novelty of Paul's work was the development of wholly new synagogues that were not only Christian but Greek.

Winter states that many Jewish evangelists went before Paul all over the Empire. Jesus described these as people "traversing land and sea to make a single proselyte." Paul followed their path, built on their efforts and went beyond them with the gospel he preached. The gospel allowed the Greeks still to be Greeks and not be circumcised and culturally assimilated into the Jewish way of life. The *first structure* was later to be called the New Testament *church*.

The New Testament has little to say about the *second structure* used by the Jewish proselytes as they operated all over the Roman Empire. We can assume that Paul used somewhat the same procedure. While ministering in the church at Antioch, Paul and Barnabas were called by God to a special ministry. They were sent out by the Holy Spirit. This *evangelistic team* was led by the Holy Spirit and was economically self-sufficient when necessary. On occasions it was dependent on other churches that had arisen as a result of his evangelistic labors. *Paul's team* consisted of Christians who *voluntarily became members*. Their ministry was more than an extended outreach of the Antioch church. It was a separate structure. It is the *second of the two redemptive structures* in New Testament times.

In the Roman culture we see development of the *diocese* within which *parishes* were formed on a local level. The monastic tradition appeared in its various early forms but probably had no connection with Paul's evangelistic band. Though most Protestants have an in-built prejudice against the *monastic structure,* they had a significant part in the vital continuity of the Christian tradition across the centuries. An illustration of their importance would be recognition of the relationship between Gregory the Great and Augustine of Canterbury. Though

Gregory was powerful as bishop of the diocese of Rome, *he had
no church structure for sending a missionary to England* where
Celtic Christianity had been deeply wounded by the invasion of
Saxon warriors from the continent.

Winter summarizes these concepts and says:

> Let us now call the synagogue and diocese
> *modalities* and the missionary band and monas-
> tery, *sodalities*...a modality is a structured
> fellowship in which there is no distinction of
> sex or age, while a sodality is a structured
> fellowship in which membership involves an
> adult second decision beyond modality member-
> ship and is limited by either sex or age or
> marital status. In this use of terms, both
> the *denomination* and the local *congregation*
> are modalities, while a mission agency or a
> local men's club are sodalities (1974a:127).

The Antioch church would be described as a *modality* and
Paul's evangelistic band as a *sodality*. The church (modality)
included men and women of all ages while Paul's evangelistic
band (sodality) was a group of *men* who decided to join for a
special purpose. A men's association, women's missionary organization, committee for evangelism are all examples of sodalities *within* a modality (the church).

A Reformation Mistake:

During the Reformation, Luther abandoned both the diocesan
structure and the monastic orders. The Lutheran diocesan structure evantually developed, *but the sodalities were omitted*.
Winter says:

> This omission, in my evaluation, represents
> the greatest error of the Reformation and the
> greatest weakness of the resulting Protes-
> tant tradition. Had it not been for the so-
> called Pietist movement, the Protestants
> would have been totally devoid of any organ-
> ized renewing structures within their tradi-
> tion. The Pietist traditon...was very de-
> finitely a *sodality* inasmuch as it was a case
> of adults meeting together and commiting
> themselves to new beginnings and higher goals
> as Christians without conflicting with the
> stated meetings of the existing church. You
> can see this phenomena very clearly in the case
> of the work of John Wesley: he absolutely pro-
> hibited any abandonment of the parish churches.

You can see this in the widely influential
so-called East African Revival, which has
now involved a million people but has very
carefully avoided any clash with the func-
tioning of local churches. Rather, the
churches that have not fought against this
movement have been greatly blessed in it
(1974a:131).

The Protestants had no mechanism for missions for almost
300 years until William Carey proposed "the use of *means* for
the conversion of the heathen." His key word *means* refers
specifically to the need for a *sodality,* for the organized
initiative of the warmhearted. The resulting Baptist Missionary Society is one of the most significant organizational developments in the Protestant tradition: it set off a rush to
the use of this kind of "means" for the conversion of the heathen,
and we find in the next few years a number of *societies* forming
along similar lines.

Almost all mission efforts in the nineteenth century,
whether they were sponsored by interdenominational boards or
denominational boards, were substantially the work of initiatives
that were independent of the ecclesiastical structures to which
they were related. There seemed to be two opposing streams of
influence toward the latter half of the nineteenth century which
nevertheless did not completely nullify each other.

Winter sees Protestant blindness about the need for mission
sodalities as a tragic influence in mission work today. *Protestants are modality-minded,* and their missions tend to think
that merely modalities, e.g. churches, need to be established.
Mission agencies (even those that were the most independent from
churches) tend to see their mission work simply as establishing
churches (modalities) rather than also planting new missions
(sodalities) in other lands.

There can be many different relationships between the
modality and sodality. The *efficient organization* of a mission
society (sodality) *properly related to the church* (modality) is
of *primary importance* for effective *cross-cultural missions.*
The relationships vary in different countries depending upon the
nature of the church. Most Christians recognize the need of new
believers becoming baptized members of a local church. Few
Protestants, even missionaries, realize the vital necessity of
a sodality in order for the church to accomplish the primary
task of evangelism.

Winter gives four illustrations of church (modality) -
mission (sodality) relationships (1974b:21).

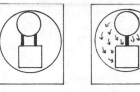  

Type A   Type B   Type C   Type D

Diagram 5:1. Types of church (modality) -
mission (sodality) relationships.

The circle represents the church, the square represents
the mission. The left solid line in Type A indicates the mission being administered by a board appointed by the church, and
the solid line on the right represents a unified budget which
prevents local churches from affecting the percentage of the
church budget that goes to missions. The small arrows indicate
unstructured relationships between the churches and missions,
especially concerning the provision of money for missions.

In Type A the church (modality) strictly controls the mission
(sodality). In Type B the church also controls the mission, but
the budget is flexible. In Type C the church has no direct control of the mission but gives considerable financial help, and in
Type D the church has no control of the mission. In America, the
Interdenominational Foreign Mission Association (IFMA) affiliated
missions are type D, the Evangelical Foreign Missions Association
(EFMA) affiliated missions are represented by all four types,
while the Division of Overseas Ministries (DOM) of the National
Council includes mainly Type A structures.

What type of church-mission structures are best for Third
World Missions? My current research of Asian Missionary societies
indicates that there is a great variety in administration and fin-
cing. I have found no example of Type A or Type C in Asia. Many
are Type D as the Japan Committee - Wycliffe Bible Translators,
the Friends' Missionary Prayer Band, the Philippine Missionary
Fellowship and others.

Many missions in Korea are Type B. The church denominations
are large enough to have their own missionary societies. Though
the mission policy and control is strongly church oriented (as
represented by the solid line), the financial support is not
rigidly controlled (as represented by the small arrows). Mission giving is usually in response to specific projects. Certain
local congregations or districts will provide designated funds

for missions, administered through the missions committee of the
general assembly or denominational headquarters. Though denominational missions in Korea have certain advantages, there is need
for interdenominational cooperation for a missionary training
program. There is also need for greater liason in assigning missionaries to other countries. If responsible and effective mission
programs become established in Korea, the congregations will respond if challenged by leaders with faith and vision.

The sodality (mission) is the *means* for carrying the gospel
to other countries. Though there are degrees of mission autonomy,
the sodality is dependent upon the church. Dr. McGavran says:

> The church, or rather the Christians, are
> the very ones who are evangelizing the world.
> Para-church organizations--like interdenomina-
> tional missionary societies--rest on the church.
> The churches support them. The churches pray
> for them. The churches generate the young
> people who dedicate their lives to the propa-
> gation of the gospel. Back of every success-
> ful missionary, there is usually a church in
> which he grew to Christian manhood or Chris-
> tian womanhood. The successful missionary,
> as he goes abroad, begins new churches. The
> role of the church in the evangelization of
> the world is very great (1973:38).

A Vision is Needed:

But how can Asian pastors get a world vision of missions
and communicate this to their members? The importance of missions
in both the Old and New Testaments must be taught. God spoke
to Abram, "And I will bless them that bless thee, and curse him
that curseth thee: and in thee shall all families of the earth
be blessed" (Genesis 12:3). God's promise to Abram was not only
to bless his descendants but all the families of the earth.

The same promise was repeated to Isaac with the words
"...in thy seed shall all the nations of the earth be blessed"
(Genesis 28:14).

Isaiah 45:22 states, "Look unto Me, and be ye saved, all
the ends of the earth: for I am God, and there is none else."
Thus from the beginning the promise of blessing through Messiah
was intended to include the *whole world*. When we come to the
New Testament, this is confirmed. On the very night when Jesus
was born in Bethlehem, the angel of the Lord said unto the shep-
herds, "Fear not: for, behold, I bring you good tidings of great
joy, which shall be to *all people*" (Luke 2:10). God loves *the
world*, not just one nation. He gave His only Son for the whole

world (John 3:16).

Addressing the All-Asia Consultation at Seoul in 1973,
Kyung Chik Han said:

> Home missions is not enough; it must go
> together with world missions. No matter
> how young a church might be, her mission
> is to preach the Gospel to all the world.
> I am glad to note the fact that when the
> Presbyterian Church in Korea was first
> organized in the year of 1912, its
> leaders not only sent a missionary to
> Cheju Island which is the largest and the
> most remote island of Korea, but they also
> sent three missionaries to Shantung, China.
> I think this was in harmony with the best
> traditions of the Christian Church. It
> also reflected literal obedience to the
> Great Commission of Christ.
>
> We are persuaded that any church in any
> land, or age, when faithful to this world-
> wide task is also greatly blessed in turn
> by its missionary activities. On the other
> hand, when a church is so near-sighted and
> introverted that she is preoccupied with
> her own affairs, such a church never grows.
> And it does not receive the blessing of God.
>
> Most churches in Asia are called younger
> churches. They are the products of the
> missionary obedience of the church in Europe
> and America. Most of these younger churches,
> I suppose, are not quite self-supporting
> churches in the strict sense. That is, most
> of them still receive aid in one way or other
> from the mother churches. Does this not reflect
> the fact that they have still to become mis-
> sion-minded churches? When they do they will
> be blessed by God. Truly indigenous and truly
> mission-minded churches seem to be not only
> self-governing, but self-supporting as well
> (1973a:35).

Pastor Cheng has a missionary vision and communicates it
to his congregation in the Grace Gospel Church in Manila,
Philippines. This church supports 46 missionaries (Asian Outreach 1974). Such a "vision is caught, not taught." Cheng
teaches his people, "Where there is no vision, the people perish"
(Proverbs 29:18). The Living Bible uses the phrase, "The people

run wild." Running wild means a lack of control among individuals
and confusion in a group. Cheng says, "I have seen a church
blessed by God with wealth, and with a large membership, but
lacking missionary vision. As a result, the members were at odds
with each other. Not until they rose up to launch a missionary
program at home and abroad did all the darkness disappear" (April,
1974).

Where there is no vision, there is no work. Cheng relates
the experience of Wu Yung on a speaking tour in Europe. He visited
a small church with 30 or 40 attending the service. Yet that church
had sent out three missionaries to the Far East. Mr. Wu Yung was
greatly impressed for this church was just as small as many of the
churches in Taiwan. After returning to Taiwan, he initiated the
founding of a missionary society called "Chinese Missions Overseas."

Progress in World Evangelization:

Is there steady progress toward the goal of world evangelization? With recent famines and droughts in several countries,
there is a new concern for the "population explosion," especially
in certain developing countries in the Third World. There are today in India more non-Christians than when William Carey left England for India in 1792. However, since that time, more people have
been won to Christ and more Christian churches have been planted
in the world than in the preceding 1792 years combined. C. Peter
Wagner in "A Bicentennial View: Missions in America's Third
Century" says, "By a conservative estimate, 55,000 people are now
becoming Christians every day and 1,400 new Christian churches
are planted every week" (1976:3).

Citing information from Ralph Winter in *Evangelical Missions
Quarterly* (January 1974b) Wagner continues his optimistic view
for the future.

> Current trends are highly encouraging.
> Pessimists might point out that every
> year there are more non-Christians in the
> world, and this is true. They also could
> dwell on the fact that, worldwide, the
> percentage of Christians to total popu-
> lation shows little increase in recent
> years. But this is not the most signi-
> ficant kind of date for a current assess-
> ment of the progress of Christian missions.
>
> The bulk of the 2.7 billion unreached peoples
> of the world are to be found in Asia and
> Africa. While much evangelization needs to
> be done among the masses of nominal Christians

in Europe, North and South America and
Oceania, the progress of Christian mis-
sions must be tested worldwide, where the
Christian message is impacting non-Christians.

According to the best information we have, the
progress has been dramatic and the *percentage*
of Christians to total population in Africa
and Asia is rising rapidly. For example, in
1900 in Asia, there were 75 non-Christians for
every Christian. This year there are only 22.
In Africa in 1900 there were 28 non-Christians
for every Christian, but today there are only
2.5.

Or to look at it from a slightly different
perspective, let's picture a group of 100
Christians in Asia and another group of 100
non-Christians, both back in 1900. Today
that group of Christians would have grown to
870 but the non-Christians would have grown
only to 240.

Likewise, in Africa. One hundred Christians
in 1900 would now be 2,900, but 100 non-
Christians would be only 250. In fact, by the
end of the first quarter of century three, we
can reasonably expect that the majority of
Africans will be Christians (1976:3).

Ralph D. Winter helps to clarify our mission vision in
"Seeing the Task Graphically" (1974b:16). In Diagram 5:2.
Winter shows the growth of non-Christians in Africa and Asia from
1965 to 1985.

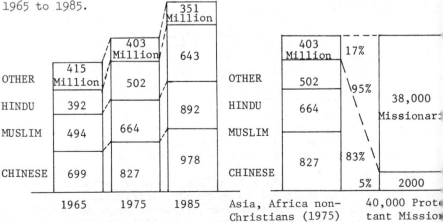

Diagram 5:2. Growth of non-   Diagram 5:3.
Christians in Africa & Asia

Diagram 5:3 shows the amazing fact that the 403 million non-Christians, who are 17 percent of the task, are the object or the attention of 38,000 missionaries who are 95 percent of the force. Meanwhile, the Hindu, Muslim and Chinese blocks, some 1,993 million people, are the object of the attention of only 7 percent of the missionary force.

Winter exclaims, "Please do not suppose that too many missionaries are devoted to the 403 million! The major lesson here is that we need to exert more effort on behalf of the bigger problem: if it is *reasonable* (and we believe it is) to send 38,000 missionaries (from all Protestant sources) to 403 million people, then it is *unreasonable* to send only 2,000 to reach 1,993 million. If we were to give the larger group equal effort per million, it would require 212,000 missionaries--almost 100 times as many as the 2,000 we are now sending!" (1974b:17).

Strategy for Evangelism:

Recognizing the rapid growth of new Christians and the establishment of new churches and the large percentage still unreached, the question is who will take the gospel to these millions of non-Christians in Africa, Asia and the rest of the world? A further question concerns the most effective structure to accomplish this mission.

Winter repeatedly states that "87 percent of the non-Christians are in the cross-cultural category" and cannot be reached by near-neighbor evangelism (1974c:230). Donald McGavran, referring to the International Congress on World Evangelization, wrote that "Dr. Winter proved beyond any reasonable doubt that in the world today 2,700,000,000 men and women cannot hear the gospel by "near-neighbor evangelism" (1974d:4). Many accept this as an unchallengable theorem in the School of World Mission at Fuller Theological Seminary in Pasadena, California. The task of reaching these people seems almost too complicated and difficult to begin. However, Winter emphasizes that "Two thousand years give us only one answer: the para-church structure" (1974b:12).

Confusion arises from a misunderstanding of Winter's use of the term "near-neighbor evangelism." This term refers to those in our *same* culture, as extended family members and neighbors, who can be won to Christ *without* crossing cultural barriers. These people may be geographically "near" or "far." Geography is not a factor in this cross-cultural emphasis.

We miss the point of the above quotation if we understand "near-neighbor" to refer not to a friendly neighbor, but to hostile people, with a different ethnic background. A church has not yet been established in their village, tribe or homogeneous unit. Without the existence of a local church, it is impossible for these people to be evangelized by the church. The weakness is not necessarily the failure of the local church to reach out, but the absence of churches among this particular group in society.

Charles R. Taber, Visiting Professor of World Mission and Anthropology at Milligan College and a former missionary in Ghana, Africa, stresses the importance of the national church in his article "Unevangelized Peoples: Whose Responsibility?" (1974: 7-9). His concern is one of missionary principle and strategy: whose primary responsibility is it to evangelize these peoples, that of the churches which already exist within the national boundaries, or that of the traditional missionary sending Western churches?

In an article looking back on the Consultation on Frontier Mission held in Chicago in December 1972, Taber recalls arguing strongly "that the *primary* responsibility belonged to the national churches, and that independent missionary initiatives from the West without prior consultation and cooperation with existing national churches were to be avoided whenever possible. In the subsequent discussion, Dr. Winter took issue with me, arguing that in many cases it would be more appropriate and effective to rely on independent Western initiatives" (1974:7). Taber then summarizes Winter's key points as follows:

1. It is a fact of observation that in many of the cases, the problem has existed for many years without the national churches showing any signs of accepting it as a challenge or a responsibility. Many national churches are totally indifferent or even hostile to the other ethnic groups within their national boundaries. In the face of such great need and apparent apathy, dare we stand around and miss ripe opportunities out of exaggerated deference to churches lacking in missionary vision?

2. National boundaries in much of the Third World, notably in Africa, are quite arbitrary and incoherent from an ethnic point of view. A single national state may contain very diverse ethnic groups, whose forced coexistence within the state reflects no sense of unity or even reasonable cordiality between them.

3. Most ethnic groups which are both quite different and geographically contiguous have long traditions of bitter enmity, hatred, and mutual contempt which would constitute a great barrier rather than a potential bridge for evangelism.

4. In many cases, people from entirely outside the
    situation, who have no vested interests or feelings
    in the age-old conflicts, can more effectively
    reach unevangelized peoples than their hostile
    neighbors, even though the latter be fervent
    Christians (1974:8).

Taber recognizes a great deal of truth in these points.
Neighboring people are often enemies; traditional enemies have
often been forced to coexist in a single state, churches within
one population are frequently indifferent to their neighbors
and in some cases Western missionaries have been able to do jobs
that nationals were either unable or unwilling to do. Taber
(as would Winter) argues against this position as an *exclusive*
or *primary* approach. Taber's reasons are as follows:

1. National self-consciousness and unity, although by
    no means universal today, are definitely the trend
    of the future, and ought to be respected wherever
    possible.

2. There is quite an assortment of unevangelized or
    inadequately evangelized enclaves in our own country,
    and existing churches are either indifferent to them
    or ineffectual in reaching them. In this situation,
    is it our expectation that Africans, Asians or Latin
    Americans should come here on their own initiative,
    without contact or cooperation with existing Ameri-
    can churches, to do the job we are not doing? (Here
    Winter would say "yes").

3. Growing anti-Western feelings are rapidly placing
    a question mark in many countries over purely
    Western initiatives, especially when these can be
    interpreted as trespassing on the domain of exist-
    ing and recognized national bodies. My experience
    and observation also led me to doubt that the racial
    and cultural barriers between Americans and the un-
    reached peoples of the Third World are any easier
    to surmount than those between neighbor-enemies.

4. Evangelism across ethnic boundaries does not
    require massive people-to-people contacts. All
    that is initially required is that one or two
    individuals who have the gospel make effective
    contact across the barrier. The classic instance
    was the Apostle Paul. Who could have guessed
    from his fanatically orthodox Pharisaical back-
    ground that he would be the effective apostle to
    the Gentiles...in the first century church?

It seems to me that accepting as an unchanging
given the persistence after conversion of a historic enmity belittles the transforming power of
the Holy Spirit.

5. Theologically, this point of view represents a
   deficient view of the national church. The Church
   Growth Movement has a high view of the church. I
   find it hard to reconcile this with the position
   that, although the goal of mission is to establish
   indigenous churches, it is itself a kind of extra-
   ecclesiastical, self-impelled activity. I am all
   for a pragmatic recognition of realities, but this
   must not be at the cost of losing sight of the ultimately supernatural character of the church (1974:
   9).

Taber wisely recognizes that his difference from Winter's
comments at the Consultation is partly a matter of *emphasis* and
different field *experiences*. No longer suggesting less emphasis
upon Western missions, Taber now is suggesting that "in a context where national churches do exist, the sending of Western
missionaries to open new fields ought not to be an automatic
reflex, nor ought it to take place at all without an accompany-
ing effort to establish close and cordial relations with national
churches" (1974:9). To this Winter would agree, but he would not
regard the denominational structures any more supernatural than
the so-called "para-church structures."

George W. Peters, Professor of Missions at the Dallas
Theological Seminary supports Taber's view and emphasizes evange-
ism through the church. Speaking at Lausanne he said:

> According to the divine order...*the key to
> church renewal of any kind is the leader-
> ship and the pastor*. Here the fire ought
> to begin to burn, from here it most rapidly
> and most progressively spreads.
>
> There is another divine ideal. *The church is
> God's supreme agent of evangelism*...we are all
> deeply concerned about and committed to the
> evangelization of the world...How is this to
> be accomplished? Automatically we are think-
> ing of mission societies and missionaries will
> be demanded for years to come. They must
> send, they must go!
>
> However, it must be emphasized with equal force
> that the world will not be evangelized solely

or mainly by mission agencies and professional
missionaries. The biblical and main key is
the local church mobilized and trained in evangelism. The *mission agency and the missionary
are the advance guard to establish an outpost.*
They are the supplement of the church in world
evangelism. This is a principle that must be
taught and preached until it will sink into
the fiber of the life of the church (1974:
201 italics are mine).

I believe the difference between Winter and others such
as Taber and Peters is primarily one of emphasis and of terminology. Cross-cultural missions are imperative, "the advance
guard to establish an outpost," consisting of evangelizing
churches. Instead of an "either-or" emphasis of either missions
or churches to do cross-cultural evangelism, it must be "both-
and."

Actually, this is Winter's conviction, though it may not have
been clearly explained earlier, as evidenced by the differing
interpretations of other missiologists. At Lausanne Winter said:

In summary, the master pattern of the expansion
of the Christian movement is first for special
E-2 and E-3 efforts to cross cultural barriers
into new communities and to establish strong,
on-going, vigorously evangelizing denominations,
and then for that national church to carry the
work forward on the really high-powered E-1
level. We are thus forced to believe that
until every tribe and tongue has a strong,
powerfully evangelizing church in it, and thus,
an E-1 witness within it, E-2 and E-3 efforts
coming from outside are still essential and
highly urgent" (1974c:216).

Mission/Church Relationships:

The relationship of the national church with foreign missions
is, therefore, not a topic for mere theoretical speculation
or academic discussion. This relationship affects the growth
of the church and the evangelization of the world. Recognizing
the need for more missions to unevangelized "peoples" it is also
true that some missions have stayed too long in a country and
some left too soon. What is the right relationship?

There is no *one* relationship that is ideal for every
situation. Some missions are large and others are small.

Some have historically emphasized evangelism and others have concentrated on developing an indigenous church. Some missions have a large budget and others have a budget that is comparatively small.

Some populations are receptive to the gospel and the church is growing. In other countries the government has a firm policy restricting visas and the work missionaries can do. Some countries are closed to missionaries from certain nations and some do not permit foreign missionaries from either the East or the West.

Churches are different in various countries. Some are indigenous and growing while others are indigenous and not growing. Some churches may still be dependent upon financial help from the West. Some areas may have many churches and few mission established institutions but the opposite is often true. If the church gained control of all mission properties, they could not even pay the taxes and utilities!

At the Green Lake conference in 1971, Louis L. King, the Foreign Secretary of the Christian and Missionary Alliance gave an address entitled "A Definite Statement on Church-Mission Relationships" (1971:175-190). In this address he mentioned seven forms of relationships between the sending church (mission) and the receiving church as follows:

> Mission dominance, or paternalism
>
> No mission, only the church
>
> Modified mission dominance
>
> Dichotomy, cooperation of autonomous equals
>
> Modified dichotomy
>
> Full fusion (or functional integration)
>
> Partnership of equality and mutuality

Using the square to represent the church and the circle to represent the missions, these relationships are illustrated in Diagram 5:4.

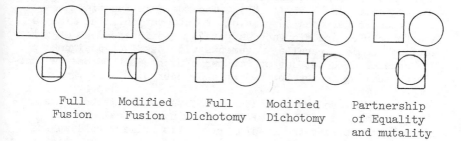

| Full
Fusion | Modified
Fusion | Full
Dichotomy | Modified
Dichotomy | Partnership
of Equality
and mutality |

Variety of church-mission relationships Diagram 5:4.

Most would agree that mission dominance is outdated, though it may have been necessary for an early beginning of missions in the 18th century. The modified mission dominance in the 19th century indicated an improvement, but is not now acceptable in the 20th century. No mission, only the church, precludes any relationship.

Most attention is given to the relationships of fusion and dichotomy. King says that advocates of fusion emphasize 1) The oneness of the church; 2) The church IS mission; 3) A "Proper" Church; 4) Financial Assistance a "Right" and 5) Independence. Most of the ecumenically oriented missions and churches have a "fusion" type relationship.

Though spiritual unity does not require organizational oneness, yet this Biblical principle cannot be ignored. The missionaries need to be responsible members of the national church and work *with* and *through* the existing church. Sometimes the national church wants to own all mission properties, control the missionaries' work, and not allow any new mission organization into "their area." This is the comity principle established early by missions entering a new country to prevent overlapping of work and the neglecting of unoccupied areas. King mentions that even groups that have "fused" often experience a "neo-colonialism" as the few Westerners present have a strong influence in decisions as they control the continued flow of money from the West. The fusion view may be full (integration) or modified (functional integration).

King continues with the view of dichotomy. Webster's dictionary defines dichotomy as "division into two subordinate parts" using the illustration from botany of one branch becoming two, and from logic of division into two subclasses opposed by contraction as white and not white. King has his own definition of dichotomy as "cooperation of autonomous equals." With his *new* definition he says this "allows the mission and the church to maintain their own organizations" (1971:187). The ideal is functional co-operation rather than separation or integration. The mission and the church are distinct, separate, and independent organizational bodies, parallel movements with distinct assignments. The mission does not set up its own churches but becomes a functional serving agency to the national church.

George W. Peters lists the benefits as: 1) It best protects the autonomy and selfhood of the emerging national church; 2) It best protects the missionary in his primary calling and in his freedom and initiative as a "sent one" for a particular task, and 3) It best protects the image of a board of missions as being an agent of a unique task and particular assignment. King believes this relationship is best.

Modified dichotomy allows the mission's resources in personnel and finances to be divided. One segment would be for maintaining liason and vital support with the national church and the other for pioneering and planting by the mission.

The last view "Partnership of equality and mutality" as proposed by Peters was not discussed in the Green Lake Symposium. In *A Biblical Theology of Missions,* Peters describes this relationship. Because of Paul's emphasis upon fellowship with the churches he had established, Paul would have avoided both extremes of dichotomy (parallelism) or merger (fusion). Paul labored in partnership with the churches. Peters states:

> We will not find it easy to enter into true
> partnership, for partnership eliminates the
> over-against, the side-by-side, the one over
> the other, and the one submerging in the
> other. Partnership in missions is a sacred
> and comprehensive concept of equals bound
> together in mutual confidence, unified purpose
> and united effort, accepting equal responsibili-
> ties, authority, praise and-blame; sharing bur-
> dens, joys, sorrows, victories and defeats.
> It means joint planning, joint legislation,
> joint programming, and involves the send-
> ing and receiving churches on equal basis.
> Only the closest bond in Christ, savored by
> a rich measure of humility, love, confidence
> and self-giving, will actualize partnership.
> Partnership of equality and mutuality in
> missions is as much an attitude, a spiritual,

> social and theological relationship, a
> philosophy of ministry, a way of life and
> missions, as it is a defined pattern of
> church-mission relationship for adminis-
> tration and legislation (1972:238).

The receiving and sending churches are partners in finances,
strategy planning in world evangelization, capital investments
and personnel. Their partnership is a united effort. Partnership is also reflected in joint programming with mutality and
equality in planning, decision and action. With such a base
the sending and receiving churches can make a missionary thrust
into the world.

I believe these views all have degrees of merit depending
upon the prevailing circumstances. King tended to present the
idealistic view of the missionaries as people concentrating on
evangelism and church planting, and a low view of the younger
church, guilty of all the ingrown concerns of the Western
churches. He does not mention that the small number of churches
in nations where the Christians are usually less than 10% have
already sent out nearly 3,000 missionaries.

Missions/Church/Missions Model for Continuing World Evangelization:

After studying the advantages and disadvantages of each of
these relationships, I propose the following diagrams to illustrate the need for missions and churches to both do evangelism
and church planting, and to establish younger missions.

In Diagram 5:5, we see how Western missions have established
churches in Asia. The square represents the sending mission
and the circle represents the receiving church. During the
last 175 years, most of the younger churches have been established by missions from churches in Europe and America. These
early missionaries had a *vision* to cross cultural barriers
to do evangelism and church planting. They endured many hard-
ships and made mistakes, but they had a passion to preach the
gospel to those who had not heard. Western missions provided
the necessary *support* (McGavran calls this "muscle") and a
strategy was developed.

For some, the indigenous church became a satisfactory goal,
and missions lost their original vision of taking the gospel
to the whole world. Some national churches neglected evangelism
and reflected the attitude of foreign missionaries who now seemed
interested primarily in the care of Christians, providing schools,
hospitals and a higher living standard.

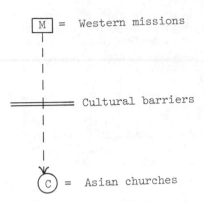

Diagram 5:5. Western missions
establishing Asian churches

Missionaries without vision and commitment to their original goal cannot blame the national church for a lack of evangelistic zeal. The church seeks improvement and the mission is often ready to serve and develop the church. Wagner refers to this as the "syndrome of church development" (1973:96). The national church may even oppose a different mission coming into "their area" to do evangelism, fearing another mission may divide their church in an effort to establish a "new church."

R. Pierce Beaver studies this trend and comments:

> At this moment each church in each land
> considers itself to be sovereign there,
> and few welcome the coming of new mission-
> aries into the country no matter how inade-
> quate present evangelism may be in relation
> to the territorial size and population of the
> country and the extent of available resources
> of the church there. Effective mission through-
> out the world in the future demands the giving
> up of false pride and the baseless assertion
> of full sufficiency. There is no church large
> or small, ancient or very young, in any country
> today which appears thoroughly adequate to
> its responsibilities in evangelism and minis-
> try. Certainly the American churches are no
> longer adequate to our own situation. We
> should welcome Asian and African missionaries
> who might come with a fresh statement of the
> gospel and a new approach to our dechristian-
> ized masses (1970:50).

The goal of evangelism and church planting is added to
this illustration in Diagram 5:6. This is not the responsibility of the indigenous church *only*. Some say the national
Christians can do evangelism better than Western missionaries.
However, all Christians have the responsibility to witness.
Western or Asian missionaries can *neglect* evangelism, work
independent of the national church, or work *with* the church.
I believe that it is best for missionaries (Asian and Western)
to do evangelism and church planting with the national church.

Because of the cultural *difference*, this becomes FM-2
or FM-3 for the foreign missionaries, but HM-1 "near-neighbor
evangelism" for the indigenous Christians who are working among
people of their own culture. The established "mother-churches"
should reproduce many "daughter-churches." Many mission-
church problems of relationship can be avoided if both agree
on the *goal* of evangelism and planting new churches.

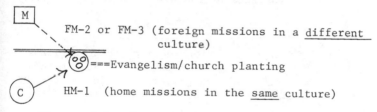

FM-2 or FM-3 (foreign missions in a <u>different</u>
                            culture)

===Evangelism/church planting

HM-1 (home missions in the <u>same</u> culture)

Diagram 5:6. Western missions and Asian churches
                 cooperating in evangelism and church planting.

In this way, the mission and church experience "koinonia"
which is one of the goals desired in the "fusion" relationship.
The missionaries are also members of the national church and
work *with* the national Christians. Some missionaries want to
be "independent" but this is not a desirable strategy for effective evangelism and church planting. If a foreign missionary
evangelized *alone* and established a church *alone*, then he
would need to become the pastor. As the mission would expect
a national Christian to pastor the church, the national would
have the joy of evangelizing and establishing the church together
with the missionary. Such a church would be less Western in
its form.

If the missionary is content not to do any evangelism,
he is a different type of missionary from those who pioneered
and established the first churches. Missions need missionaries who will do evangelism while working *with* the indigenous church. The best way to teach new Christians the importance
of evangelism is to *show* them.

Diagram 5:7. has an additional square, referring to the
organization of an Asian mission agency. The Western mission
must not be content with fruitful evangelism and even the establishment of an indigenous church. Winter emphasizes the fact
that "we cannot promote second-generation churches without pro-
moting second-generation missions. The great new fact of *our* time
must be the emergence of Third World *missions*. This is the next
phase of missions today" (1972a:145).

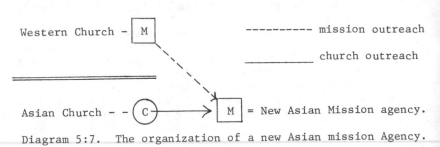

Diagram 5:7. The organization of a new Asian mission Agency.

The goal of world evangelization requires the establishment of Third World Missions. As the nationals have limited
experience doing cross-cultural evangelism, the mission has an
added responsibility of helping to select and to train Asian
missionaries.

Many Asian Christians are becoming more aware of their
responsibility to become world Christians. This includes the
privilege and responsibility of becoming partners in world evangelization. Asian Christians are to be commended for obedience
to this new vision. Though Asian missions are usually independent of Western missions, there are various ways in which
cooperation is helpful. With the rise of nationalism we must
remember that Western and non-Western Christians are both members
of *one* Body and together seek to obey the Great Commission given
by our risen Lord.

An Asian missionary being sent to another nation is illustrated in Diagram 5:8. They may be invited by an Asian church
or association, but sometimes they go because there is a special
need. Asian missionaries are even going to Western countries.

Missionaries from Asia face the same subtle temptation that
comes to Western missionaries. A younger church invites Third
World missionaries to assist in their church development. The
new missionary may become an active teacher, music director,
or even pastor a local church in a rural area. These things
are good, but must not become a *substitute* for further

evangelism and church planting. Western missions have a responsibility of helping younger missions to develop correct strategy.

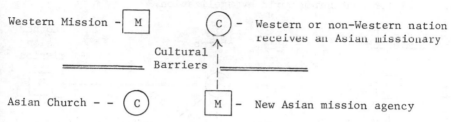

Diagram 5:8. An Asian missionary going to another culture.

Diagram 5:9. shows the responsibility of the Asian missionary to cooperate with the receiving church to do more evangelism. This is FM-2 or FM-3 for the Asian missionary who must cross cultural barriers similar to those experienced by Western missionaries. The receiving church does HM-1 evangelism among their own people, planting new churches as a previously agreed *goal* for both the missionary and the church.

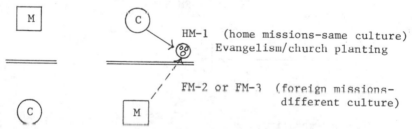

Diagram 5:9. The Asian missionary and receiving church cooperating in evangelism and church planting.

The Asian missionary can also help another younger church to get a vision for sending out their own missionaries. They may send missionaries to other countries or to people of other cultures and religions within their own country. This is illustrated in Diagram 5:10.

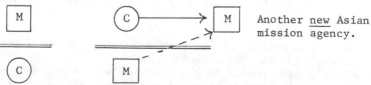

Diagram 5:10. Asian missionary counsels younger church to establish a younger mission.

We have considered step by step, the church/mission relation ships necessary for world evangelization. If each of these parts are connected, we then have the following "Missions/church/mission model for continuing world evangelization."

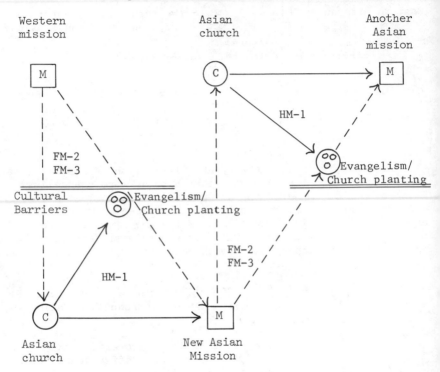

M   - Mission (sodality)

C   - Church (Modality)

⑨   - Evangelism/church planting

---   Mission outreach

HM-1 Home Missions One - "near-neighbor" evangelism-church planti

FM-2 Foreign Missions Two - cross-cultural evangelism (radically
                                            different culture)

A mission plants/assists an indigenous church in evangelism/churc planting, *and* counsels the national church in organizing another Third World Mission agency to plant/assist another indigenous national church to also do evangelism/church planting, etc. Missions and churches both need vision, people, strategy and money.

Diagram 5:11. Missions/church/missions model for continuing world
                    evangelization.

The main thing is not the structural relationship of the mission and church, but their spirit of commitment to a common goal. Too often *many* secondary goals have been *substituted* for the primary goal. If both groups have the desire to evangelize, they will.

Often the churches can evangelize alone, but don't. McGavran emphasizes the fact that the Eurican Missions can provide added "muscle" (vision, people, strategy, money) to assist the national church. Fusion can reduce added muscle from the West. It was wrong for the younger church to be a slave of the mission, just as it is wrong for the mission to be the slave of the younger church. We are all members of *one* Body with *one* goal and *one* Lord. The best structure is the one that zealously prevents paralysis, and allows each member to respond in obedience to the Head.

Businesses in the secular world learn to successfully practice management by objectives. The church is slowly learning this lesson. Our *first goal* is to establish indigenous churches, our *second goal* is to help the church to organize their own mission agency that *together* we may fulfill the Great Commission. Missions, missionaries and churches in *both* the East and the West can make the subtle error of *substituting* nurturing Christians and neglecting evangelism. This goal oriented fellowship of Spirit-filled Christians can be a model to keep the church in the will of God.

Association of Church Missions Committees:

How then can local congregations receive an enlarged vision for evangelism and missions? A recent organization called "The Association of Church Missions Committees (ACMC) is a unique service of churches helping churches in missions. This organization is interdenominational, dedicated to strengthening the role of the local church in world evangelization. They have this emphasis as they believe "the key to the success of the Great Commission task lies in the church." This is a model that can become international. Asian Christian leaders have a concern for missions, but want to see missions as effective evangelistic, church planting movements.

In response to Winter's report on "Two Structures of God's Redemptive Mission" Kyung Chik Han stressed that the greatest issue of the Consultation was to discover how Asians could evangelize Asia as quickly as possible. We must, he said, encourage the church itself to be more evangelistically minded as was the Apostolic church. That is, we should be careful not to discourage modality missions by overemphasizing sodalities (1973b:80), but *modality missions* are in fact type A, B, or C sodalities to Winter (see page 82).

The Korea National Strategy Group at Lausanne reported:

> An important first agreement was that the local
> church must be at the heart of our evangeliza-
> tion. The best evangelistic activities will
> come to nothing if those brought to faith in
> Christ are not brought into the local church
> fellowship...it was recognized that with all
> the strengths of the Korean church--cross-
> cultural evangelism is our weakest area.
> There is agreement as to the vision for, the
> urgency of, and the necessity of this kind of
> evangelization...Believing that God has richly
> blessed our Korean Church and that He has given
> us the potential and thus the responsibility
> to play an important role in the evangelization
> of our own country, of Asia, and of the world,
> this Congress has increased our awareness of
> needs, helped us to consider ways to meet them,
> and strengthened our dedication and determina-
> tion to do, under God, all we can to "let the
> earth hear His voice" (Hunt 1974:1,399).

For these reasons, the Association of Church Missions
Committees organized in 1974, is the kind of organization
that can help Latfricasian Churches develop a mission program.
The objectives of the ACMC are five-fold:

1) Encourage and aid local churches, both denominational
   and independent, *to establish a strong missions committee.*

2) Keep local churches *informed* of what God is accom-
   plishing around the world today.

3) Increase church-awareness of the *principles and
   practices* of missions.

4) Provide tools for more effective *evaluation and
   administration* of church missions programs.

5) Challenge local churches to a *growing responsibility* for reaching the unreached with Christ.

The philosophy of ACMC is "churches helping churches in
missions." This perspective affords a cross-fertilization
of information, enthusiasm, and ability unparalleled anywhere.
ACMC is a *laymen's* organization, concentrates on the *goal* of
world evangelization, provides inspiration by *reporting* on
God's activities around the world, and advocates total *local
church* involvement in missions. Missions is not optional for

pious Christians but the ultimate test of whether or not Christians really believe the gospel. Missions must be seen as an integral part of total church obedience. "The *whole* church taking the *whole* gospel to the *whole* world" must be more than a slogan.

Application in Asia:

How does this relate to younger churches and to Third World Missions? What insights can be received from the scriptures and from nearly 2,000 years of church history?

1. *Biblical understanding* that God loves the *world* and desires to reveal Himself to all as Saviour and Lord must be emphasized. The Reformation theology brought the church back to salvation by faith but failed to relate this to a worldwide mission for the church.

2. The Great Commission was given to *all Christians*. Believers are members of the mystical body of Christ, the Church, and must act in obedience to Jesus, the Head.

3. Christians need to become *responsible baptized members* of local churches. Nurture, fellowship Bible teaching, worship, witness are all aspects of the church.

4. As the body has two legs, the local church has responsibility for *home missions* (HM) and *foreign missions* (FM).

5. Home missions (evangelism/church planting) *require constant emphasis*. Many Korean churches have women evangelists called "Bible women" whose main responsibility is evangelism. A Korean seminary graduate works as an "evangelist" for about three years before he can be ordained. Many of these young men plant new churches, which is one of the reasons for church growth in Korea.

6. Foreign missions also require continual *emphasis by a group of committed Christians*. A *missions committee* needs to be organized in *each* church. As the music committee is responsible for music and the trustees or stewards are responsible for finances, this group must be responsible for foreign missions. They will study missions, discuss missions, pray for missions and stimulate giving for missions. The National Women's

Association of the Presbyterian Church of Korea
is an excellent illustration of what a church
related mission sodality can do. The post-
Reformation double century tragedy must *not* be
experienced in the Third World.

7. Each denomination must organize a sodality as
a *Board of Missions* or a *Missions Committee* that
is responsible *only* for foreign missions. Evangelism at home and abroad are not identical. Funds
for evangelism *and* missions are usually inadequate
to meet all the needs, and highest priority goes
to needs visible to the members of the congregation
and its officers. The heads of local worthy evangelistic programs can daily present their budget
needs. Therefore a *separate* group (sodality)
emphasizing foreign missions needs to be organized.

8. The foreign missions *sodality* must have *authority*
to *raise funds* and *administer* these funds for
missions according to church approved *policy*. In
countries where denominations are large, these
members will probably include some influential
Christians. The primary requirement is that these
people must have a *vision* for foreign mission work.

9. *Diaspora missionaries* are urgently needed to reach
their own people living in other countries. This
type of mission work should increase rapidly and
plant scores of truly indigenous mission-minded
churches.

10. *Cross-cultural* mission work has *three* major
categories: 1) evangelism/church planting; 2)
nurture; 3) service. Working as a doctor, nurse
etc. is valuable service but does not usually
plant *new* churches. Teaching in a seminary or
working in an established church is valuable
Christian nurture but seldom produces *new* churches.
Evangelism is the presentation of the gospel with
the *intention* of making new believers. Asian missionaries need to learn how to *plant cross-cultural
indigenous churches.*

Kor Cheng, pastor of the Grace Gospel Church in Manila
that sent 47 missionaries to eight Asian countries in 1975,
believes that in order to have success in missionary work, the
local churches should take the initiative. Cheng recounts
the following steps used in starting missionary involvement
in his church.

1. We spent a period of several Sundays expounding from
    the pulpit the *missionary message* in order to create
    a missionary vision and burden among the members.

2. We *prayed* for missionary work in our public and
    private prayers, asking the Lord to show us what
    step we should take.

3. I arranged a *personal talk with each of the leaders*
    of the church so that all of them would have the
    same mind and the same response.

4. We made a *proposal to the Board of Deacons* for their
    approval. After it had been accepted, a *mission-
    ary committee was organized,* and committee mem-
    bers were appointed to do *research*.

5. We promoted missionary endeavor in all the *Sunday
    School classes* and other groups in the church so
    that these people would interact with their ideas.

6. We announced the *formation of the mission board* in
    the church and had it approved at a congregational
    meeting. With the support of both the board of
    deacons and the congregation, we mobilized every
    member in the church to be involved in missionary
    work.

7. Finally, we planned an *annual missionary conference*
    so that the members would have the opportunity be-
    fore God to give their money and their lives in
    missionary service, and in doing so there would
    be no lack both in money and in manpower in our
    missionary effort (1973:n.p.)

Growing churches are missionary sending churches. In
the Western world many missions are completely independent
of the established church. With an increasing number of "independent" churches and the possibility of buying "mailing
lists," independent mission societies are multiplying in the
West. The most prominent single characteristic of these
nearly 150 new agencies is the fact that almost without exception they are not part of the official government of any church
denomination. Winter observes that not only their number but
their structure leads us to ask about the relations between
these new "missions" and the "mission" of the church (1971b:90).

The number of unaffiliated missionaries increased 900%
going from 1,000 missionaries in 1945 to 10,000 in 1969 (1970a:
56). Many are honest and sincere, yet some are irresponsible
and their work is negligible.

In the non-Western world, Christians are in the minority.
Christians need the fellowship, nurture and Bible teaching
received in the church, and the church could not exist without
Christians. Winter writes that "Churches need missions because
modalities need sodalities" (1971b:193). Without structures for
home missions *and* foreign missions, the church cannot fulfill
the Great Commission.

Sometimes Winter is unnecessarily criticized by those who
do not understand the great variety of mission sodalities and many
different church relationships possible. Concerning the church
in Korea, I fully agree with Winter that "Most crucial of all is
the need for *mission* sodalities within the younger churches"
(1971b:200).

William Carey's call for "exerting ourselves in the use of
means for the obtaining of those things we pray for" (Sect. V:81)
was a significant factor in beginning the Protestant missionary
movement. The *use of means* applies to Third World Mission
Agencies today. Effective Asian modality-sodality relationships
must be developed in order for the church to become an effective missionary sending agency.

6
Effective Sending Agencies

The diversity among Western mission agencies is also characteristic of Third World Mission organizations. Sending missions may be highly structured with a strong central headquarters or have no apparent structure, being responsible only to God as they feel led by the Holy Spirit.

Responsibilities of Sending Agencies:

Sending agencies in the Third World are usually churches (modalities) with sodalities as a Board, Committee or Department of Foreign Missions. Some, however, are sent by a more autonomous mission sodality. The difference is determined primarily by the source of finances, the kind of missionaries sent, (laymen or ordained) and the type of mission work planned.

Selection of Missionaries:

Some qualifications of missionaries have been suggested in a previous section. Missionary candidates will need to be selected following a time of training, preparation and experience. The local church should recommend the candidate to the Mission Board, Committee or Society, who must make the final decision.

Though Third World Mission Societies will normally send
Asian missionaries, others also need to be considered. As
many Western missions have personnel from non-Western nations,
so should Asian missions consider including Christians from
the West. This "international flavor" is more representative
of the oneness in Christ of believers from every nation.

Third World missionaries may choose missions as a career,
but this movement is still too new to indicate any pattern.
As most missionaries are working among their own people in another
country (Diaspora missionaries) their cross-cultural experiences
are limited. Many may actually have the gifts of evangelism and/
or a pastor, rather than the missionary gift needed for a cross-
cultural ministry. A Korean pastor who organized and pastored a
church in Hong Kong for Koreans, could easily return to Korea
and become the pastor of a local church.

The Korean church has not intentionally sent out any short
term missionaries, but some "career" missionaries have immigrated
to America rather than returning to their mission field for a
second term of service. This is not entirely the fault of the
missionary.

Missionaries who do not remain on the field as expected,
have experienced disappointments and frustrations beyond their
endurance. While it is true that some may not have the missionary gift, it is also possible that they lacked adequate training
before going and did not receive proper direction and supervision
on the field. Their goals may have been unclear. Maybe no time
was planned for learning the language which is so necessary for
effective communication and a satisfying ministry. Insufficient
funds for living, transportation, children's education, the
ministry, etc. may have brought discouragement. The lack of a
clear goal planned and accepted by the missionary and the sending
and receiving agencies is the primary cause for failure.

Ordained missionaries can do one type of missionary work
and laymen can do another. As Peace Corps people are assigned
work in various secular institutions, Christian laymen can also
be helpful in various short term ministries. "A Survey of Predicted Trends in North American Based Missions in the '70s"
reported "Greater use of specialized short-termers for education,
social concern, field office work...Increasing number of highly
motivated non-professionals finding new avenues of overseas
ministry" (Dayton, 1973:78).

This is very significant also for non-Western missions.
Short termers include three groups: 1) Pre-career people who
are eager to do something overseas as they prepare for their secula
vocation; 2) Mid-career people who can make a unique contribution
for a brief period of time; and 3) Post-career people who have

retired but still have ability and energy for further work or a
new vocation.

Short termers are usually able to provide their own living
expenses so they become no financial burden to the Asian Mission
Society. If these short term workers have a fulfilling ministry,
they may encourage additional Western staff and also more finances.
The most important factor will be the selection of a clear goal
that is acceptable to all involved. The greatest difficulty will
be communication, as English would probably be used by these
short term workers.

Several national industries invite retired executives from
the West to give counsel on a short term agreement. Missions
could gain much by following this same principle. Secretaries,
teachers, audio-visual technicians, printers, plus a variety of
"experts" may be helpful on a short term basis. Linguists may
assist in translations, a pilot may help establish an indigenous
"Missionary Aviation Fellowship," doctors, dentists, teachers and
other professional people may make a significant contribution to
evangelism and missions as associate members of a Third World
Mission Society.

Promotion and Accountability of Adequate Finances:

Many missionaries think the lack of adequate funds is the
biggest hindrance to a more effective ministry. Though more money
may be helpful, the *greatest need usually is to clarify the objective and to establish a clear goal*. After this has been decided,
one can then explain how additional funds would help to achieve
this goal in a shorter period of time.

"Partnership in Mission" is a popular slogan for the promotion of missions and is now the name of an organization funded
by the National Liberty Foundation in Pennsylvania. What kind
of partnership do we mean? There are partnerships where one
partner is strong and the other weak, where one partner is silent,
partnerships with limited liability and partnerships where everything is held in common, such as a family with a joint banking
account.

The Whitby statement of 1947 describes "Partners in Obedience"
--in obedience to the will of God in the fulfillment of a common
task (Hogg 1952:341). How does this divine ideal relate to the
material side of missions?

Many practical problems arise when one discusses money.
Everyone seems to get touchy and defensive. There are two poten-
tially clashing principles at work. One is the legitimate and
necessary accountability of a mission society to its supporters,

and the other is the legitimate and essential desire of the overseas church to set and determine its own priorities and make its
own decisions. There is no easy answer to this problem as both
sides are somewhat ambiguous. Each wants to receive undesignated
funds and then decide how they should be used. Budget preparation
and discussions have very important psychological implications.
This is especially true in East-West joint projects, as the Westerners' desire for reports may be interpreted by an Asian as
lack of trust.

Another important aspect of partnership in finances is the
channel for transferring funds. Does the Western mission send
money to the mission treasurer or directly to the national church
or Third World Mission treasurer? Often money is sent to the missionary who is "neutral" rather than support one faction of a
national church or organization (Strong 1972:287).

ACMC National Conference:

Some mission minded people in the Western churches expressed
need for insight into how churches in North America can better relate to Third World Agencies. The "Association of Church Mission
Committees" (ACMC) National Conference met in Wheaton, Illinois,
July 25-27, 1975 and received a "Report of the Ad Hoc Committee
on Relations With Third World Missions." This report gave many
insights, yet it recognized the need for further study and researc

The emphasis upon a *dynamic* relationship in the report was
excellent. In order to accomplish the goal of world evangelization, this partnership must be "vital" in the sense of being
alive, evidenced by interaction, movement and shared goals. It
demands close and continued contact, mutual trust and confidence.
There is a need for joint policies, pooled resources and common
action. The strength of churches in North America must be made
available to Third World Mission Agencies without that strength
becoming either an embarrassment or an occasion for developing
weakness.

The need for all Christians in all churches in all nations
to bring their tithes and offerings to God is a necessary step
in fulfilling the Great Commission. As the church is one, all
have a common opportunity and responsibility to help in the
growth of the Body of Christ.

The committee reported that reputable Third World Agencies
will be self-supporting at the primary level of organization
and administration, but did not indicate the specific source
of these funds. Referring to the fact that foreign funds are
frequently needed for theological education, one should expect
that at this stage foreign funds may be needed by the agencies
for missionary training. There may be a further need to assist

in the sort of preliminary survey activity that is essential
to strategic and effective missionary service.

The use of mission funds is the greatest single point of
friction between Western missions and the churches they planted
in the Third World. Tensions have developed because of: 1) The
disparity between Western and national standards of living; 2) The
partiality towards one's own kind, whether Western or national
administering the funds; and 3) The Western penchant for attach-
ing strings to their gifts. These issues need to be candidly discussed and a financial policy established acceptable to both,
before the transfer of any funds.

In order for local congregations in North America to become
involved with Third World agencies, the following recommendations
were made by the Ad Hoc Committee on Relations with Third World
Missions presented at the ACMC National Conference, July 1975 at
Wheaton, Illinois.

1) Churches will need to become aware of this new avenue
   of service by Western missions they already support.
2) Key national workers involved in the work of Third
   World agencies will probably need to visit these
   churches and give reports.
3) Western missions will be asked to assist in all nego-
   tiations, being sensitive to cultural differences.
4) Neutral agencies as the "International Missions Commission" of the "World Evangelical Fellowship"
   should be approached to serve as the "Introducing
   agent" in those situations where no Western mission
   exists with which the church has had a prior relationship (ACMC 1975:14).

The committee was very sensitive to cultural differences.
As the new birth does not depersonalize the convert, neither
does Christianity establish a Western model as normative. Third
World Agencies will also differ among themselves.

Christians in most Asian churches give to the church without receiving any advantage from the government. Christians
pay taxes the same as the non-Christians, and often more because
they have an economic position higher than the average and also
are motivated to be more honest. One hesitates to imagine what
might happen to contributions from American Christians if they
received no tax benefit from the government.

As long as this tax deduction continues, we are thankful.
It becomes necessary to know and to obey the regulations for
tax deduction. Generally speaking, gifts sent *directly* to
individuals or projects overseas are *not* tax-deductible. Gifts

must go to a recognized tax-deductible organization in the States
that can then transmit funds for an overseas ministry as budgets
are approved.

The committee drafted a Code of Ethics For Evaluating Third
World Agencies, which should also apply to Western Agencies! The
basic thesis is that *no church should support any mission that
it has not thoroughly checked beforehand.* The key points are
as follows:

1. *Statement of Faith:* This should be evangelical in
   doctrine and supported by all the members.

2. *Statement of Purpose:* its general purpose is to
   serve the cause of Christ. Specific objectives
   should be stated.

3. *Board of Directors:* "the agency needs an active
   Board of Directors, consisting of at least five
   well known, broadly representative, reputable
   individuals who control the work. They should
   hold regular meetings, create policy and maintain
   effective control. A Board of Reference cannot
   be an adequate substitute" (ACMC 1975:16).

   **Though the above is ideal, I think it is difficult
   to achieve this completely in either the East or
   the West.** Most new movements are the result of
   one man's vision who solicits the cooperation of
   his friends. It is vitally important to know if
   this Board has received government authorization.

4. *Reputation:* "the agency should have a good reputation among other missions, especially in the
   country in which it works. It should be known
   for its efficiency and its willingness to cooperate
   with the efforts of other established and function-
   ing ministries. The reputable agency will generally
   be non-competitive with respect to an association
   of missions or a fellowship of churches (ACMC
   1975:17).

5. *Finance:* "the agency should publish regular,
   detailed, easily understood and audited financial
   statements and make copies available upon request.
   They should be prepared by an outside professional
   Certified Public Accountant. New agencies should
   be able to demonstrate with a CPA's Statement that
   a proper financial system has been installed. One
   should be reasonably assured that the agency uses

funds efficiently and that designated gifts are
devoted to the purposes specified. The financial
statements should enable one to distinguish between
ministry activities and fund-raising activities,
between members serving on the home staff and
those actively engaged in the ministry. It needs
to be kept in mind that if home staff are listed
as missionaries, administrative costs are drastic-
ally increased. One should beware of the "cheapest"
missionary dollar. Reputable agencies provide for
essentials (health insurance, retirement, cooperative activities, such as with the "World Evangelical
Fellowship," etc.) that simply cannot be provided
by a 5-8% operation" (ACMC 1975:17).

This seems to me to be one of the most ethno-
centric policies in this report. If the Society
has a responsible Board of Directors as described
in item #3, and if the reputation is good (item
#4) there may not be a need for this *Western* policy
regarding finances. One should learn what financial reporting the Board (and the government?)
requires before introducing item #5.

6. *Recruitment and Training:* "the agency should be
    able to show that it carefully recruits its mis-
    sionaries and national workers and takes all neces-
    sary steps to ensure that they know their respon-
    sibilities, are capable of carrying them out, and
    regularly subject their work to review and evalua-
    tion" (ACMC 1975:17).

7. *Management:* "the agency should give evidence of
    sound management, not moving from crisis to crisis,
    but steadily monitoring its organizational develop-
    ment while it grows in members and financial strength.
    In addition, no agency is worthy of support that
    fails to provide for the responsible supervision of
    its workers. One tangible evidence of its maturity
    will be the degree to which it can demonstrate what
    has been accomplished toward developing a financial
    base within its own country. Does the budget reflect
    this activity? How many prayer cells has it recruited?
    How much money have they contributed? (ACMC 1975:17).

This is extremely important. "Matching-funds"
is a policy used by many corporations in America,
and could be used effectively by Western churches.
The churches resemble a corporation and could give
a percentage as one half or two-thirds *after* the

national Christians have raised one-half or one-
third for a specific project or an approved budget.
If the nationals contribute finances, they will
require a financial report. Western cooperative
agencies should receive a copy of this report.

Some Third World Mission leaders in Asia believe
assistance by the Western church is needed but
the receiving and giving should be done anonymously.
If members of the Asian church know help has been
received from the West, they would not give. Other
Asians say that operational funds from the West
should never be publicized. They state that Asian
missionaries must take the lead while our Western
counterparts take a back seat as far as Asian missions is concerned.

I believe that Westerners need to learn to ride
in the back seat, but the car owned and driven by
the Asian missionary needs to be jointly purchased
and this truth should not be hidden if the reputation of the Asian society is to be preserved and
the giving from the West stimulated.

8. *Promotion:* "the agency should be able to provide
   accurate reports of its work that provide con-
   vincing evidence that it is actually fulfilling
   its stated purpose" (ACMC 1975:18).

   This evaluation takes time. When completed, the
   mission committee may be tempted to take a unila-
   teral decision either for or against an agency.
   However, the committee recommends a reciprocal
   agreement drafted and signed by both including
   the following items: statement of faith, permission for promotion, pledge against exploitation,
   allocation of funds, launching new projects, how to
   deepen mission integrity and keep communication open.

The committee concludes their report with suggestions for
strategic giving. This list of sixteen organizations and eighteen
projects is helpful but very incomplete. Some of the information is inaccurate. Third World Agencies with English speaking
leaders are not necessarily ones doing the most effective evangelism. This illustrates again the significance of a thorough research and evaluation of both Western and non-Western mission
agencies. There is a need for some office to handle confidential
information about mission organizations. It is difficult for
each church to independently learn about worthy organizations
and projects overseas.

Evaluation of Missionary Activities:

Using the grid explained on page 15, I have prepared a report on Asian missionary societies which is included in the Appendix. The largest number of Korean missionaries (160) were sent out by the University Bible Fellowship. With the exception of one missionary family in Bangladesh and one single evangelist in Japan, the others are lay-missionaries. Their main activity is evangelism among Koreans in other countries.

A partial listing of Korean missionaries is included (beginning below) with the names of the missionaries and the sponsoring organization, the country of ministry, date of departure, and the classification of ministry, indicating cultural differences, primary activity, and those on furlough. A missionary couple is reported as two missionaries. A single person (unmarried) is indicated with the letter "s."

This report includes 22 missionaries working among Koreans in Japan. There may be others that have not been reported to me.

Also included are the names of seven missionaries on furlough in the United States. These are all from the FM-3 category. Another FM-1 missionary is on furlough in Korea. A * indicates missionaries on furlough.

As a pastor is also concerned about evangelism, it was difficult to distinguish whether the main activity of the diaspora missionaries was evangelism or Christian nurture. However, most Koreans interviewed, said that these overseas Korean pastors were involved primarily in work as a pastor.

Also omitted from this list are Korean pastors working in Canada and the United States. This represents another large number, but as many of them immigrate, they are not included in this report of Korean *missionaries*.

Korean Missionary Report - 1976

Organization	Missionary	Country	Departure	"Classification
Ewha Womans University				
	Chaeok Chun	Pakistan	1961	FM-3-E * s
Korea Evangelical Church				
	Yong-Han Chun	Japan	1955 ?	FM-1-N
	Hee-Baik Choi	Japan	1955 ?	FM-1-N

Korea Evangelical
Church continued:

Ik Soo Choi	Japan	1955 ?	FM-1-N
Suck-Ho Lee	Brazil	1970	FM-1-N
Suck-Kyu Kim	Brazil	1974	FM-1-N
Jung-Shik Pak	Okinawa	?	FM-2-E

Korea International
Mission, Inc.

Samuel I. Kim	Thailand	1956	FM-3-E *
Hong-Shik Shin	Thailand	1971	FM-3-E
Hung-Bin Lim	Brunei	1971	FM-3-E

Korean International
Mission For Christ, Inc.

Suk-Rin Pak	Argentina	1973	FM-1-N

Methodist

Sung-Wook Kim	Sarawak	1965	FM-3-E *
Sung-Joo Lee	Japan	1970	FM-1-N
Duck-Wha Kim	Japan	1972	FM-1-N
Sung-Joo Kim	Japan	1971	FM-1-N

Presbyterian (Hap-Dong)

Byung-Soo Paik	Japan	1973	FM-1-N
Sung-Man Yang	Brazil	1970	FM-1-N
Sung-Man Kim	Brazil	1970	FM-1-N
Man-Soo Suh	Indonesia	1971	FM-3-E
Whan Cho	Guam	1972	FM-1-N
Hyung-Tak Kim	Japan	1972	FM-1-N
Kim	Ecuador	1976	FM-1-E

Presbyterian (Tong-Hap)

Ung-Sam Kim	Taiwan	1968	FM-1-N
Sung-Tae Pak	Taiwan	1971	FM-1-N
Yoon-Suk Kim	Indonesia	1972	FM-3-E
Hyung-Choon Yang	Japan	1972	FM-1-N
Young-Hee Chung	Japan	1972	FM-1-N
Byung-Koo Lee	Japan	1972	FM-1-N
Chung-Woon Suh	Indonesia	1973	FM-3-E
Young-Il Kim	Samoa	1974	FM-1-N

Presbyterian (Kordyo)

Young-Jin Kim	Taiwan	1955	?	FM-2-E
Kil-Soo Chung	Brazil	1967		FM-1-N
Byung-Chul Cho	Japan	1969		FM-1-N
Hwan-Choon Yoo	Taiwan	?		FM-2-E
Chong-Chul Lee	Brazil	?		FM-1-N

Salvation Army

Hee-Dong Chang	Singapore	1967	FM-3-N *
	Hong Kong		

University Bible Fellowship

Sung-Gyoon Chung	Bangladesh	1974		FM-3-E
1 ?	Japan	1974		FM-2-E s
1 ?	France	?		FM-1-E s
1 ?	Peru	?		FM-1-E s
3 ?	Switzerland	?		FM-1-E s
1 ?	Upper Volta	?		FM-1-E s
152 ?	West Germany	?		FM-1-E s

World Omega's Revival
Missionary Society

Chin-Su Toh	Australia	1976	FM-1-N
Byung-Cha Choo	Bangladesh	1976	FM-3-E s
Young-Ha Lee	Paraguay	1976	FM-1-N
Suh-Ae Chung	Japan	1976	FM-1-N s

Full Gospel Central Church

Sung Joon Pak	Brazil ?	1976	FM-3-E
2 ?	Japan	?	FM-1-N
1 ?	Vietnam	?	FM-1-N
4 ?	West Germany	. ?	FM-1-N

Mission for Vietnam

Sang-Oh Kim	Vietnam	1970	FM-1-N *

Independent

Young-Chul Kim	Okinawa	1965 ?	FM-2-E
Immanuel Yoon	U.S.A. (Indians)		
		1974 ?	FM-3-E

* Missionary on furlough   s indicates single (unmarried)

With the above explanation clearly understood, my research of 18 Korean agencies reveals 259 Korean missionaries in the following categories: 224 or 86.5% are FM-1 missionaries, 11 or 4.2% are FM-2 and 24 or 9.3% are FM-3 missionaries.

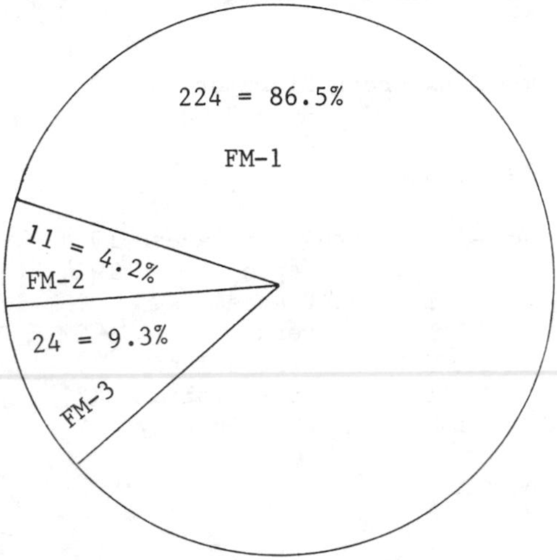

Diagram 6:1. Cultural difference experienced by 259 Korean foreign missionaries, 1976

The evaluation of the Korean missionaries would appear as follows:

Cultural Difference	Location		Primary Activity				
	(HM)	(FM)	E	N	S	W	Totals
M-1	0	224	160	31	0		191
M-2	0	11	6	0	0		6
M-3	0	24	12	1	0		13
Totals	0	259	178	32	0	(49)*	210

Diagram 6:2. Primary activity and cultural difference of Korean missionaries, (Chun and Nelson 1976).

*Note: Wives not included in activity totals.

The questionnaire used did not clearly indicate the activity of the wives. There is need for further research on the unique role of the missionary wife. The statistics reported under E-N-S are, therefore, of men and single women only. The special category (W) includes the number of married women. It is hoped that this method of reporting will show a realistic picture of the missionary activities. The analysis of individual organizations is in the appendix.

As some Korean missionaries go overseas independently to serve as pastor in a Korean community, some go abroad for study following missionary work, and some immigrate to Canada or the United States, there is no one source for this information. These facts have been obtained from interviews, letters and printed reports from the following people: Sunhee Kwak, Paul Chun, In Won Choye, Dal Jin Park, Joseph Chang, Won Yong Koh, Synn Suk Yang, John Kim, Samuel Kim, David J. Cho, Yong Ki Cho, Chung Woo Lee, Min Woo Lee, Chang Hwan Park, Hae Suk Lee, Paul Rader and Donald Sansom.

Missionaries on Leave:

There is a great flexibility in policy for Western missionaries on leave (furlough). During the 18th and 19th centuries it often took three to six months for a missionary to reach his "field." These career missionaries frequently stayed for seven years before returning home. Amy Carmichael went more than the second mile and spent her entire life in India without a furlough.

Missionaries with families usually had to send their children to boarding schools in other cities or countries. Some parents and children adjusted well to this unnatural situation but others did not. Concern for children who need to learn how to live in two cultures is a constant problem for parents and often produces "missionary casualties." The parents voluntarily decide to work in another country, but not their children. Furloughs provide a necessary time for children to adjust to their own "foreign culture."

With modern transportation, it is possible for the missionary to be home within a week. Some boards bring their missionareis home more frequently for a shorter period of time. The distance of travel, the climate on the field, health, education, need for deputation are all factors related to the missionary's furlough. The nationals usually think the missionary goes for a long holiday and there are places to rest within the country. However, many missionaries spend most of the year at home traveling to raise funds, and anticipate rest *after* returning to the field.

Does this mean that the missionary should do no deputation while on furlough? Absolutely not. He has a responsibility to report what God has done in response to the prayers and giving of congregations. This can also be a significant time of recruiting new missionaries.

The missionary family should have time for rest while on furlough. They also need a complete physical examination. Time is needed to visit relatives and renew friendships. Some further study in the field of missiology would be of significant value. New experiences in a cross-cultural ministry motivates one to seek new knowledge and added understanding. If the mission could recommend or donate recently published books on mission, it would be helpful.

New missionaries need special training before going to the field, and one of the most qualified teachers is the missionary who has experienced a cross-cultural ministry. Teaching in seminaries, speaking at seminars and conferences for pastors and young people will give much needed information, understanding and inspir tion regarding 20th century missions. Some missionaries can exten their influence by writing articles or books about their experienc in another country.

The missionary's *salary should be continued while on furlough* In some cases it may be necessary to increase it. Anxiety about his living and family responsibilities must not be permitted to detract from his furlough ministry. The sending agency has an important responsibility for their missionaries. Soldiers would never go into battle without the support of their people.

The church is responsible to "lengthen the cords and to strengthen the stakes." (Isaiah 54:2). A missionary sending church grows and is a fellowship blessed by God. Because the missionary task is so important, there will be spiritual oppostion. It would be foolish for Satan to try to stop all missionary activity. The subtle strategy is to redirect this emphasis to other good and important goals. Few can criticize the church engaged in many *good* activities. However, nothing must be permitted to become a *substitute* for cross-cultural evangelism. Making disciples among peoples of other nations is the heart of the Great Commission and the *objective* of missionary sending agencies.

7
Effective Receiving Agencies

Paul's evangelistic band (sodality) was sent off with the blessing of the Christians in the Antioch church (modality) to witness and to plant churches. This band of men apparently was free to evangelize as led by the Holy Spirit. These godly men made plans but willingly changed them in obedience to clearer guidance from the Holy Spirit. It is encouraging for "ordinary" Christians to know that "spiritual" missionaries Paul, Silas and Timothy also made wrong plans. Acts 16 records their desire to go to Asia and then later into Bithynia, but the Holy Spirit did not permit them. The vision "come over into Macedonia and help us" (Acts 16:9) brought the gospel in the direction of Europe.

Logistics:

When thinking about Third World Mission Societies today, we need to recognize the two major categories of home missions and foreign missions. Each of these areas has two distinct aspects that require careful analysis. Home missions-one (HM-1) refers to near-neighbor evangelism among people of the *same culture* in the same country. Logistics required would be the same as when starting a local church. The planting of "daughter-churches" with the goal of becoming a reproducing "mother-church" is a useful model for evangelism in many countries.

Home missions-two (HM-2) is cross-cultural evangelism in
a *similar culture* and Home missions-three (HM-3) is cross-
cultural evangelism in a *radically different culture* but both
are within the same country. Cross-cultural evangelism can occur
within any country as India, Indonesia, the Philippines and others
When a missionary evangelist goes to another culture in his own
country, there are more logistical needs than for HM-1 near-neighbor evangelism. Logistics for home missions are relatively simple
in contrast to problems encountered when doing foreign missionary work.

Foreign missionaries are of three distinct types. *Diaspora
missionaries*, those working among their own nationality (same
culture) in another country can be described as FM-1. They have
logistical problems to overcome, yet they are still working among
people of their own kind. In a recent study of Asian Missionary
Societies at the Fuller School of World Mission, it was learned
that 72.1% of the Asian *foreign* missionaries responding to a questionnaire were in this category.

Foreign missionaries in a different culture (FM-2 and FM-3)
experience many more difficulties. They must adjust to people
with an entirely different language and culture. These Third
World missionaries gain a new perspective to some difficulties
experienced by some Western missionaries who are also FM-2 and
FM-3.

Paul's team members obeyed the Macedonia vision and simply
went. They didn't need a notarized letter of invitation from a
person, church or organization recognized by the national government. They did not need to wait for a background investigation
to see if they had any communist connections before they could
receive a passport for travel. Paul was a Roman citizen, and
he frequently made mention of this advantage in his travels.

Paul's team members did not need to secure a health cer-
tificate to prove that they had received the proper vaccinations
required for international travel. There was no question about
the sending and receiving agencies being in countries that had
diplomatic relations, or a friendly attitude towards the admit-
tance of Christian missionaries. Paul, Barnabas and Timothy
needed no visas for their missionary travels.

Neither was there any special concern about securing foreign
currency to purchase the tickets for travel to another country.
The legal transfer of money to support this evangelistic band
was also no problem as Paul's team frequently worked to provide
their own needs. Many countries today do not allow foreigners
to secure employment that would be in competition with their
own people.

These are a few of the logistical difficulties that must
be overcome before 20th century missionaries from either the East
or the West can minister the Word of God in another country. Both
Western and Asian missionaries find it difficult to enter some
countries and impossible to secure visas to enter others.

The receiving agency can often help prepare these legal
documents. The receiving agency may be an individual, a church,
a denomination, a council of churches or an evangelical fellowship. They often extend the invitation necessary for securing
a passport and visa. In response to an invitation from Emperor
Haile Selassie of Ethiopia, for example, the Korean Presbyterian
church sent two missionary couples, a medical team and a minister
with training in agriculture (Moffett 1968:4). Sometimes the host
church assumes full or partial financial responsibility for the
Asian missionary. Usually their salary is the responsibility
of the sending church and Western churches may assist with travel
expenses.

Even when the sending church provides full financial support
for their missionaries, the governments frequently will not permit the transfer of dollars out of the country. Dollars, pounds
or marks are used for international trade and governments plan
to use this money for economic development and defense. How then
can a national church transfer yen, won, pesos, etc. to their
missionaries living in another country?

Sometimes these younger churches still receive some financial
assistance from a Western mission or from churches related to
the World Council of Churches. Instead of having the full designated budget sent to the younger church, a portion of these dollars
is designated for the support of their Asian foreign missionaries
working in other countries. The national Christians of the sending country in Asia actually provide the missionary support, but
it goes into the local seminary or hospital account in lieu
of designated funds from abroad being redirected to support their
missionaries. This is a very complicated aspect of sending Third
World missionaries.

Sometimes the national church does not want to invite
another mission into the area where they claim comity. If
this area were entirely evangelized, this would be no problem.
But if the area is not yet evangelized and the national church
has no viable plans for aggressive evangelism and planting of
more churches, there is need for more evangelistic missionaries.

Sometimes missionaries of *other* denominations do enter
these areas. Roman Catholic missionaries, or Protestant missionaries or people belonging to various sects sometimes come
in though, and gather the harvest neglected by the established
national church.

Independent missionaries may easily be misunderstood and
cause suspicion. The independent missionary may give the impression that he is more concerned about the unevangelized in
this area than the existing "liberal" church, which may be true.
Frequently the new mission society has a sizeable budget for evan
gelism and may employ many dissident ministers of the established
national church. One is amazed to see how easily a Presbyterian
national pastor can become a Baptist or vice versa. If the independent missionary is working alone or pioneering a new work,
he seldom has time for language study. His preliminary work then
is done through an interpreter. He needs to secure a capable man
preferably one who has traveled abroad. He doesn't covet such
people working in the established church, but merely offers them
a double salary. He must secure people to help him do "the
Lord's work." This new missionary may emphasize a certain doctri
or create dissension among members of the established national ch
He may satisfy his supporters by reporting that he started six ne
churches within six months, but actually these may be splits from
the nearby established national church. No wonder the national
church may resist inviting a new mission into their area!

Does this mean that new groups should not come? No.
Is there a need to establish new churches? Yes. But the ideal
is to establish *new* churches in cooperation *with* the established
national church. This may call for a new kind of missionary,
but such a relationship is vital to maintain the unity of the
body of Christ and to extend the Kingdom of God.

It is best for independent missionaries to work in an
area where churches have not yet been established and build a
solid work there. It will take time to learn the language,
win converts, organize churches and train local leadership.
However, this is not impossible. There are both advantages
and disadvantages of working with the established church. The
emphasis here relates primarily to logistics. In a later section
we will see how this relationship affects the ministry.

Orientation to the Culture:

It is necessary to remember that a missionary is a person
working in *another culture*. This cross-cultural aspect distinguishes a missionary from a pastor or evangelist working among
people in his own culture. Another culture may be similar or
radically different, within one's home country or in a foreign
country. A Christian in the church of South India doing evangelism among the people living in Himachal Pradesh is working
in a *different culture* (HM-2) within his home country of India.

Both the Western and non-Western missionaries must recognize
the need for orientation to another culture. Asian missionaries
are also foreign missionaries. William Henry Scott recognizes
that "It is significant that the designation "foreign missionary"
is composed fifty percent of the word *foreign,* for at least half
of the missionary task is being a good foreigner" (1973:383).

Being a good foreigner is something like being a good guest,
and certainly the missionary of all foreigners is a guest. As a
good guest he appreciates what his host offers him and keeps
quiet when he doesn't. He tries to adjust himself to his host's
way of life and politely acknowledges his inferiority when he
can't. It is a humbling experience to enter a world in which
you are a foreigner, an outsider, and a kind of freak.

Orientation to a new culture requires *interest* and *respect.*
Unless a person is interested, he will not want to learn the customs in a new culture. There will be no desire to get information about the people and the country. It is important to get
acquainted with their ways, their music, their art, their national
pride and their way of thinking. Dick Hillis says, "This means
you must read, read, read" (1972:84).

Knowledge alone is inadequate. One must show *respect.*
The culture of every country is different, but that does not make
it wrong. The sooner that simple fact is learned, the greater
fruitfulness the missionary will enjoy. It is important to develop a sensitivity to the desires of the people, to appreciate
their problems and to recognize their progress. Books are helpful but making friends with the nationals is more interesting.
Even though the language barrier is so obvious, yet love and
respect can be communicated. In a sense, love becomes a supra-
linguistic way of communicating.

Reyburn emphasizes this insight and says:

> The African wants above all other things to
> be treated as a self-respecting person shar-
> ing in the spiritual and material rewards
> of modern life. He does not demand that he
> become the only one entitled to first-class
> citizenship, but he does demand that he be
> included in this category...the individual
> missionary who treats the African with the
> respect which the African expects is making
> the greatest contribution in this field
> (1958a:88).

Missionaries are frequently criticized for maintaining a style of living distinctly different from the people to whom he ministers. This can be said of many city pastors in Asia also. Asian missionaries will have a natural desire to live as Western missionaries, especially if their work is in the same institution or church. Why should Asian missionaries live on a lower standard than Western missionaries? Though one may try to give an intellectual explanation, the bad feelings remain. This is a difficult but important mission policy that must receive serious thought by leaders of Third World Mission societies. One solution is for Asian missionaries to work in an unreached area where there are no missionaries from the West.

Identification:

C. Peter Wagner considers one of the unquestioned axioms of missionary orientation to be that an effective missionary must constantly strive to "identify with the nationals" (1975b:91). Because this axiom has been unquestioned, dangers of over-identification of a foreign person or organization have not been clearly indicated.

Identification is important. Paul's ability to be made all things to all men" that he might "by all means save some" (I Cor 9:22) was the thing that made him a missionary in contrast to Peter. Paul could identify with the Gentile "nationals" and was called the "apostle" to the uncircumcision. In modern missiological terminology, Paul was a home missionary in a second culture (HM-2) while Peter was an evangelist in his own culture.

We now have advanced understanding in cross-cultural relationships. Modern linguistic techniques, extensive writings on customs and cultures and new depths of anthropological sensitivi all help the new missionary to identify more rapidly. While appreciating these above contributions Wagner says:

> The fallacy goes like this: the *more you*
> *identify with the nationals, the more effec-*
> *tive a missionary you will be.* Be careful
> of this. It is almost as foolish as argu-
> ing that the more salt you put into the soup,
> the better it will taste (1975b:91).

Social sciences have made us increasingly sensitive to the importance of human roles. Because we learn our roles so gradua and perform them so automatically in our society, we are often u aware that they exist at all.

It is important for the new missionary to realize that social roles are defined from within a culture, not from the

outside. This is no problem to the person living in his own culture but becomes significant to one doing a cross-cultural ministry.

There is a need to recognize the etic and emic roles in a
society. The etic role views society as an outsider, while the
emic view is that of an insider. Many unconsciously believe that
a missionary achieving an emic role will become more effective.
However the risks involved are usually too high.

The dangers inherent in the insider's role are well known
to social scientists. Each role has a web of complex relationships
to numerous other roles in society. Cultural behavior is best
learned through growing up inside the culture itself. Bodily
motions, facial expressions and attitudes plus the obvious and
unconscious linguistic errors are frequently interpreted by
others in ways the missionary didn't expect.

The resulting frustrations and disappointments may prove to
be too high a price to pay for any benefits that an insider's
role might provide. It is a pathetic case when a missionary *per-
ceives himself* to be an insider when he is obviously not regarded
as such by the nationals. Not only does he suffer from self delusion, but he often is more despised by the nationals than he
would be as an outsider.

The missionary who assumes an outsider's role in categories
of behavior is not failing to "identify with nationals." Rather,
he has chosen a certain *kind* of identification. As an outsider,
his cultural blunders will more readily be excused, the differences in life style will be understood and fewer obstacles are likely
to clutter the channels of gospel communication.

Paul Crane, a missionary doctor who lived many years in
Korea writes:

> The Westerner working in Korea needs to
> keep certain philosophic principles in
> mind. First, a Westerner can never become
> a Korean. He will never be completely
> accepted by Koreans as a "person"...A
> Westerner is most respected when he is
> first true to his own philosophy, ideals
> and beliefs. To compromise one's moral
> and religious beliefs is to invite scorn.
> Most Koreans have now studied and know
> what Westerners claim to believe. They
> judge them by their inability to live up
> to their own, not Korean standards.
> Koreans graciously excuse many gross
> social errors in foreigners (1967:175).

William D. Reyburn keeps this subject in proper perspective when he says:

> The central point is that identification
> is not an end in itself. It is the road to
> the task of gospel proclamation. Likewise
> the heart of the controversial matter of
> missionary identification is not how far
> one can go but rather what one does with
> the fruits of identification. Going native
> is no special virtue (1960:3).

It is quite obvious that Asian missionaries have numerous advantages in identifying with other Asians. They have an understanding of the extended family system and the way decisions are made, as well as the economical difficulties many experience in order to survive and educate their children. Those who are recent converts can still remember their previous life style as a Buddhist, Hindu, animist or adherent to other religions.

Asian missionaries experience many advantages but also have certain handicaps. Because of their similarity as Asians, they are expected to identify immediately and completely. There is less sympathy for the Asian who cannot yet speak the language well. The Asian is often expected to know all the customs and to live in smooth harmony with his host people.

J. Herbert Kane, former missionary to China writes:

> People of these countries don't make the same
> same allowance for Oriental missionaries that
> they do for missionaries from the West...
> Orientals...are expected to think and act
> alike...one missionary doctor who went from
> the Philippines to Thailand was given such a
> rough time that she had a nervous break-
> down and was invalided home. The people ex-
> pected her to speak Thai *perfectly*. When
> patients came to the mission hospital they
> expected to be treated by a "foreign" doctor,
> only to find a Filipino instead! (1974:370).

The adjustment to another culture is never easy, and few can appreciate the difficulties until they have had a comparable experience. How much of one's own national culture and food should be retained? For example, how long should Koreans live in another country without rice and "kimchi?" Some may expect to live as the nationals, yet some expect to live as the other Westerners. They too are expatriate missionaries and seek a comparable living standard consistent with their view of their

new status and role. Some Asian missionary candidates are like
mercenary soldiers, offering their service in order to receive
money from an outside organization. This principle cannot become
a pattern if thousands of new Asian missionaries are to go to
other Third World nations.

Peternalism is a natural human characteristic. As Western
missionaries planted churches with Western characteristics, it
may be equally difficult for Asian missionaries to plant a truly
indigenous church. Without missiological insights, it is nearly
impossible for a person to plan an indigenous church if he has
never seen an example. Many think they have an indigenous church
when they actually have a few nationals indoctrinated to act in
Western ways.

Alan R. Tippett emphasizes that it is not until:

> ...the indigenous people of a community
> think of the Lord as their own, not a
> foreign Christ; when they do things as
> unto the Lord, meeting the cultural needs
> around them worshipping in patterns they
> understand; when their congregations func-
> tion in participation in a body, which is
> structurally indigenous; (that) you have
> an *indigenous* church (1969:133 & 136).

Charles H. Kraft says the most important criterion of in-
digeneity is the church's "self-image" (1971:159-161). A *domi-
nated* church is one firmly controlled by both the representatives
and the concepts of a foreign culture. There is a *dependent*
self-image when carefully indoctrinated nationals see themselves
as foreign enclaves in their own nations, putting a foreign "Christian" system against the surrounding culture as if Christianity
were intended to be a competing culture rather than a redeeming
leaven designed to operate within any culture. The *independent*
self-image is a truly indigenous church. For these churches,
Christianity's battle ground is *within* their culture rather
than against it.

Qualifications of leadership are built upon ideals already
present in society, rather than upon Western culture values or
literacy, education and youthfulness. Missions must *turn over
authority and stay on*. With respect to the future Kraft says:

> The missionaries of the next 30 years -
> Eurican and Latfricasian, must be culturally
> and spiritually perceptive persons whose
> single aim is to stimulate the multipli-
> cation of truly indigenous and truly inde-
> pendent congregations and clusters of

congregations, i.e. churches which are culturally so one with the people that they no
longer seem in the least foreign (1971:171).

It is important to apply the Golden Rule to both the people
and to their culture. The Western and Asian missionaries should
both show the same respect to the host culture, as they would wan
shown to their own culture. Such an attitude of interest and respect will "cover a multitude of sins."

Orientation to the National Church:

The independent missionary may avoid any contact with the
national church and vice versa. Such an unnatural relationship
can easily create misunderstandings by both groups. The independent missionary may not consider it necessary to contact any
Christian group within the country. His desire is to simply
fulfill the Great Commission in obedience to the leading of the
Holy Spirit as recognized in his personal life and/or the mission
organization.

Perhaps the leaders of the new mission organization contacte
the established national church leaders and were told to stay
home! They did not want another organization to upset the status
quo. This concept of comity was learned from the West so one
must be patient and understanding. Another new group may simply
create division among the existing churches or may establish a
new denomination of *new* churches. Though it is not ideal to
transplant church denominations into another country, it may be
acceptable if this is the only way to reach more people with the
gospel.

Frequently the "established national church" has no aggressive plan to totally evangelize the area of their responsibility.
In such a case, others should be invited to come in. Paul rejoiced when Christ was preached with an undesirable motive (Phil
1:15-18). Though missionaries often have many faults, they
usually can be described as honest people, willing to endure
hardship in order to serve the Lord.

Third World missionaries are frequently invited by a church
or by a denomination. Recognizing their unity in Christ, each
can make a spiritual contribution to the other. Missionary Paul
eagerly anticipated his visit to Rome that he might minister to
them and they to him (Rom. 1:11,12). Any Asian missionary sent
to another country has much to share with the church, and he is
likewise helped by learning of the experiences of fellow Christians in another country.

It is important for any new missionary to know the history and growth of the national church where he is to minister. When was the church started and by what group? What factors have encouraged church growth and what has caused periods of decline? Studies of the growth of the church should include the Christian population in relationship to the total population, as well as the growth of the various denominations. If most churches are experiencing steady growth and the host church is not growing, there is a need for careful research.

The denomination may be growing but the growth may be coming from one or two groups within the society. The present vogue is to request missionaries who are specialists. A specialist is usually one with a unique skill in translation, mass media, and the like. There is a great need for missionaries who are specialists as evangelists and church planters. This requires an understanding of church growth principles which should be a minimum requirement for 20th century missionaries.

There is a tendency among certain groups to regard the missionary as a fraternal worker or a fraternal brother. He surely must be this. The difficulty is not in the relationship experienced but in the *goal* which is established. This will be considered in the section concerning the selection of the missionary's assignment.

Language Study:

By the use of linguistic sciences, one can now measure the comparative ease or difficulty in learning another language. Even so, missionaries usually say that the most difficult language to learn is the language they are studying. Donald McGavran asked a class of mid-career associates studying at the School of World Mission how many thought the missionaries in their organization had an adequate understanding of the language to communicate effectively cross-culturally. Not one gave a confident affirmative answer.

Learning another language is difficult for most adult missionaries. Some may not have an aptitude for language study, but usually the problem is trying to study in the midst of many distractions. The missionary may have an immediate assignment to do the work of another person on furlough. The mere survival of a family in another country takes more time and energy than when living at home. Culture shock also affects one's attitude toward the people and this sometimes reduces the ability to establish good human relationships with the language teacher.

Some countries do not have language schools or the method of teaching may be ineffective. These schools are frequently expensive and some missionaries lack a budget for study. A substitute plan is to employ a tutor to study at home, but this is often ineffective. There are countless interruptions at home, the lack of class competition reduces motivation and the teacher may be more eager to learn English than to teach his national language. A mother of young children has added frustrations, studying either at home or in a school.

Though there are many difficulties, it is important to learn the language if the missionary is to have a *satisfying* ministry over an extended period of time. Though it is often easier for Asians to learn another Asian language, they have the handicap of being expected to learn *quickly* and to speak *perfectly*. Failure to meet such a high standard can bring much frustration.

Reyburn's article,"Don't Learn That Language," appears to be a cop out for the missionary who fails to apply himself to this frustrating discipline (1958a:151-178). The emphasis howeve: is to learn not merely the words and grammatical constructions of the language, but to learn sentences that can immediately express a thought. Such an approach removes it from a mere classroom discipline to an exciting experience in a new society. One who begins conversing in another language will experience some immediate satisfaction plus a motivation to learn more. Donald N. Larson is correct in saying that "The degree of difficulty in learning a new language is in inverse proportion to the richness of opportunity" (1973:76).

Some missionaries live alone or on compounds, and seldom have occasion to use the language being learned except in the classroom. Often the wife has the advantage of being forced to speak the new language to her cook or to the one caring for the children. Her faster progress may become another emotional obstacle to her husband's learning.

Single people who can live with a national family, have an added opportunity for learning. This is often a satisfying experience for single people but very difficult for a family. Language learning is difficult due to the linguistic complexity and social tensions which involve degrees of alienation. Larson summarizes these ideas by saying "The degree of difficulty is in inverse proportion to the favorable nature of the students' socia and psychological environment during language study" (1973:76).

Some mission assignments require an excellent knowledge of the national language while others can be done acceptably in English. Often Western missions give an added incentive for language study by allowing only their members who have achieved a certain proficiency in speaking to vote during mission meetings. Most missionaries should allow from six months to two years for concentrated language study.

The Silent Language:

A new aspect of communication has emerged as a result of Edward T. Hall's book, *The Silent Language.* Hall recognizes three levels of communication which he calls the "Crucial trio of the *formal, informal,* and *technical"* (1959:51). The "formal" relates to what people are overtly aware of in an event, the "informal" is that which is learned by imitation or observation and the "technical" refers to what is recorded on paper. This could be illustrated by observing the distance between people during polite or friendly conversation.

Robert C. Gordon develops this concept in an article, "The Silent Language Every Missionary Must Learn" (1973:230). Cross-cultural workers need to be concerned about learning unstated rules of behavior. This silent language affects the missionary's acceptance by others and thus his ability to communicate.

Gordon then lists questions a person will be able to answer after understanding the people he is working among.

1. How late can one arrive without insulting a dinner host? A business contact? A government officer? A pastor? A School teacher?

2. Is there a technical time, a formal time, and an informal handling of time? What are the meaningful units of time? Five-minute segments? Fifteen-minute segments? Hours? Movements of the sun?

3. Do specific activities correspond to certain segments of the day?

4. What time of day is best for a relaxed informal visit? When should one never attempt business? Does the culture formalize such rules--8 to 5 for good business; 12 to 3 for siesta; 12 to 1 for lunch? Or is one time as good as any other?

5. How long should you wait before concluding someone does not want to see you?

6. How much notice should be given for a committee meeting? Religious services?

7. What length of time is required to establish a satisfactory social relationship?

8. Is there a sense of future in the outlook of the
    people? Or do they live for the present? Do
    they relate life to the past?

9. Do awards or rewards stimulate performance?
    What are effective rewards?

10. What territory does an individual man (woman)
    control? An elder or chief?

11. Can you predict where men will sit at a normal
    function given their rank or status within the
    society?

12. What system of learning is stressed? Rote?
    Logic? Example?

13. How do people play? When do they play? What
    does laughter mean?

14. What kind of person does the society fear most?
    Respect most?

15. Is law enforcement rigid with manipulation of
    penalties (as in the U.S.)? Or is enforcement
    according to the "spirit of the law" but pro-
    secution rigid and strict?

16. Are bribes criminal, or merely a means of obtain-
    ing some flexibility within an otherwise overly
    rigid enforcement-prosecution system?

17. What determines who is served first (for example
    at a post office)? Sex? Age? Arrival sequence?
    Rank? Race?

18. Is it possible to be truly "social" in African
    culture while living indoors (1973:236)?

All of these things are ways of communication. Lest one
becomes tense with fear of commiting some unforgiveable mistake,
the missionary should remember the Golden Rule toward the other
person and his culture, the supra-linguistic language of love,
and the fact that no one is perfect. People can easily identify
with others who make mistakes, especially if they can laugh at
themselves instead of blame others. This principle of communication is often forgotten in a cross-cultural ministry as well
as between parents and children in the home. There is no substitute for the attitude of *respect* from a person motivated by
love.

Selection of the Missionary's Assignment:

The independent missionary or mission society beginning a
new work in another country usually begins with zero. This is
extremely difficult and one could question the wisdom of such
action today. With the church on six continents, there are many
advantages of relating with, or at least of counselling with some
group of Christians before beginning a "pioneer work" among an
unreached segement of the population.

It will take time for a new missionary to become established
in a totally new area. If the people are not literate and there
is no church, one could say a specialist is needed who could do
linguistic evangelism.

Most new mission groups begin in areas where there are already
Christians. If they feel immediate results are necessary to maintain the continued interest of their supporters, they may begin
working with an interpreter. If they have no funds for national
workers, a few pastors may be willing to identify their congregation with this new society. Though this may describe some individ-
ualistic oriented Western missionaries, this pattern is not common
among Asian missionaries. Asians have a higher respect for the
established church and are more concerned about maintaining good
relationships with other Christian groups. Their difficulty would
be in the area of seeking too much cooperation with an established
church that has stopped growing.

Before a missionary leaves his home country, there should be
a clear understanding of the missionary's work. Will the primary
emphasis be on evangelism/church planting, Christian nurture or
service? The conciliar movement places high priority on service
and encourages a variety of social actions. Evangelism is often
interpreted to mean church development.

Unity in Christ and the relationship of fraternal workers
is also emphasized. Representatives of Asian church leaders
that met in 1960 in Hong Kong in a consultation sponsored by the
World Council of Churches and the International Missionary Council
said, "A missionary must be received as a brother. There must be
a mutual sense of responsibility" (Engel 1969:310). This is a
significant improvement over the paternalistic attitudes preva-
lent during 19th century missionary work. The question concerns
the purpose of the church and its place in bringing others into
a redemptive relationship with Christ.

Another temptation is for Asian missionaries to become
totally absorbed in an institutional ministry. Such an assignment can be easily described and offers emotional security. If
the missionary is paid by the sending church, this provides the

institution with the services of one staff member free. There
are economic factors plus aspects of "church politics" that become involved even in the assignment of missionaries.

The 1960 consultation of Asian leaders that met in Hong Kong
also discussed the relationships of the sending and receiving
churches. The sending church:

> should not do anything to prevent the mis-
> sionary from becoming wholly and without
> reserve a member of the church where he lives,
> belonging to it, acknowledging its authority
> over him, and playing a full part in its life.
> While we recognize that there are complex
> problems which still have to be solved in
> applying this principle, we believe that it
> is of universal application. It is through
> these missionaries it has sent that a church's
> commitment to mission is localized and made
> specific (Engel 1969:310).

If the receiving church has an aggressive plan of evangelism
and church planting, this presents no problem. But what does the
missionary do if the church is not growing and is not concerned
about seeking and finding lost men and women? Some Western missions maintain a mark of individualism and operate with some type
of dichotomy. This frees the mission and/or church from "captivi
by the other. Ideally, the two organizations, the mission (sodal
ity) and the church (modality) should agree on the common *goal* of
evangelism with the intention of planting new churches.

Mr. U. Kyaw Than, while a member of the Burman Baptist Convention and General Secretary of the East Asia Christian Conference referred to the issues of partnership in personnel, in finan
in policy and in administration discussed at the I.M.C. at Whitby
in 1945 and said:

> Partnership then was purely partnership in
> the ecclesiastical or domestic framework...
> as that of sending and receiving "ecclese-
> astical employees." You don't send mission-
> aries *between churches*. Crossing of geograph-
> frontiers alone does not constitute mission.
> Mission must involve crossing of the frontiers
> between faith and unfaith (1971:368).

McGavran continually emphasizes the importance of bringing
in the harvest. In an article "Logistic and Mission" he says:

World evangelization is in large part an
exercise in logistics--getting the forces
to the place where they are needed in time.
Missions should be viewed not merely as
extending a thin red line of men to proclaim the Gospel to all men whether they
believe or not; but as discriminating dis-
patch of sufficient, well-trained laborers
to fields which are now ripe, where churches
can be multiplied, where indeed they are
being multiplied (1966:7).

How does this apply to Third World missionaries? I see
the need for clear goals agreed upon *before* the missionary goes
to work in another culture. One of the functions of the sending
mission (sodality) is to make a clear policy for the work of
their missionary before he is sent out.

Some missions and churches have the goal of inter-church
aid by exchanging personnel. The emphasis is upon unity in
Christ and international witness of the gospel. If the image
of Christianity is that of a Western religion, the cooperative
effort of Christians from several Asian countries would have
significant influence for Christ. This pre-evangelism influence
is good, but needs to be followed by concentrated evangelistic
efforts with the intent of winning many to Christ. Not only
would the established churches be enlarged, but *new* churches
should and could be planted in new areas. Evangelism occurs
when people are won to Christ, new believers are baptized and
churches are established.

Other missions see their primary goal as evangelism and
church planting. The role of the mission board is to protect
these evangelistic missionaries from being absorbed into a
church structure that is indifferent to the Great Commission.
Many churches in Asia are growing. It is imperative that evangelistic minded missionaries be united with like minded churches.
This will require some creative thinking as there are few good
Western models to follow.

Evaluation of the Missionary's Activities:

Few business organizations could operate with the vague-
ness that characterizes the Christian movement. Some pastors
refuse to keep membership rolls as this could lead to a cause
for pride. In reality, many pastors with this type of thinking
are seeking to avoid a feeling of failure by concealing the
facts of little or no growth.

Others feel it is unspiritual to plan because one cannot
be certain of tomorrow (James 4:13-17). If there is no plan to
achieve a goal, there is no fear of failure. Fortunately, this
kind of thinking is changing. People are beginning to ask
questions about missions, evangelism and church planting that
were seldom thought of a century ago.

A common cause for failure in business or in missions,
is the neglect of carefully describing the person's work. This
"job-description" needs to be understood by both the employer
and the employee. A person may be working hard and yet not do
the work considered most important from the viewpoint of the employer. David A. Womack says, "The greatest enemy of the success
of Christian missions has never been the opposition of heathen
cultures, but the lack of unified goals and the failure to plan
strategically" (1973:17). This has a direct application to mis-
sion/church relationships.

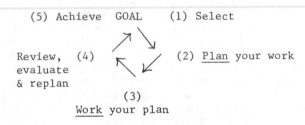

Diagram 7:1. Goal planning and achievement.

The above illustration shows the steps necessary to achieve
the goal. A goal must be *selected* (1) after discussion by all
concerned; a *plan* (2) of action must then be carefully prepared;
the sending church, the missionary and the receiving church *work*
(3) according to the accepted policies; recognition of success,
partial success or failure is learned by *review and evaluation*
(4) together. Success is a cause for rejoicing together and
brings much encouragement. Failure can also be a way of learning as new plans are made which then make it possible to *achieve*
(5) the desired goal.

If the goal is to provide medical treatment for 60 inpatient
and 250 outpatients monthly in a Christian hospital, one can meas
ure the results by checking the records. If the goal is to teach
four subjects in the seminary, one can check the hours of instruc
tion and the number of students enrolled. If the goal is to esta
lish one new church within 12 months in a village where no church
exists, one simply finds out if the church was started.

Each major goal has many intermediate goals that can and should be evaluated. How effective is the witness expressed with the medical care? What are the seminary students motivated to do? How does the response in Village A compare with the response in Village B or Village C? It is very important to plan carefully and to evaluate honestly.

Not only is evaluation of the mission work necessary, but also periodic times of missionary self-examination. Dick Hills says "Be a Better Missionary Because You Check on Yourself" (1972: 84-87). In these days of rash Christian activism on the one hand and indifference, lethargy and failure on the other, Christians must use some kind of a system to check themselves regularly.

Hillis suggests six topics for self-evaluation: (1) Language--have you lowered your standard? (2) Orientation--how well do you know the people? (3) Culture--have you learned to accept customs as different and not wrong? (4) Ministry--have you allowed the overwhelming opportunities to bring only frustration instead of fruitful work? (5) Spiritually--have you continued a vital and fresh spiritual life allowing the Word to become incarnate? (6) Love--have you allowed this to be neglected or replaced by intellectualism? "Self-examination may be a disappointment, but one can become a better person because he checked on himself" (1972:87).

The missionary's assignment needs to be evaluated by himself, by the host church and by the sending church. If the goals are not being achieved, there may be changes needed by all involved. For example, if the missionary's salary is no longer adequate because of unprecedented inflation, the supporting church should be aware of this and make adjustments. If the missionary neglected sending reports because he "failed," this also needs to be discussed. If the host church failed to give sufficient encouragement or if some policies needed review and change, a time of evaluation would be helpful to all concerned. Third World Missions have an opportunity to excel in this science of management that is still relatively new and not yet practised by many Western missions.

Many missionaries go to the field called to preach, teach, do evangelism, church planting, translation etc. Unfortunately, many are assigned jobs as mission treasurer, building supervisor, host for mission guest house, etc. With an emphasis that missionaries are to serve and not be served, that missionaries have no rights, etc. it is unspiritual to complain when foreign guests come to "see the work" and demand to be served.

What happens in the heart of missionaries whose primary work is public relations with tourists? If such a person remains polite to his guests, he may vent his anger and frustration upon his wife. If not, he may return to his homeland with a bleeding ulcer.

J. Melvin Miller diagnoses this condition in his article "Mission Priorities and Personnel Placement" (1972:78-83). A missionary with a recognized spiritual gift of teaching is being unfaithful in his ministry if this gift is neglected because the mission has no treasurer. Miller describes a "new resources" theory of management.

> We should fit the mission to the missionary
> and his gifts more than we do, rather than
> always fitting the missionary to the needs
> ..."new resources" is a management theory
> just now being applied to missions manage-
> ment from industrial management. In large
> organizations managers often become dissatis-
> fied with themselves, discouraged and depressed.
> This "new resources" theory suggests that the
> way to excite the manager who is discouraged
> and bogged down is to give him new resources,
> financial, technical, or human, to revitalize
> his interest and help the man to perform su-
> perbly--for himself and the organization (1972:
> 83).

This plan gives new resources to reactivate the missionary and his gifts for Christ. A Korean seminary professor went to Indonesia as a missionary. But was he assigned to a ministry of teaching in a Bible school or seminary? No, he became pastor of an established Indonesian church. As he experienced no special growth in the church, his wife organized a kindergarten and he began an English Bible class. In this way they contacted some people who were not Christians and a few made decisions for Christ. However, this missionary does not plan to return to Indonesia for a second term, even though he learned the language well. He plans to continue teaching in a seminary in Korea. One could seriously wonder if his assignment allowed him the most effective use of his spiritual gifts.

Inter-Mission Relationships:

"No man is an island" and this surely applies to Third World missionaries. Often they are required to live in three cultures: their own national culture, the culture of their host nation and also a transplanted Western missionary culture. The Western missionary culture may be the most difficult to relate with because of a different economic standard and social practices.

Is it good strategy for an Asian country to send seven
missionary families to seven different countries or to send them
to one or two different countries where they could evangelize and
plant new churches in an unreached area? Donald McGavran emphasizes

> ...finding a suitable population...sending
> a *band* of missionaries. Sending one Asian
> missionary to one nation and another to another,
> there to work as part of a Eurican team in
> some institution built by Eurican funds, is
> not a fruitful custom. It forces Asian mis-
> sionaries to adjust not only to the people being
> evangelized but to Eurican colleagues. Asian
> missionary societies should send out bands of
> Asian missionaries who will find comradeship
> and spiritual support from fellow workers who
> come from the same sending churches, eat the
> same kind of food, speak the same mother tongue,
> and are free to devote their whole energy to
> evangelizing those to whom God has sent them
> (1975:431).

This strategy would require a certain kind of Asian missionary. Many of Korea's FM-2 and FM-3 missionaries have worked in
hospitals, seminaries, universities, Bible societies, pastored
national churches, directed literacy programs, etc. Perhaps
they did not have the spiritual gifts necessary for planting
churches among unreached people. Continued research is necessary to see what Third World missionaries are able to do most
effectively.

There is the danger of Asian missionaries transplanting
their own denominational emphasis. The post World War II surge
of new Western missions and missionaries are not members of the
ecumenical movement. There is a tendency for independent and
interdenominational missions to misinterpret the goals and motives
of ecumenical missions in order to justify their own separate
existence. Actually, the theology among many Third World churches
is quite conservative in contrast to the liberal element often
found in the West. Independent missionaries coming to Korea were
amazed to see the life and growth of the Korean "ecumenical"
church. This did not fit into their preconceived stereotyped
image.

Third World missionaries need to avoid a "dichotomy mentality"
that one group is all good and the other group is all bad. These
prejudices need to be buried beside Western attitudes of colonial-
ism, paternalism and imperialism.

A person with a Biblical ecumenical view must include the independent missionary worker even if he does not yet want to be included in this broader Christian fellowship. Christians need each other. Christians need to recognize their unity in Christ, their common fellowship as Asians and their common obedience to the Great Commission given to all by their risen Lord.

There is a great *need for additional research and continual consultations between sending and receiving agencies. The unity within the diversity must be recognized and developed.* The effective use of spiritual gifts must be encouraged. Above all, there must be a recognition that *there is no one way* best for all of the sending and receiving agencies of Third World missionaries. The emphasis must be upon a cross-cultural communication of God's message rather than a propagation of Western Christendom. This must happen in order to effectively reach the 98% in Asia who do not yet affirm faith and allegiance to Jesus Christ.

8
Effective Cross—Cultural Training Institutions

Selection of the proper people for missionary work is of
primary importance. Some of the essential qualifications were
considered in Chapter 4. In addition to those personal and spiritual qualities, *specialized training* is needed for an effective
cross-cultural ministry.

Necessity:

Beyond Korea's borders, it was recognized at the Lausanne
Conference that with all the strength of the Korean church--cross-
cultural evangelism is still the weakest area. The Korean
National Strategy Group reported that "There is agreement as to
the vision for, the urgency of, and the necessity of this kind of
evangelization...there is a need for a stronger program of training academically, practically, and spiritually for cross-cultural
evangelization" (Hunt 1974:1,399).

James Wong says the church in East Asia is optimistic in
its goal towards world evangelization.

We believe that we are going to see the
beginning of a vast missionary enterprise
in the hands of Asian leadership. For us
it is the sunrise of missions. Asians are
beginning to assume the major responsibility

of evangelizing Asians across cultural, ethnic
and geographical boundaries. The greatest
challenge and need is not to motivate them
for evangelism but to train them in the know-
how of evangelism. The training of Asian Christian leadership (beyond the formal academic
program at theological seminaries) for evangelism and church planting should be given top
priority of attention...Efforts are being made
to coordinate and train more Asian missionaries
to be recruited each year. The projection is
that, by the end of this century, the churches
in Asia will train and send 10,000 missionaries
to reach the unevangelized areas of the world
(1974:1,323).

Won Yong Koh, a Korean pastor believes that God is raising
up many young people who are tasting revival and wanting to become missionaries, but face two major problems of finances and
training before they can be sent overseas. The Korean church
has spiritual vitality, many candidates are well educated and
most Orientals have a similar cultural background so they don't
have the problem of cultural overhang. However, the problems
of finances and training must be overcome (1972:218).

Recognizing the need for a training center in Asia, the All-
Asia Mission Consultation Seoul '73 resolved "to work for the
establishment of a center for Asia in cooperation with Korea Inter
national Mission for missionary orientation and research in Seoul"
(Chun 1973:350). The Seoul Declaration on Christian Mission
affirmed by the Asia Missions Association on August 31, 1975 supported this decision.

There are significant potential mission
forces emerging from various countries of
Asia, Africa and Latin America. We realize
the urgency to mobilize and train these forces. This is the purpose that has called into
being the Asia Missions Association, and that
has inspired the foundation of the East-West
Center for Missionary Research and Development (1975: Sect.IV).

One can clearly see that the Asians recognize the need
for a cross-cultural training institution. The location, curriculum, faculty and budget are a few factors that require seriou
thought.

Location and Language:

The selection of the site for the training center will influence many policy decisions. Will Asian missionary societies have *one* place where candidates from several countries will receive specialized training? Or will each country have its own national, or regional center? Will it be advantageous for some denominations to have their own training center? Each of these proposals has distinct advantages and disadvantages.

The East-West Center For Missionary Research and Development is a cooperative project of the All-Asia Mission Consultation and Korea International Mission Inc. This is the vision of David J. Cho, one of the energetic organizers of the All-Asia Mission Consultation, Seoul '73, where this project was approved. The goal is to train at least 10,000 Asian missionaries at the Center by the year 2000 A.D. This would be an average of over 400 Asian missionaries per year.

Korea has the advantage of having a strong growing church widely scattered throughout a responsive population. The church is considered conservative and there are many national leaders with graduate degrees from the West. The Korean government is strongly anti-Communist, and ready to receive visitors from non-Communist nations.

Korea has the disadvantage of being located at the north-east region of Asia. Transportation would be expensive for missionary candidates coming from central or south-east Asia. The winter weather is very cold in Korea. This would require a difficult adjustment for Asians coming from warm climates. It would also increase the operational cost of the Center to continue through the winter. The Korean church is conservative and the larger groups have strict denominational loyalties. Historically, inter-denominational efforts in Korea have been difficult.

Language is another significant factor in an international center. Would teaching be done in Chinese, Korean, Japanese or some other Asian language? The trend is for delegates attending international conferences to use English. Missionary candidates from India or the Philippines may speak English well, but it would be difficult for trainees from other nations.

Interpreters are frequently used for translating Korean into English and vice versa. This assumes a majority present being Korean and not Japanese, Chinese, etc. Perhaps lecture notes could be printed in advance, using the major languages of those present. There may be discussion groups according to one's national language. Though various plans may be substituted, a good knowledge of English is still necessary in order to have an effective international conference or seminar.

The faculty would experience the same difficulties as the missionary candidates. When they attempt to carefully explain spiritual truths to people of another culture using a language other than their mother tongue, they would have a new appreciation for the frustrations of Western foreign missionaries.

National or regional centers would have fewer difficulties. Logistical expenses of travel, board and room would be less than in an international center. Communication would be in the one national language. More teachers and students would be able to participate. Many qualified teachers are not fluent in English. Many missionary candidates preparing to do evangelism and church planting do not speak English well.

Home missionaries working in other cultures within the countries as the Philippines, Indonesia and India need to learn *another* language to minister effectively. Is it advisable to require them to also learn English *before* they can attend a missionary training institute? I doubt it.

National training centers also have the advantage of offering training to those who may not know for certain if they have the missionary gift. They are committed Christians, eager to learn more about missions, to become world Christians, and are willing to become involved within their own country. For such people, training in a distant international center would be less than ideal.

Denominational seminaries can also be developed as places for cross-cultural missionary training. Western theology should be replaced with an indigenous Christian theology which can be more readily communicated to other Asians. Anthropology should be added to the curriculum as it will help both ministers and missionaries to communicate the gospel. The large number of Christian workers contacted in a seminary could become the place for preliminary missionary candidate training.

Samuel H. Moffett reports that one of their best seminary professors, Chang Hwan Park, has gone to Indonesia as a missionary. The Presbyterian seminary (Tong-hap) in Seoul, is planning an Institute of Missions. This will train and orient Korean missionaries, and challenge the whole Korean church to face outward as well as inward with the good news of Christ (1971: newsletter).

Another new center also located in Seoul, Korea is the Asian Center for Theological Studies and Mission Church Growth Institute (ACTS). This evangelical, international and interdenominational center has the goal of training missionaries, pastors and theological seminary professors in missions and church growth. Some

will work within their respective nation and others will go to
other countries. By providing opportunity for a recognized
academic degree, it is hoped that Asians will study and develop
an Asian theology of mission rather than go to Western countries.
This project is still in its developmental stages.

What patterns are most effective for cross-cultural training of missionary candidates? I recommend that *each seminary*
develop a department for missions and church growth. This represents the main purpose of the church at home and abroad. With
present funds and faculty members, this new emphasis in curriculum
could be arranged with a minimum of difficulty.

Those interested in becoming missionary candidates should
enroll in a denominational or *interdenominational* training center
located in each country. If the candidate intends to be sent
abroad by a church or denomination, he should continue his in-
service-training in that local church on the weekends. This provides opportunity for further observation and counselling. Following a period of six months to one year of training, the candidate is recognized by the church, denomination or mission society
and commissioned as their missionary.

The *international center* may also be used as an interdenominational training center. If Korea is to send scores of trained
missionaries to other Asian countries, there is need for cooperation in this field of specialized training. If they expect to
work together in another country, they need to develop understanding and cooperation during their training. Denominational barriers
of pride and prejudice must be broken down in preparation for their
witness to God's love for all through Jesus Christ. Koreans preparing to serve and suffer together in their witness and efforts
to establish new churches in Indonesia or Thailand, must learn
to fellowship together in Korea.

The international center could also be a place for specialized linguistic training for Bible translation. It could be a
place for missiological research and publications for Asian
missionaries, mission societies, and national churches.

I see these cross-cultural training institutions as a pyramid. At the
bottom 1) there is need for scores
of Bible Institutes and seminaries
that emphasize church growth and
missions. Those interested in becoming missionary candidates should
enroll in denominational or interdenominational national or regional centers. 2). Only a
small number would attend the
international center 3).This

Int. Center

National and
Regional Centers

Bible Inst.
and Seminaries

Diagram 8:1. Proportional need
of training centers.

center would provide a place for research, publications, specialized training and seminars for planning and reviewing strategy
for world evangelization.

The key to interdenominational cooperation is selection of
proper members for the Board, faculty and staff. A leader of
Third World Missions cannot be one seeking recognition and promotion. Leaders in the East and the West are men and women who
learn to consistently serve others. This is never easy. Asians
who discern a proud domineering spirit in the Western missionary,
also see this among their own brethren. God will exalt the one
who humbles himself. Pride divides but love (humility) unites.

Curriculum:

The ordinary person thinks of curriculum as the total of all
subjects being taught in an institution. If the maximum subjects
possible within the school year is twenty four, it is easy to
"adjust the curriculum" by adding or replacing an equal number of
subjects. Frequently this is done according to the availability
of faculty members.

However, the curriculum is *not* the total of all subjects.
Curriculum is a course of study, the direction taken to achieve
a desired goal. Schools to train mechanics and ministers may
have a few of the same subjects, but the *course* is different.
A minister and a missionary likewise need a different curriculum
as their goal is different. A missionary needs special subjects
to prepare for a cross-cultural ministry.

Charles R. Taber observes the fact that most mission boards
and theological seminaries do not provide sufficient training
for a missionary to do effective Christian work in a cultural
milieu which is foreign to him. Taber suggests the need for
knowledge and competence in at least three areas: (1) the biblical
theological, and historical dimensions of his mission; (2) the
cultural and social milieu in which he is to work; (3) the basis
of human communication (1967:267).

While recognizing the effectiveness of some of the seminary
curriculum, there is need for profound restructuring. It is important to know the controversial theories of the relation of the
human and divine in Jesus Christ when studying the incarnation,
but there are other equally important facts especially in cultures
that may not question these philosophical theories. It is important to realize that in the incarnation, the absolute and un-
conditioned entered into a temporal and finite cultural setting
and immersed Himself in it totally to communicate with man.

The doctrine of inspiration is an essential part of revelation, but attention should also be paid to the fact that God used specific, human languages for communication. Likewise, the theology of salvation and the doctrine of the church should be made relevant to people with a different worldview.

Frequently church history is studied without noting the causes for growth or non-growth. Seminary students in India may learn all about the church in the West while remaining unaware of the history and development of the Christian movement in India.

Likewise missions can be taught without recognizing essential doctrines and movements in both the Old and New Testaments. Asian missionaries must find their own biblical mission mandate.

In the introduction to his new classic work *Initiation des Missions en Colonie Francaise* Maurice Lendardt, himself a missionary ethnologist with the Paris mission in New Caledonia for over forty years, wrote the following words:

> The experience of Pentecost renews itself
> in each apostolic vocation. A missionary
> called to the evangelization of a people, thinks
> of this people in a universal sense, that it is
> one of a group of souls. The other aspects,
> which are ethnic, social, political, appear to
> the missionary as almost accidental, a peculiar-
> ity of the domain of things which pass (1953-4:93).

The different worldview facing the missionary produces many unexpected results. There is a danger of unconsciously identifying the Christian faith with the Western culture. One can compare Western ideal situations with the lowest practices observed in another culture. Ignorance of the extended family system can hinder inter-personal relationships. A student may ask to be excused from school to attend her sister's funeral in the country. The missionary may later discover that the "sister" was a cousin and severely punish the student for lying. Yet in the student's worldview, the cousin was actually a "sister."

Failure to recognize the respected leaders in a village and their responsibility for group decisions, refusal to relate Old Testament practices of marriage to people in polygymous cultures receiving the gospel for the first time, an indifference to the reality of spirits and powers in the non-scientific and non-material-istic worldview, has hindered the effective ministry of many mis-sionaries.

One or two anthropology courses will not eliminate all of the prejudices in our minds toward those of another culture. Nor is

it just a matter of faith and prayer. But one or two courses
for missionaries should be planned so as to impart insight and
sensitivity to the missionary candidate before he goes to the fiel
The more training one has the fewer mistakes he is apt to make on
the field.

Alan R. Tippett believes the first requirement in planning
a training course is to be aware of the need and to set the goals
that meet it. This problem ultimately resolves itself into six
basic questions which must be answered:

1. Is the anthropological training given to mis-
    sionary candidates adequate and relevant?

2. What is a missionary candidate entitled to expect
    in his training?

3. What is the problem faced by the professor of
    missions?

4. What is the indigenous church entitled to expect
    of men sent to them by the church for cross-
    cultural mission?

5. Has anthropology any contribution to make to
    mission theology?

6. What is the missionary role in "directed cultural
    change" (1968:7-19)?

Tippett sees anthropology not as a luxury, but a vital neces
sity for a viable cross-cultural ministry. The missionary's know
ledge, attitudes, emphases and methods will determine the effectiveness of communication.

One of the most recent and complete reports on the curriculu
for training missionaries was done by a committee appointed by th
administrators of the William S. Carter Symposium, held at Millig
College, Tennessee, in April 1974. The committee members were
Gerald H. Anderson, Charles Forman, Linwood Barney, Tetsunao
Yamamori and Alan Tippett (Convenor) who examined the question
of guidelines for a curriculum suitable for the training of missionaries in cross-cultural understanding.

The statement and guidelines were published in the Milligan
Missiogram being specified as tentative and calling for feedback
from readers (1974:1-3). The statement is as follows:

1. The training of cross-cultural missionaries for the changing times and conditions of the mission fields of the work in our day, requires more and more understanding and empathy. For many years the discipline of anthropology... has been inadequately utilized in the majority of educational institutions where missionaries are trained. With the availability of this kind of education in our day, the sending forth of missionaries untrained in anthropology is no longer justifiable.

2. We recognize that the missionary situation in the world has changed dramatically since World War II, and that the old methods need revision, and the training provided for missionaries needs to be more relevant to the new situations... they need to be trained within a well-developed and relevant cross-cultural curriculum.

3. The attached model is recommended for consideration by an institution planning or adjusting its curriculum for the training of missionaries...It is assumed that each missionary candidate will have received his general education, together with his theological and biblical training. The fields set our in the model are related to preparation for service in Christian *cross-cultural* mission...The model is arranged in three columns (1-3) representing a sequence of increasing diversification (i) for a larger faculty, or (ii) for a training program for a wider range of mission fields. We do not say that all these subjects should be taught before the candidate leaves the institution: e.g. Language learning might be taken in a special institution or on the field - but it should be taken somewhere (1974:1-2).

This statement and the suggested model on the next page represents hours of careful planning by men who have accumulated decades of experience as cross-cultural missionaries. This suggested curriculum gives much emphasis to various aspects of theology and anthropology. This is important. However, an equally strong emphasis should be given to church growth and mission strategy. Instead of assuming these important subjects will be included in other courses, I recommend adding specific courses in Church Growth Principles and Procedures and Strategy of World Evangelization. With these additions, the curriculum suggested on the following page is a model that should be seriously considered by every faculty of a School of World Mission or of an institution for training missionaries.

1. SIMPLIFIED	2. MORE DEVELOPED	3. MORE DIVERSIFIED
1. History of Missions	History of Missions to the Reformation History of Missions since the Reformation	Expansion of the Early Church Missions - Middle Ages to Reformation History of Modern Missions & Ecumenics
2. Theology of Mission	Theology of Mission - Gospels Theology of Mission - New Testament Church	People of God in the Old Testament Theology of Mission - Gospels Theology of Mission - New Testament Church
3. Principles and Practice	Principles and Practice Indigenous Church	Principles and Practice Indigenous Church Theological Education by Extension
4. Cultural Anthropology	Cultural Anthropology Social Structure and Authority Patterns	Cultural Anthropology Social Structure and Authority Patterns Contemporary Trends in Missiology
5. Comparative Religion	Hinduism and Buddhism Islam	Hinduism and Buddhism Islam Other Eastern Religions
6. Applied Anthropology	Applied Anthropology Theory of Anthropology	Applied Anthropology Theory of Anthropology Data Collecting (Research Method)
7. Traditional Religions	Phenomenology of Traditional Religion Traditional Religious Practices & Praetitioners	Phenomenology of Traditional Religion Traditional Religious Practices & Practitioners Nativistic & Revitalization Movements
8. Church Growth Case Studies	Case Studies from Africa Case Studies from Asia and Latin America	Case Studies from Africa Case Studies from Asia Case Studies from Latin America
9. Language Learning	Language Learning Language and Culture	Language Learning Language and Culture Translation
10. Missionary Internship	Missionary Internship Mission Project	Missionary Internship Mission Project Reading Courses
11. Global Awareness and World Affairs	Global Awareness and World Affairs Cultural Dynamics	Global Awareness and World Affairs Cultural Dynamics
12. Spiritual	Formation and Growth of	the Missionary

Faculty:

Though this may appear obvious to some, the faculty needed in cross-cultural training institutions should be people who have had cross-cultural missionary experience. Attending graduate school in a Western country incurs certain cross-cultural experiences which are helpful. However, men and women who have ministered the Word of God to people in another culture can be more effective teachers. Asian missionaries properly trained are the best faculty members. Western missionaries with church growth and anthropological insights can also have a unique teaching ministry.

The shortage of competent faculty members is a most serious obstacle for every center of learning. People with the breadth of field experience, depth of academic preparation and outstanding personal and spiritual qualities are difficult to find. However, mission boards, seminaries and directors of missionary training centers, must make every effort to secure qualified people. This is essential if missionary candidates are to receive essential training.

Though cross-cultural training should be required *before* missionaries begin their career, it should also be *continued* during their first furlough. New problems experienced will require added knowledge and skills. An *annual* conference of Asian missionaries and directors of Asian missionary societies would be a very valuable experience. This could occur first on a regional or national basis and also biannual seminars at an international center as in Seoul, Korea. This would provide an opportunity to recruit new missionary candidates and to update seminary mission teachers and pastors on the current situation on mission fields.

Budget:

Though money is an essential part of every missionary project, it is unfortunate to see ideals compromised in order to secure financial assistance. The agency, church or individuals providing money for the construction and operation of cross-cultural training centers may have valuable missionary insights or may be guilty of Christian paternalism that can hinder the progress of missions as economic imperialism can stifle the development of a country.

The ideal training center would be one entirely financed by non-Western Christians. This sacrificial giving would require modest, indigenous style buildings and an efficient administration accountable to a national Board of Directors. An Asian Center financed and directed by Asians for the sole purpose of training Asian missionaries to do evangelism primarily in Asia, establishing new churches among unreached people, would have countless advantages.

However, do not Western nations have some responsibility
in assisting the development of Asian missions? Some see this
responsibility as an obligation and others view it as a privilege.
Donald McGavran says:
    Why should not the man power of Africasian
    churches be wedded to the financial resources
    of Eurican churches to meet more effectively
    the needs of the world? The Great Commission
    could become the strongest link binding Afric-
    asian and Eurican churches together (1973a:329).

    The Ad Hoc Committee on Relations with Third World Missions
in their report to the Association of Church Missions Committees
in 1975, indicated that foreign funds may be needed by agencies
for missionary training and to assist in the sort of preliminary
survey activity that is essential to strategic and effective missionary service. As foreign funds are still needed to assist
Third World churches at the level of theological education and
inter-agency, continent-wide associations, surely assistance for
missionary training is reasonable (1975:13).

    The East-West Center in Seoul has a tentative budget of
$5,000,000 for the major construction works. Though the land has
been donated, the major funding for this large international missionary training center will have to come from the West. From
my experience in Korea, I have learned that though it is difficul
to finance the construction of an institution, it is much more di
ficult to administer an institution that is intended to provide
service. Such projects need careful thought by the Board of Direc
in consultation with prospective donors.

    Cross-cultural training institutions are clearly needed. Ho
ever, if they are to be effective, careful thought must be given
the curriculum, faculty and missionary candidates. Cooperation
between Christians in the East and West is essential. Any appear
ance of preparing "mercenary missionaries" must be avoided. Eng
need not become the "trade language" for Asian missionaries. The
financial help from Western countries can and should be expected
success of the Asian missionary movement must not depend upon mo
from the West. I believe these guidelines are necessary for pol
decisions concerning training centers. Many centers are needed
provide the training essential for effective cross-cultural evan
gelism and church planting.

9
Effective Mission Infra—Structures

The preceding chapters emphasized subjects necessary for a viable cross-cultural mission. The proper relationship of these structures is also essential. I am indebted to Ralph D. Winter for Diagram 9:1 shown on page 156, "The Chief Structural Elements For World Evangelization."

1. *Recruits:*

When Kor Cheng, pastor of Grace Gospel Church in Manila spoke at the First Asian Student Missionary Convention in Baguio City, Philippines in December 1973, he referred to the problem in recruiting missionary candidates.

> No doubt, finance is a major problem in mis
> sionary work. However, the biggest problem
> is personnel. It is very hard to recruit
> qualified candidates. The solution to this
> problem lies in the local church encouraging
> its young people to obey the leading of the
> Holy Spirit so that they will dedicate their
> lives for the work of the ministry. On the
> other hand the seminaries and the Bible col
> leges should stress world missions in their
> curricula to challenge students to become
> missionaries (Cheng 1973).

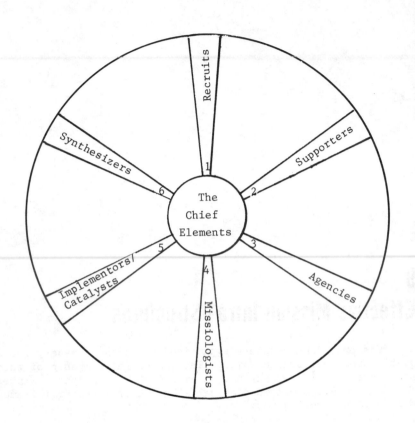

Diagram 9:1. "The Chief Structural Elements For
          World Evangelization."

          Student movements in Korea represent large potential for
Asian missionaries. Ewha Womans University in Seoul sent three
women to Pakistan and others were prepared to go but could not
receive a visa. With the largest student body of women in the
world, this Methodist University has the potential of recruiting
and sending scores of missionaries during the next decade.

          The University Bible Fellowship (UBF) led by Chung Woo Lee,
is a sodality sending over 200 Korean lay-missionaries to West
Germany, United States, Switzerland, Bangladesh, Japan, France,
Upper Volta and Peru. This movement is entirely indigenous and
growing. Campus Crusade For Christ, Inter-Varsity Christian

Fellowship, The Navigators and other student organizations also represent significant potential for Asian missions.

Pastors with experience in evangelism and Christian nurture are needed as diaspora missionaries to reach their own people resident in several nations. In some places a small group of Christians already gather for worship in houses. These need pastors for shepherding, and also to encourage evangelism among their own ethnic group. The Korean church is responding to this opportunity, yet scores of additional diaspora missionaries are needed especially in Latin America, Asia, the Middle East and in Europe.

Doctors and nurses are often able to enter countries closed to other missionaries. A recent unpublished survey of Asian missionary societies states that the Japan Overseas Christian Medical Cooperative Service has eight missionaries working in Nepal as part of the "United Mission to Nepal." Joon Lew, medical director of the World Vision Special Skin Clinic in Seoul, Korea has a vision of sending doctors to countries as Afghanistan, providing Christian care for people suffering from leprosy. Medical missionaries as this could receive full support from other doctors and nurses.

Asian missionaries can be recruited in missionary conferences sponsored by a local church, a denomination, or by regional, national, or international student conferences. Seventy seven students, volunteered for missions during the conference in Baguio attended by 800 young people. These need to receive counseling and specialized training to become effective cross-cultural missionaries. Such training is now possible. The science of missiology provides new insights unknown when Western missionaries first crossed the ocean with the gospel in 1812.

A new movement in the States called "Fellowship of World Christians" has prepared a valuable booklet, "Everything You Need to Know to Become a World Christian" (Graham 1975). This booklet provides information on the biblical basis of missions, historical development, facts and figures on the present state of the world Christian movement, function, structure and characteristics of mission agencies, local church mission committees, schools and institutions that train one for missions involvement, living and communicating in another culture and how to become a world Christian. This information is very helpful to anyone considering missions as a vocation.

. *Supporters:*

There are many patterns of support for Third World Mission agencies. Because the church represents a smaller proportion of the Christian population than in Western countries, the money

for missions comes primarily from the churches. The four main
patterns of support for Asian missionaries are: A) Wholly Asian;
B) Asian and Western; C) Wholly Western; and D) Self-supporting.

A. *Wholly Asian*

1. A church *denomination* may provide full support as the Baptists in Japan and Hong Kong, the Kinki Evangelical Lutherans in
Japan, and the Christian and Missionary Alliance Church of the
Philippines (CAMACOP). This structure is very effective when the
mission is planting churches of the same denomination in another
country.

2. Several *individuals* provide indigenous support for the missionaries in Japan and Bangladesh sent by the University Bible
Fellowship in Korea. A group of praying, concerned individuals
in India provide full support for the 75 missionaries in North
India sent by the Friends' Missionary Prayer Band.

3. A church denomination *and* individuals support missionaries
sent by the Foreign Missionary Committee of the Presbyterian
Church of Taiwan, the Immanuel General Mission in Japan, the
India Evangelical Mission, and others.

4. *Several* churches and individuals support the Indian Mission-
ary Society and interdenominational missions as the Japan Oversea
Christian Medical Cooperative Service, the Japan Committee of
Wycliffe Bible Translators, the Indonesia Senkyo Kyoryokukat (in
Japan), and others.

5. *Several* churches support the National Missionary Society of
India, organized in 1905 and currently having 51 missionaries
within India and two in Nepal. They plan to send six more soon.

6. A church *board* of the Sam Duck Presbyterian Church in Daegu
Korea was organized in 1971 and supports a missionary couple in
Indonesia doing literacy evangelism. The mission board of the
Grace Gospel Church in Manila, Philippines was organized in 1966
and this church now supports 47 missionaries in eight Asian coun

7. A *presbytery* of churches in Daegu, Korea organized the Dae
Presbyterian Foreign Mission in 1962 and supported a missionary
who worked for three years in Indonesia. As the missionary returned to Korea to continue teaching in the seminary, this mission is looking for another qualified candidate.

8. A concerned *pastor*, Heavystone Choi, contacted other Korea
pastors and organized the World Omega's Revival Mission Society
(WORMS) in 1973. This newly formed organization has already sen
three missionaries and has three others preparing to go.

B. *Asian and Western*

1. *Individuals* in Asian and Western countries support organizations as the Indonesia Missionary Fellowship organized in 1961
that now has five missionaries outside of the country and 72
missionaries in Indonesia.

2. An Asian *church and* individuals give directly to the support of societies in India as Bharosa Ghar Mission and the Hindustan Bible Institute and Western individuals send money through
a committee.

3. Asian churches and individuals give directly to the support
of Asian missions and Western individuals send money through a
committee for the Philippine Missionary Fellowship, Ambassadors
For Christ India, Overseas Missionary Fellowship, and others.

4. Asian churches and individuals give directly, and Western
churches and individuals send money through a committee. This
is the way the Korea International Mission, Inc. receives funds.
A similar pattern is used to support the Burning Bush Mission in
Taiwan, affiliated with the Mustard Seed Inc.

5. Asian and Western churches contribute on a proportional
basis for mission work of the Salvation Army, the Philippine Baptist Church, and others. This is also the policy of the Presbyterian Church in the United States and some others in the conciliar movement.

C. *Wholly Western*

1. *Individuals* of the Japanese community in the U.S.A. support
the Japanese Evangelical Missionary Society organized in 1950.
They are presently supporting one couple in Brazil and four couples
working in Japan.

2. Churches and individuals in the U.S.A. are being approached
directly by leaders of various Asian missionary societies, appeal-
ing for finances. Though they usually represent a genuine need,
it is important for Western donors to request and to receive a
bonafide report of the mission's activities.

D. *Self-supporting*

1. "Tent-making" is the policy of 157 missionaries sent out
by the University Bible Fellowship in Seoul, Korea. Foreign
missionaries sent out by the Hindustan Bible Institute must also
live by faith as money cannot be sent out of India.

2. *Diaspora* missionaries are often sent by their denomination
to establish self-supporting churches among their own ethnic
group in other countries. This is a successful model and is
practiced by many Korean and Chinese missionaries.

Each of these patterns is necessary and these models have emerged out of necessity. Undoubtedly there are many other variations of these four distinct patterns that will be discovered by those doing further research.

It is important to discover the most effective patern that will provide adequate funds for the missionaries and also become a spiritual blessing to those giving. Few Christians or churches have suffered financial lack due to excessive giving to missions. The Grace Gospel Church in Manila increased its giving from ₱ 28,500 ($4,070.00) for the support of 9 missionaries in 1966 to ₱ 320,000 ($45,714.00) in 1973 to support 46 Asian missionaries.

Some Western churches also want to become more involved. At the risk of simplicity, I suggest the practical policy of giving less than 50% to a ministry or project that receives the majority of support from Christians of that nation. They know the importance of the work and the integrity of the workers better than any foreigner. A responsible organization will provide financial reports to their own people and copies must be made available to others when requested.

Secret and indiscriminate giving can spoil the reputation of sincere people. Lavish and irresponsible giving can produce mercenary missionaries as easily as it produced rice Christians in the past. With increasing nationalism, there is also a new awareness of our oneness in Christ. This research reveals the fact that there is no one structure ideal for every cross-cultural mission organization. As we recognize the various organizational patterns, it is possible to adjust or create the method *most useful* in each country in working toward the goal of world evangelization.

Another practical problem facing missionary societies in Asia, is how to send money to workers in other countries. In some countries it is impossible. In countries where it is possible but difficult, some of the following channels have been used:

1. *Bank:* many organizations send a limited amount of funds through the bank. The Presbyterian office in Seoul sends money through the Korea Exchange Bank. Though funds for personal support are permitted, large amounts for special projects are prohibited.

2. *Branch office:* funds received by a branch office in the West can be used for air travel and special mission projects difficult to support from within the country.

3. *Western mission board:* some Asian churches continue to receive money from the West for special projects and institutional budgets. Often these funds are provided locally in lieu of Western funds that can be channeled to the support of their Asian church missionaries in other countries.

4. *East Asian Christian Council (EACC):* The Board of World Missions of the Presbyterian Church in the U.S. adopted the policy in 1973 of designating up to 5% of its personnel budget annually for the partial support of non-U.S. missionaries, ordinarily from the Third World, in countries other than America. These funds will be used in the following ways:

a) to provide funds to ecumenical missionary support programs of ecumenical agencies, such as WCC and EACC for the sending of persons from one country to another.

b) to aid non-U.S. churches, mainly in the Third World, to send missionaries to other countries by providing a share of the support, travel and allowances for these missionaries. The Board's proportion of these costs will be approved by the Board in each agreement...(Presbyterian Church in the U.S., 1971).

Each of these methods has certain advantages and disadvantages. It will be interesting to see what new methods can be arranged by Asians to surmount this unique problem not experienced in the West.

Financial support comes in a variety of ways. Unfortunately, this is often seen as the primary difficulty for the expansion of Third World Missions. The psychology of Western dependence is difficult to overcome, but it must be encouraged. The examples of men of faith as Adoniram Judson, J. Hudson Taylor, David Livingstone and others can speak to leaders of this new missionary movement. God continues to bless individuals and churches that emphasize missions and evangelism, so there is reason to believe that non-Western missions will continue to grow.

3. *Agencies:*

Though sending and receiving agencies were analysed in chapters 6 and 7, it is helpful to see their relationship to other elements for world evangelization. Winter gives additional insights on mission organizations in "The Anatomy of the Christian Mission" (1969:14-17). The "vertical structure" refers to the Foreign Board of Missions of the Christian Reformed Church, or Assemblies of God, or Southern Baptist Convention, etc.

These groups usually reproduce their own church denomination
on the mission field.   This vertical-vertical mission pattern
is used by diaspora missionaries and Asian missionary societies
as CAMACOP (Christian and Missionary Alliance Church of the
Philippines), Kinki Evangelical Lutheran of Japan, and others,
as illustrated in Diagram 9:2.

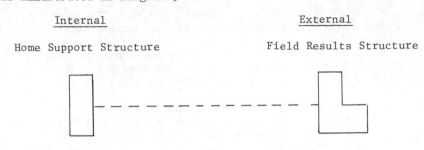

Diagram 9:2.   Diaspora missions, CAMACOP, etc.

        Winter then uses the horizontal line to represent an *interna*
field result described as "service missions."   For example, the
United Presbyterian overseas missions establishes churches,
schools, hospitals, etc.   This structure is illustrated in
Diagram 9:3.

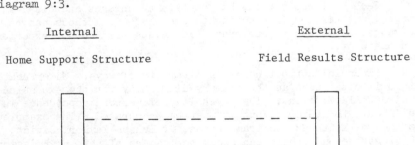

Diagram 9:3.   United Presbyterian Overseas Mission

        Some interdenominational missions that receive funds
from several churches and individuals may emphasize establishing churches but also have limited "service missions."

This describes many missions related to the EFMA (Evangelical
Foreign Missions Association), and Asian missions as The Philip-
pine Missionary Fellowship. This structure is illustrated in
Diagram 9:4.

Diagram 9:4. E.F.M.A. and Philippine Missionary Fellowship

        Another interdenominational mission may emphasize "service
missions" rather than planting new churches. This describes the
experience of workers with the Japanese Evangelical Missionary
Society that plants new churches but also emphasizes students,
radio, T.V. and Crusade evangelism as illustrated in Diagram 9:5.

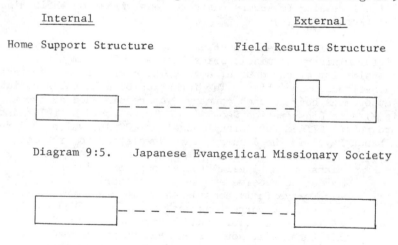

Diagram 9:5.   Japanese Evangelical Missionary Society

Diagram 9:6.   Japan Wycliffe Bible Translators

        Some interdenominational missions concentrate entirely on
"service missions." The Japan Committee of Wycliffe Bible
Translators are working in Nepal and Indonesia and the Japan
Overseas Christian Medical Cooperative Service in Nepal are
examples of this type, and illustrated in Diagram 9:6.

Usually the concern is primarily with the *internal* home
support structure. Leaders of denominational churches may oppose
their members giving money to interdenominational missions. Some
pastors of local churches likewise fear that money for local expenses will be inadequate if foreign missions is emphasized.
The goal of 50% for missions has been achieved by only a few
churches.

As denominational leaders and church pastors are concerned
about the internal structure for financial support, the mission
committee chairmans of local churches and directors of internation
missions should likewise carefully study the *external* field result
structure. Is the goal of missions evangelism, Christian nurture
or service? How many people are involved in each type of ministry
What percentage of the budget is committed to each? This information must be collected and evaluated in order to update and
improve the mission program. The senders have a responsibility
for the fruitful ministry of their missionaries--the sent ones.

The Japan Overseas Mission Association was organized in March
1973 with ten charter members. The goal of J.O.M.A. is to bring
about united action among Japanese churches in fulfilling the
Great Commission. Promotion, research and fellowship are included
in the J.O.M.A.'s ministries. With closer cooperation, they expec
to find it easier to secure passports and visas for their missionaries (Furuyama 1974).

The receiving agency must also accept responsibility for a
fruitful ministry of missionaries invited. Sometimes this is the
responsibility of one church, a group of churches, a denomination
or a national association. The formation of National Association
an autonomous body in each country, was recommended at the All-
Asia Mission Consultation Seoul '73. These would be related to a
Coordinating Office for Asian Evangelism (COFAE) which is directe
by Chandu Ray. In the January, 1974 Newsletter Ray reports:

> Plans for National Associations for Asian
> Mission to receive and send missionaries are
> being prayerfully considered in many countries.
> From all the correspondence that has reached me
> and the recent tours that I have undertaken in
> this behalf, it would seem that many are ready
> to encourage their young men to go beyond the
> borders for the sake of Christ. What we lack,
> because of rigid currency controls, is a finan-
> cial pool for travel of Asian missionaries.
> Perhaps a central fund for movement of persons
> will evolve during this year. Over one hun-
> dred persons are under training (1974 *News-
> letter*).

Two missionaries from an Asian missionary society working
in Indonesia refused to accept the authority of the inviting
church. As the goals of cooperation for evangelism and church
planting had been agreed upon before the missionaries were sent,
this action was inexcusable. As a result, those two missionaries
were not invited to return and were replaced by others.

Responsibility always involves authority and requires obedience. As missionaries tend to be independent, submission to authority is not easy. Clear goals need to be established, agreed upon
and regularly reviewed. A missionary can be busy, yet ineffective.
Recognizing the importance and urgency of the task, disciplined
planning and living is required.

4. *Missiologists:*

The new science of missiology seeks to relate courses in
theology, anthropology, history, geography, linguistics, etc. to
missions and church growth. The increasing number of mission
journals, research centers, church growth publications and seminars,
and growing enrollment in Schools of World Mission, are indicative
of the increasing influence of missiologists.

Following the Berlin Congress on Evangelism in 1966, many
national and regional congresses were convened. This gave evangelism an added emphasis and also encouraged greater cooperation
among evangelical pastors and mission leaders.

Seoul '73, however, added a new dimension, using the word
mission for the first time to describe an overseas seminar. The
All-Asia *Mission* Consultation was a significant first for leaders
of Third World *Mission* agencies and *mission* minded pastors. The
formation of the Asia *Missions* Association in 1975 was another
meaningful emphasis in the right direction.

Research is important and the publishing of research is
essential. Only in this way can those involved in missions and
evangelism gain benefit from the progress of worldwide learning.

Each nation should have its own periodical on missions
and church growth. Ideally, this should be edited by a national
with articles written by nationals and printed in their own language. Selected writings by others could be translated. This
publication should be well prepared and widely read by mission
and church leaders, seminary students and laymen concerned about
world evangelization.

An international edition for Asia could be printed in English, selecting significant contributions from missiological
journals and church growth publications from the East and the West.

This should be printed quarterly. It would be ideal if a Christian publishing company could recognize the importance of printing many books and articles related to missions, as the William Carey Library is doing in South Pasadena.

Writing, publishing and distribution of Christian literature is difficult in many non-Western countries. Without a subsidy, books are too expensive for the average Christian. He is more concerned about daily necessities of life and the children's education, than buying Christian publications. But with increasing literacy and a rising standard of living, especially in the larger cities, more are able to purchase Christian books written by their own people.

5. *Implementors/Catalysts:*

Many good ideas are lost simply because people or circumstances hindered their development. Roland Allen, an Anglican missionary to China, probably influenced by Nevius' insights, developed a biblical base for indigenous church principles. Allen's great book *Missionary Methods: St. Paul's or Ours?*, kept in print by World Dominion Press for fifty years, has been one of the most influential documents on mission methods ever written. Unfortunately, World War I created havoc and confusion for many mission agencies, especially those in Europe. This was one of many circumstances that caused the mission leaders to neglect the indigenous principles emphasized by Allen. Missiologists today are seeking to implement principles and policies recognized half a century ago.

A mission executive or pastor can be extremely busy and yet fail to develop mission strategy to implement effective policies. The late General Eisenhower was a very busy man who planned his work so that only the important and urgent matters came to him. Soon he discovered an interesting fact. The really important matters were seldom urgent and the most urgent matters were seldom important. Leaders of missions and churches need to conscientiously plan time to discuss and to establish mission priorities.

Winter has developed the concept of sodalities and has shown their importance in a mission structure. Chandu Ray, formerly an Anglican bishop in Pakistan, is being used of God to implement these insights in Asia today.

Following Seoul '73, Ray emphasized that these groups or "sodalities" be brought together for planning wider cross-cultural evangelism through teams, selected personnel, within the denomination framework in the first instance. At such gatherings a survey should be made of the people in the area, what is their cultural history and present milieu; religious beliefs and systems; standards and modes of living; political consciousness and administrative framework; language and dialect; education, etc.

From these representatives should come strategy and recommendations for selecting, commissioning and sending forth and receiving missionaries. Only then will the movement be truly integrated and become a two-way mutuality. The whole Church will thereby authorize and allow such agencies to carry out the functions on their behalf and raise the required funds for the program (1973 Newsletter).

The William Carey Institute (WCI) and the Missions Advanced Research and Communication Center (MARC) emphasize many new concepts developed in the School of World Mission and Church Growth Institute at the Fuller Theological Seminary in Pasadena, California. The "Fellowship of World Christians" (FWC) described on page 157 and the "Association of Church Missions Committees" described in Chapter 5 are two recent developments of the William Carey Institute.

MARC published the 10th edition of *Mission Handbook: North American Protestant Ministries Overseas*, edited by Edward R. Dayton, in 1973. With increased interest in the church and missions in countries other than in North America, a *World Christian Handbook* is being prepared. Dayton recently met with David Barrett, senior editor on the *World Christian Handbook*, and reports that this monumental project is nearly ready for publication (1976:7).

The Sixth Edition will be published by Macmillan. It will not only include statistical material on the church in all the different countries of the world, but will have detailed descriptions of the status of Christianity in each of these countries as well as essays on many different aspects of Christianity. An extensive directory of churches and Christian organizations will be included.

It is planned that MARC will make available the computerized data base which has resulted from the gathering of all this information as well as microfilm versions of the computer printouts. The *World Christian Handbook* will represent the most complete and exhaustive study of Christianity that has ever been done. It is hoped that it will give new understanding and impetus to the growth of the church worldwide (MARC 1976:7).

5. *Synthesizers:*

With increased international travel and communication, leaders in the Third World are more aware of activities worldwide. The independent worker has an increased disadvantage. As members of the one body of Christ, each has something to learn and to contribute.

The World Vision pastors' conferences that began in Korea
during the Korean war, now number over 100. Thousands of men and
women have been brought together to learn from each other and from
speakers from various nations. The director of this ministry for
World Vision International is Samuel Kamaleson, a Methodist pastor
evangelist from Madras. With new international leadership, this
organization founded by Bob Pierce in 1950, is experiencing rapid
growth under the leadership of W. Stanley Mooneyham, the man who
coordinated the Berlin Congress on Evangelism in 1966 and the Asia
Congress on Evangelism in Singapore in 1968 while an associate
of Billy Graham.

In addition to sponsoring 80,000 needy children, providing relief and development for suffering people plus a score of other
good works, the time may have arrived for the ministry of evangelism and pastors' conferences to add a new dimension. The new third
dimension could be sponsoring regional, national and international
seminars for leaders of Third World Mission Agencies.

This new movement for world evangelization has God's blessing.
It will continue and it will enlarge. But it will also make unnec-
sary mistakes costing lives, money and time. The urgency of the
task does not permit this unnecessary waste.

Some missiologists are discussing the possibility of an Edinburgh II in 1980. This would not be a conference for church leade
to discuss evangelism. It would be a World Missionary Convention
for *mission* leaders to research, study, discuss and plan strategy
for *cross-cultural* evangelism.

The Convention would not need to be large, luxurious and
expensive. Invited delegates should be carefully selected and mo
of them should travel at their own expense. There should be time
for Bible study, prayer, reports, discussion, disagreement, recon
ciliation, planning, etc.

The International Congress on World Evangelization (ICOWE)
which met at Lausanne, Switzerland in July 1974 was preceded by
many regional and national conferences. Edinburgh II on 1980
will likewise require preparatory national and regional conferenc

Ralph Winter's article, "1890 and that Certain Elite" (1976)
develops the proposal for a 1980 World Missionary Convention and
the events subsequent to it. The entire first half gives the lon
historical view and rationale for the conference, in a word, the
drifting away from *evangelistic* structures to *nurture* structures.

The latter part gets to the nitty-gritty of *how* this thing
is going to come about. It admits that the ad hoc group that
created the CALL--e.g. the professors at Wheaton in 1974 listed

on the back cover of the pamphlet--are not and cannot be the final steering committee.

The Call, as it was carefully formulated by those professors in 1974, consists of just two sentences: "It is suggested that a World Missionary Conference be convened in 1980 to confront contemporary issues in Christian world missions. The cross-cultural missions, broadly representative of the missionary agencies of the various Christian traditions on a world basis" (1976:152).

The echo of this Call has been heard in various periodicals, in small gatherings and in many face to face conversations throughout the intervening 24 months. The idea has actually moved about more rapidly than the exact wording and implications of the Call, so that in some discussions not all the elements have been present.

Winter clarifies the essential elements of the Call. The first sentence chooses quite intentionally the exact name of the 1910 conference. The second sentence describes the most important characteristics of the 1910 meetings:

1. that "representatives of missionary agencies" should constitute the conference.

2. that "missionary" in this context means "cross-cultural" outreach, not efforts for renewal within the church, nor local outreach in the same cultural sphere of existing churches.

3. that the meeting should involve simply a *conferring* as befits a *conference*, not a meeting which in any remote sense could or would *bind* any agency sending representatives.

4. that representatives of no cross-cultural Christian mission agency will be excluded due to its being related to one or another of the "various Christian traditions."

5. that, finally, the meeting will be a world level meeting. (1976:152).

The Lausanne Committee for World Evangelization, a worldwide synthesizing organization, is an example of this sixth element. This committee grew out of the International Congress On World Evangelization held in Switzerland in 1974. The committee has met in Mexico and in Georgia, and continues to give priority to evangelism. Emphasis is given to the development of regional and national committees, rather than creating a large international superstructure. The newly elected chairman is Leighton Ford, vice-president of the Billy Graham Evangelistic Association.

The two vice-chairmen are Akira Hatori of Tokyo, a Japanese evangelist broadcaster, and Nelson Fanini, pastor of the First Baptist Church of Niterio, Rio de Janeiro, Brazil.

In order to plan strategic evangelism, it is necessary to know who the unevangelized are and where they are located. At the meeting in Atlanta, Georgia, the Lausanne Committee for World Evangelization requested that:

> Ed Dayton of the MARC Division of World
> Vision International undertake to form an
> ad hoc subcommittee which will continue the
> valuable research on unreached peoples of
> the world already begun, and expand the oper-
> ation of the system for the collecting of
> data using the resources of the Lausanne
> Committee for World Evangelization and any
> other available and that Dr. Dayton be asked
> to report in person to the next meeting of
> the Lausanne Committee for World Evangeli-
> zation (MARC 1976).

These significant decisions are all necessary structural elements for world evangelization. Structures and organization are not synonymous with salvation and eternal life. Yet they are necessary *means* for communicating the gospel cross-culturally.

The Reformation rediscovered the message of salvation by faith but lost a sense of urgency and method for proclamation. We now have new missiological insights and improved understanding of how to effectively cross cultura barriers to make disciples of all peoples ("ta ethne").

The industrialized West is tempted to over emphasize the power of money, manpower and organization. The non-Western Christians, lacking these "resources," have experienced the reality of God's spiritual power, as many have been converted from animistic religions. With a new spirit of cooperation and agreement on the *goal* of world evangelization, there is new confidence that the Great Commission may be fulfilled with this generation.

Part Four

Evaluation, Review, and Future of Missions in Asia

10
Analysis of Selected Organizations

During the spring of 1976, Donald McGavran, Dean emeritus of the School of World Mission, directed a seminar on Asian Missionary Societies. The results of this survey were summarized in a report printed by MARC (Chun and Nelson 1976). Historical background information and current data for an evaluation of selected missionary societies is based upon that research.

As this study of principles and practices of Third World Missions has special emphasis on Korea, I will begin with several examples of Korean missionary societies. Each agency has something to contribute to a model for Asian missions.

1. The largest number of Korean missionaries are sent out by the *University Bible Fellowship* (UBF) in Seoul. This indigenous movement was organized in 1961 by Chang Woo Lee and Sarah Barry. Chua Wee Hian reported a $15,000 budget underwritten by the students and graduates of this organization.(1969:20-23).

This interdenominational fellowship is a sodality with no church relationship, though many of their members attend various local churches. In addition to Lee's responsibilities as director of U.B.F., he also writes *Daily Notes* in Korean for the Scripture Union. These are used by many Christians and become the foundation for Bible teaching and disciplined training for students. "Missionary volunteers are required to spend six months in concentrated life together training at a center in Seoul" (Chun 1973:20).

The principle of individual training is practised, as emphasized by the Navigators organization.

Most of their missionaries are self-supporting, arranging their own contact for employment in other countries. In an interview with Lee, he reported 205 missionaries that have a "spiritual relationship with U.B.F. These lay missionaries are widely scattered with 45 in the United States, 152 in West Germany, 3 in Switzerland, 1 each in Peru, Upper Volta and France, a full time evangelist in Osaka, and a missionary family in Bangladesh (Lee 1975).

These young people are to be commended for their dedication and zeal in witnessing to others of their own nationality residing in other countries. Though most of these laymen have received no formal theological education, they do experience disciplined training at their center. The missionary in Bangladesh is a graduate of the Presbyterian seminary (Tong-Hap) in Seoul. U.B.F. missionaries direct new believers into established churches and fellowships.

2. The earliest group to send out missionaries from Korea was the *Presbyterian Church*. Ki Poong Lee went to Chejudo in 1907 and other missionaries soon went to Siberia, Japan, Manchuria and China (Chun 1973). The primary emphasis was to evangelize Koreans living in other countries and many indigenous churches were established.

Following Liberation in 1945, Korean missionaries have gone to Taiwan, Thailand, Pakistan, Japan, Sarawak, Bolivia, Mexico, Okinawa, Singapore, Iran, Brazil, Argentina, Ethiopia, Hong Kong, Vietman, Indonesia, Guam, Canada and the United States. Most of these workers are diaspora missionaries, working primarily among their own ethnic group. Korean churches were established in these scattered communities and were usually self-supporting.

Unfortunately, the cross-cultural missionaries usually worked alone, rather than forming an "Evangelistic band." Frequently the became involved in institutional work or church development, rather than in direct evangelism and planting of new churches. *Excluding* Canada and the United States, I am not aware of even one new churc that has been established primarily for new believers of another nationality.

Cross-cultural evangelism and church planting require a uniqu type of missionary. Special teaching is needed. This must be don if Korea is to make a significant contribution to the evangelization of some of the unreached 2.7 billion people.

Meanwhile, diaspora missionary work should also be enlarged. Korean Christians give sacrificially and are loyal to their church. Diaspora missionaries must not be satisfied with merely shepherding a group large enough to support the local church. A vision for reaching the lost is needed. In cities where property is expensive several house churches could be established with lay leadership provided by elders and supervised by the pastor.

3. A widely publicized organization is the *Korea International Mission* (KIM), founded in 1968 by David J. Cho, pastor of the Hoo-Am Presbyterian Church in Seoul. Cho is a gifted organizer and an active promoter of Third World Missions. He was a key person in planning the All-Asia Mission Consultation Seoul '73, and also in establishing the Asia Mission Association in 1975.

Cho also organized a Summer Institute of Missions in 1973 that meets annually for two or three weeks, attended by about 60 Asians. As some are from other Asian countries, lectures are given in English and translated into Korean. Cho plans to establish the East-West Center as a place for further missionary training, research and publications.

Though K.I.M. is interdenominational and has six missionaries, most of the support comes from the Hoo-Am Presbyterian Church (Hap-Dong). As this denomination hesitates to cooperate with other groups, it is difficult for Cho to receive wide support from other denominations. This is unfortunate as Cho has an unusual vision for the development of Third World Missions. A broader base of support and cooperation is needed to make the East-West Center truly inter-denominational and international.

The Korean church represents a dynamic potential for missions. Korea was never ruled by a Western nation, so the Korean Christians do not have a psychology of dependence observed in other countries. Strong leadership is required to inspire loyalty. Cooperation is difficult, and as the churches are large, many can support and send their own missionaries. However, interdenominational cooperation for training missionary candidates is essential if Korean Christians are to do effective evangelism in other countries.

Not counting Korean missionaries in Canada and the United States, as many become permanent residents, there are 259 missionaries sent by 17 different agencies working in Argentina, Australia, Bangladesh, Brazil, Brunei, Ecuador, France, Guam, Hong Kong, Sarawak, Singapore, Switzerland, Taiwan, Thailand, Upper Volta and West Germany.

Of this number 224 or 86.5% are FM-1 diaspora missionaries, working primarily among Koreans in other countries, 11 or 4.2% are FM-2 foreign missionaries in a similar culture as Japan and

Taiwan, and 24 or 9.3% are FM-3 foreign missionaries in a radically different culture as Bangladesh, Brunei, Indonesia, Pakistan, and Thailand. A summary of research on Korean missionaries was included in chapter 6.

Japan:

Though only about 1% of the people in Japan are Christians, there is much interest there in Third World Mission activities. The *Japan Overseas Mission Association* was organized June 2, 1971 with ten charter member groups. Andrew Furuyama was elected executive-secretary. His goal is to enlarge the missionary vision and cooperation of Japanese churches.

Furuyama attended the All-Asia Mission Consultation Seoul'73 and reported 29 agencies sending 94 missionaries to various countries (1973:244-247). Eleven Japanese agencies responded to our research questionnaire, indicating 55 missionaries sent to the countries of Brazil, Bolivia, India, Indonesia, Jamaica, Kenya, Korea, Nepal and Thailand. Four types of missions in Japan seem to be in service today. We will look more closely at these types.

1. *The Japanese Evangelical Missionary Society* (JEMS) is an inter denominational Japanese Christian Fellowship founded in 1950. This society was established by evangelical Nisei ministers and lay people (first generation Japanese born in America) who received inspiration during an extended prayer session at Mount Hermon, California, that same year.

J.E.M.S. is supported by Niseis living in the United States. They have four missionary couples working in Japan and one in Brazil. This ministry includes student evangelism and also crusades, radio and TV evangelism by Akira Hatori. J.E.M.S. has a journal named JEMS printed in both English and Japanese. In this way churches and individuals are kept informed and financial support is provided.

This is another excellent model for Asian missions. People of various ethnic groups have immigrated to the United States and Canada. Many have become successful and experience a higher standard of living than their friends and relatives "back home." This enables them to have not only indigenous ethnic churches in the States, but to establish a mission society or to support missionaries with other Asian societies. With this principle, effective evangelism could be done by Asians in Asia, supported by Asians in the West.

2. *The Japan Overseas Christian Medical Cooperative Services* is another unusual sodality. This interdenominational group was organized in 1960 by 245 members of the Japan Christian

Medical Association. Though the constitution is very broad in its
nature and appears to emphasize service rather than evangelism,
this may have certain advantages. Some of the supporters may be
medical people primarily concerned with providing medical care.
Also, this group is able to enter countries as Nepal, normally
closed to the evangelistic missionary.

This organization has eight medical missionaries working in
the Christian Mission Hospital at Rajshahi, Nepal, with 26 other
medical missionaries from Western countries. Though some speak
English, their working language is Nepali. The mission plans to
send two more missionaries soon to Bangladesh.

Medical missionaries frequently have good opportunities
to witness to people resistant to the gospel. The hermit nation
of Korea was opened to Christianity primarily through the work and
witness of Horace N. Allen, a Presbyterian medical doctor trans-
ferred from China. He became the personal physician of Prince
Min, Young Ik and was credited with saving his life following an
attack on December 4, 1884 (Rhodes 1934:14).

God is concerned about salvation of the whole person. Spiritual
concern can also be expressed by caring for the sick, widows and
orphans. A Christian doctor contacts many who would never attend
church. The Presbyterian Hospital in Daegu, Korea has been responsible for establishing over 200 new churches through the outreach
of the staff with mobile units and conversion of patients in the
hospital. The Christian medical society within the hospital also
provided financial support for a Korean missionary doctor. The
medical director, Howard Moffett, continually emphasizes the responsibility of the staff to treat the *whole* person, physical and
spiritual.

3. *The Committee For Ecumenical Ministries of the United Church
of Christ in Japan (Kyodan),* provides another model of Asian
missionary work. This national committee of the church, not a
separate mission society, was established in 1956 by Rev. Gosaku
Okada. They now have missionaries working in Bolivia, Thailand,
India and Korea. The national church in Ponape, Caroline Islands
has invited missionaries and the Kyodan church has accepted this
invitation.

They presently have four couples doing various activities
as pastoral work, student evangelism, teaching in a seminary
and secular school and translation work in Thailand. They appear
to have a close relationship with Western missionaries as two
of them use English for their ministry, and work in different
countries.

It is good to see a conciliar church in Asia sending workers to other countries. They receive some funds from the West, so this is helpful in the purchase of plane tickets, transfer of local currency for living expenses, etc. One of the missionaries is involved in translation in Thailand. Hopefully, this will make it possible to reach another tribe with the gospel.

The conciliar churches have many advantages for Asian mission work. The East Asian Christian Council can assist not only in the transfer of funds, but in mission research, directing new work to the most needy and responsive places, and can frequently help in securing necessary documents for travel.

The necessity of evangelism and church planting needs to be continually emphasized, even among pastors and missionaries. As a new charcoal fire will not burn unless it is fanned, so must missions continue to stress the importance of persuading men and women to believe in Jesus Christ, to be baptized and to become responsible members of a local church. It is natural to care for those who have been converted and this nurturing is important. However, pastors and missionaries are to be followers of Jesus Who was sent to *seek* and to save the lost.

4. *The Japan Committee of the Wycliffe Bible Translators* is another interesting example of Asian missions. The work in Japan was established in 1968 by Takoshi Fukuda. They now have eight missionaries translating the Kaling language in Nepal and the Isirawa language Indonesia. Each language is used by about 2,000 people.

This work is interdenominational and receives no foreign income Support comes from various churches and individuals within Japan. During 1976 and 1977 they plan to send five more missionaries but the countries are not yet selected.

These Japanese missionaries are involved in an FM-3 ministry where the culture is radically different from their own. Though they are part of an international team with missionaries from Germany, Australia and America, they are still able to maintain their own national identity and have fellowship among themselves. This is helpful, right, and should be encouraged when Asians work with those from the West.

As these missionaries had no special linguistic training before going to the field, they are learning as they translate. The they are to be commended for their zeal and dedication, the translation of the Bible requires development and dedication of the best skills possible. The missionary training center being established in Korea by David Cho, has plans for an East-West Institute of Linguistics. This will be developed in cooperation with Wycliffe Bible Translators with a view to applying linguistic studies as a basic tool for the communication of the gospel.

Further research is needed to learn how these missionaries were trained and selected. The East-West Center in Seoul expects to develop an Institute of Lingustics in cooperation with Wycliffe Bible Translators. The Wycliffe leaders and missionaries from Japan may have helpful counsel for the development of this new project in Korea.

According to the recent survey of 11 mission societies in Japan, there are 8 FM-1, diaspora missionaries, 5 FM-2 foreign missionaries in a similar culture, and 34 FM-3 foreign missionaries in a radically different culture. These would appear on a diagram as follows:

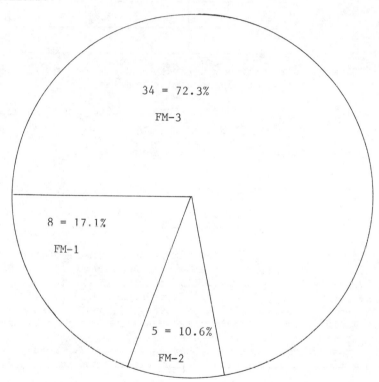

34 = 72.3%

FM-3

8 = 17.1%

FM-1

5 = 10.6%

FM-2

Diagram 10:1. Cultural difference experienced by 47 Japanese foreign missionaries, 1976.

Using the evaluation grid to analyze the primary activities in the three categories of evangelism, Christian nurture and service, we can make diagram 10:2. as seen on the next page.

	E	N	S	(W)	Total
M-1	2	2	1		5
M-2	7	0	0		7
M-3	9	6	5		20
Total	18	8	6	(23)*	32

Diagram 10:2. Primary activity and cultural difference
of Japanese missionaries.

Note: This <u>includes</u> 8 Home missionaries also doing evangelism
in Japan, 1976.

*   Wives not included in activity totals.

Taiwan (Republic of China):

Two missions in Taiwan responded to the survey and they provide interesting and different examples.

1. *The Overseas Missions Committee of the Presbyterian Churc*
in Taiwan was organized by the General Assemly in 1959. This denc
inational mission supports 41 missionaries in the following countries: Brazil (10), Canada (8), Hong Kong (2), Japan (12),
Mauritius (2), Singapore (2), Thailand (2), and the United States
(6). Their ministry is primarily evangelism and establishing
churches among the Chinese in dispersion. They did not indicate
plans to send additional missionaries in 1976-77. Perhaps they
did not notice this question or know exactly how to respond.

With such rapid growth in 17 years, one would hope that many
more missionaries would be sent out soon. Though it is difficult
for them to receive passports and visas for travel to some countries, there are many countries still open. Chinese are scattered
all over the world. Many recognize a new sense of responsibility
to evangelize their own people in the Free World, and even inside
Communist China. Perhaps someone from the Philippines Chinese
Church that supports 173 missionaries could visit Taiwan and give
them a new vision and challenge.

2. *The Burning Bush Mission* was organized by 18 pastors in 1968 as a result of inspiration by Mrs. Lillian R. Dickson, founder of the Mustard Seed Inc. The Dicksons were Presbyterian missionaries from Canada and much of their work was among the tribal people in the mountains.

In 1968 there were eight tribal missionaries sent from Taiwan to East Malaysia. Six of them are still on the field. All of the missionaries are ordained Presbyterian pastors. After being selected by the Burning Bush Mission, the presbytery was asked to give approval to send these men. Seven of the original eight belonged to the Ami Tribe and the other to the Cunum Tribe.

Keith E. Hamilton points out that sometimes persecution was a major cause of church growth, and in other instances it is a minor one. Persecution was a major cause for remarkable growth of the Presbyterian church (1939 to 1944) among the Tyal and Ami Tribes in the mountains near Hwalian Kang on the east coast of Formosa. Despite Japanese persecution, four thousand marched down out of the hills when the Japanese left the island to ask for baptism (1963:138). It is significant to note that pastors from the Ami Tribe were first to become missionaries to the Iban Tribe (Dyak) in East Malaysia.

In February 1968, Rev. Empaling, a pastor of the Iban people (Dyaks) came to Taiwan from Sarawak, Borneo to meet with the committee of the Burning Bush Mission and thirty five volunteers who were mountain pastors. The moment of meeting was very emotional. Philip Pu reported that it was almost like a reunion after centuries apart. The language structure and vocabulary was very similar (1973:260). Pu continues:

> So the Burning Bush committee tentatively
> decided to send four of the best mountain
> pastors to Sarawak. "But," objected one,
> "Why do we send away our best men? That will
> rob our church." The superintendent of the
> Iban work in Sarawak said, "We had only three
> pastors, and we sent our best one to a wild
> tribe in Malaysia." After that no one demur-
> red (1973:261).

The Methodist mission in Malaysia invited these pastors of Presbyterian churches in the mountains to work among the Iban Tribe. It was difficult to secure passports and visas, but finally the men received permission to travel. The families joined them a year later. These Presbyterian pastors worked under the supervision of Methodist pastors doing evangelism. "Two of the men were preaching where the gospel had never been preached before, and one had baptized 355 of the Iban people with more wanting baptism. But he made them wait until he was sure of their sincerity." (Pu 1973:272).

These missionaries had no problem of cultural overhang as they were working among people with a similar culture. Many of them had an animistic background and had personally experienced release from the power of the evil spirits. What they lacked in finesse, they had gained from a personal encounter with their risen Saviour. These men had become missionaries even without learning English!

The Burning Bush Mission has contributions to make to a model for Asian missions. Experienced pastors were willing to do cross-cultural evangelism with pastors of *another denomination*. This is the ecumenical movement in its highest form. But a spirit warfare is never easy. For various reasons four of these pastors (50%) became "missionary casualties" and are being replaced by ten more volunteers.

These two mission societies reported 35 diaspora missionaries (FM-1) and 8 doing cross-cultural evangelism in a similar culture. This can be illustrated in Diagram 103, below:

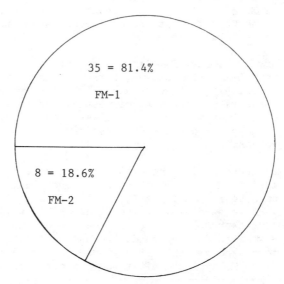

35 = 81.4%

FM-1

8 = 18.6%

FM-2

Diagram 10:3.   Cultural difference experienced by
                43 Taiwanese foreign missionaries, 1976

Using the evaluation grid to analyze the basic activities in the three categories of evangelism, Christian nurture, and service, the following diagram, on page 181, attempts to combine the primary activity of each missionary with the cultural difference.

	E	N	S	(W)	Total
M-1	18	0	1		19
M-2	4	0	0		4
M-3	0	0	0		
Total	22		1	(20)*	23

Diagram 10:4. Primary activity and cultural difference
of Taiwanese foreign missionaries, 1976.

Note: * Wives not included in activity totals.

Philippines:

1. *The Philippine Missionary Fellowship* was organized
in 1954 by the graduates and faculty of the Far East Bible Institute
and Seminary (FEBIAS). Immanuel C. Pascua is chairman of this interdenominational mission that receives support from both Western and
Asian churches. As a strict sodality movement, it does not depend
on any one denomination for support nor does it require new believers
to join any particular church.

They have 54 missionaries that emphasize both pastoring local
churches and planting new churches. They have 11 missionaries
working among tribal people, 6 are involved in a literacy program
and 4 do student evangelism. All are working within the Philippines, but in a different ethno-linguistic group. During the next
year they plan to send about 10 new missionaries to Palawan,
Ilocos Provinces, Samar, Luzon and Panay Island.

It is good to see a theological school with a strong emphasis
upon missions. This can be a good example for other seminaries
and Bible institutes in Asia. The questionnaire did not indicate
what percentage of the mission funds come from the West.

As F.E.B.I.A.S. is interdenominational, one can be concerned
about their graduates becoming fully accepted as workers with an
established denomination. What would be needed for these missionaries to become a part of local churches and then plant new churches
of this same denomination?

Interdenominational missions have many advantages but also serious difficulties. What form of church government is adopted by new churches? Does the missionary become the pastor of one or more new churches? If not, who trains the leadership? Will the new churches join a denomination of their own choosing or form a new group?

These are questions that face all missionaries starting new churches, especially in areas where there is no established church. Cross-cultural missionaries will usually impose their own background and experience on a new group. This may not always be the best. Interdenominational missions excel as service agencies, but must make several major policy decisions if they are planning to establish new churches.

2. *The Philippines Chinese Church* is another large sending agency in Asia. According to information from Joseph Young, there are at least nine Chinese churches today having a sizeable mission budget. Together they support over 173 workers in the Far East with a total budget of $161,430.00. The breakdown is as follows:

Name of church	Missionaries	Budget
Grace Gospel Church	40	400,000
United Evangelical Church	38	380,000
Davao Evangelical Church	17	80,000
Quezon City Evangelical Church	7	40,000
Jubilee Evangelical Church	6	30,000
Cebu Gospel Church	7	40,000
Grace Christian Church	24	50,000
St. Stephen Church	6	40,000
SEA Foundation	22	50,000
Elim Fellowship	5	20,000
	173	₱1,130,000 (or $ 161,430 at a rate of 7 pesos to $1.00)

There is need for further research of present Chinese mission work. Love China '75 was a "Mainland China Evangelism Study Seminar" held in Manila, September 7-11, 1975 which created a new concern and sense of responsibility for their fellow countrymen in Communist China. This is surely a significant aspect of the Asian missionary movement.

The five agencies in the Philippines included in this research have a total of 249 missionaries. There are 67 doing home mission in another culture (HM-2), plus 173 diaspora missionaries (FM-1), 4 work in a similar culture (FM-2) and 5 work in a radically different culture (FM-3). This can be illustrated with Diagram 10:5 on page 183.

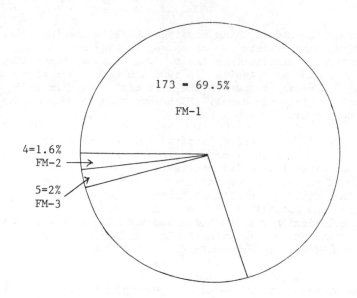

173 = 69.5%

FM-1

4=1.6%
FM-2 →

5=2%
FM-3

Diagram 10:5. Cultural difference experienced by
249 Philippine home and foreign missionaries, 1976.

Using the Evaluation grid to analyze the primary
activities in the three categories of evangelism,
Christian nurture, and service, we can make Diagram 10:6.

	E	N	S	(W)	Total
M-1	173	0	0		173
M-2	31	3	7		41
M-3	2	0	1		3
Total	206	3	8	32*	217

Diagram 10:6. Primary activity and cultural difference
              of Philippine missionaries, 1976.

Note: * Wives <u>Not</u> included in activity totals.

India:

Some of the oldest Asian mission societies are in India. The
Indian Missionary Society was organized in 1903 and now has 12
cross-cultural workers within India. The National Missionary
Society of India was organized in 1905 and reports 51 missionaries
including 8 honorary members. They are all working in India with
the exception of two in Nepal. Plans are made to send six additio
workers next year.

1. *The Hindustan Bible Institute* was organized in 1952 by
Paul V. Gupta. This interdenominational school was established fo
the purpose of training missionaries to go into the unevangelized
frontiers of India. It reports 114 workers and all but seven are
working in India. During its 24 years of history, it has planted
24 churches and established two elementary schools. They plan to
send 25 more missionaries to North India during 1976-77. Some of
their graduates also work with the Indian Evangelical Mission and
the Friends' Missionary Prayer Band.

This is another good example of a theological training center
preparing workers for cross-cultural evangelism. In addition to
work in India, they have graduates doing missionary work in Malaysia, Singapore, Burma, Sikkim and Nepal. These workers live by
faith, receiving support from the people they minister to as money
cannot be sent to them from India. This provides another significant model necessary if hundreds of Asian missionaries expect to g
into other countries to preach the gospel.

2. *The Friends' Missionary Prayer Band* (FMPB) is a movement
organized in 1958. It began at Tamilnadu as an outcome of the Vac
Bible School conducted by the South India Bible Seminary. It now
sends 87 missionaries from South India across 1,000 miles and grea
linguistic and cultural barriers to preach to those in North India

The movement is a band of prayer groups. As this work is int
denominational, there are no denominational barriers among these
"friends" who have a united concern for missions and come together
to pray.

This praying band of friends became burdened to provide the
finances necessary so one of their group could "Go and tell."
Thus, the friends chose for themselves the motto, "Go or send."
All of the workers are lay people who receive 18 months of preparation in their Missionary Training Institute located in Tuticor
before they are sent out for two year terms of service.

The plan for the coming years is to send 440 missionaries to
North India. The team is praying for 44 missionaries each year in
order to reach the goal of 440 in 10 years. In order to meet this

vast need, the leaders plan to begin 440 prayer groups which will each support one missionary. Samuel Kamaleson writes, "Within the "rest of India" there are at least 220 district headquarter cities. The praying friends purpose to place at least two missionaries in each one of these headquarters within the next ten years" (1975:433).

One is impressed by the dedicated zeal of the workers in this movement which is wholly indigenous. Their official publications, "Challenge" in Tamil and "Burn Out" in English, accent the disciplined self-giving of all in this ministry.

Their plan to place 440 missionaries in 220 district headquarters represents a strategic plan. Yet one might ask if this wide distribution permits a sufficient witness in each place. Could four workers in each of 110 districts be more effective?

Which districts have missionaries with other organizations? What areas are most responsive and may justify the temporary transfer of 50 workers to reap the ripened harvest? As the Friends' Missionary Prayer Band does not plant new churches, they must realize that they are members of a larger team doing evangelism and church planting.

There are plans to move the Missionary Training Institute to Danishpet. Soon the present faculty of graduates from the Yeotmal Union Biblical Seminary will be joined by graduates from the School of World Mission at the Fuller Theological Seminary. More adequate training can then be given to these dedicated Christian workers. Though the Friends' Missionary Prayer Band is interdenominational, most of the support comes from members of the Church of South India. Therefore mission policy of evangelism and church planting will require careful planning and honest evaluation.

3. *The Indian Evangelical Mission* was formed by the Evangelical Fellowship of India on January 15, 1965 under the leadership of Theodore Williams. The mission has a two-fold objective: 1) To take the gospel of Jesus Christ to the unevangelized areas in India and outside India, and 2) To challenge Indian Christians to realize their responsibility for world evangelization and to recognize their partnership with other Christians in the world in fulfilling this task.

The motto of the Mission is found in Isaiah 54:2, "Enlarge... stretch forth...spare not." It rests on the three pillars of VISION, FAITH AND SACRIFICE. The mission is indigenous, interdenominational and evangelical.

The mission is indigenous in finance, membership and government. It looks to God in faith for its support. This come through the freewill offerings of God's people, individuals or churches in India. No funds are solicited from abroad.

The I.E.M. is interdenominational and does not enter areas where any church is actively working. In areas where there is no church, the mission will encourage believers to form themselves into worshipping congregations. The missionaries in that area and the believers together seek the Lord's will and agree together upon the form of church order and government that they desire in consultation with the I.E.M. Board. They have established seven churches since 1965.

The mission believes in the spiritual oneness of all believers in the Body of Christ and seeks to cooperate with those of like faith everywhere. Where necessary, it will enter into partnership in countries outside India with international fellowships which agree with their principles and policies. At present the I.E.M. has entered into such a partnership with the Overseas Missionary Fellowship for work in East Asia and with the Bible and Medical Missionary Fellowship for work in West Asia (Williams 1975:435).

At the present time the mission has 38 workers within India in the Andaman Islands, Andrah Pradesh, Himachal Pradesh, Orissa, and Uttar Pradesh. There are three missionaries outside of India working in Thailand and Papua, New Guinea.

During 1976-77 the mission expects to send three more missionaries to Gujarat, India and to Indonesia. In addition to this, Williams says, "We are very much exercised about sending Indian missionaries to the Arab world and to Latin America" (*Global Report* 1976:3).

This interdenominational mission has carefully prepared policies for working with other churches, denominations and overseas agencies. This indigenous movement is well organized with accountability of funds and ministry. Surely this is a model to be adopted by several new mission societies in Asia.

India is a large country with several barriers of language, culture, and religions. Those involved in evangelism within India are certainly doing missionary work. The following graph (Page 187) indicates the distribution of 515 or 96.3% missionaries involved in home missions (HM) and 20 or 3.7% in foreign missions (FM) as reported by 10 agencies in India.

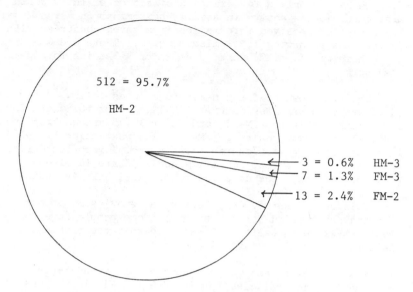

512 = 95.7%

HM-2

3 = 0.6% HM-3
7 = 1.3% FM-3
13 = 2.4% FM-2

Diagram 10:7. Cultural difference experienced by 515 home
and 20 Indian foreign missionaries, 1976

Using the Evaluation grid to analyze the primary activities
in the three categories of evangelism, Christian nurture,
and service, we can make diagram 10:8.

	E	N	S	(W)	Total
M-1	0	0	0		0
M-2	424	21	12		457
M-3	7	3	0		10
Total	431	24	12	(68)*	467

Diagram 10:8. Primary activity and cultural difference
of Indian missionaries, 1976.

Note: * Wives not included in activity totals.

These are only a few examples of scores of Third World
Mission societies active in Asia. The seminar on Asian Missionary Societies received information from seven countries with
53 agencies reporting 1,293 missionaries. There are 662 or 51%
doing home mission (HM) work, and 631 or 49% doing foreign mission
(FM) work.

The breakdown of foreign missions is as follows: 455 or
72.1% are diaspora missionaries (FM-1), 104 or 16.5% are working
in a similar culture (FM-2), and 72 or 11.4% are working in a
radically different culture (FM-3). The vast majority (91%) are
involved in evangelism/church planting, 6.5% reported Christian
nurture as their primary activity and 2.5% are involved in various
kinds of service. The detailed report is in the Appendix, page 20

This recent survey only begins to remove some of our foggy
thinking about Third World Missions. Some people have an idealis
view that escapes reality. Others see only the problems and the
vision of a new missionary escapes them.

Missiologists need to be both a catalyst and implementor of
new practices and policies for Third World Missions. One of the
best methods of learning is to share experiences, both successes
and failures. If this is done among leaders of new mission socie
ties, more rapid progress can be made toward achieving the goal
of world evangelization.

11
Potential Areas of Expansion

The Yung Nak Presbyterian Church in Busan, Korea is preparing to send a missionary to another country. Recognizing the difficulty of assuring adequate continual support, this church has established a missionary endowment fund in the local bank. The interest will be used for foreign missions. Though the circumstances vary among churches in Asia, this is a typical example of a group of Christians willing and ready to send a missionary to another country.

This pastor asked me where I thought they should send a worker. Unfortunately I had no clear answer for this important and sincere question, so contacted the editor of the *Church Growth Bulletin*. McGavran responded by emphasizing several important principles.

1. *Responsive populations abound:* In most countries several sections of the mosaic are already responding to invitations to accept Jesus Christ as Saviour and Lord. Korean missionaries should *not* think that there is only one responsive population.

2. *Train Korean missionaries* to find out which denominations are growing and in what segments of the population they are growing. A static church may be surrounded by rapidly growing churches, and remain unaware of the cause for growth or non-growth.

3. Remember that *responsiveness is in part triggered by what the advocate (the missionary) does*. In Chile, the Assemblies of God have grown only slightly, but the Methodist Pentecostals have grown enormously. The Chilean masses are responsive. A growing church is one that has discovered a way of evangelizing which appeals to the masses. Korean missionaries must not only find responsive populations, but must proclaim Christ to them, and create churches among them *in the right way*.

4. *Responsiveness is one of several factors* that determine where missionaries should be sent. Other criteria area:

a. Recognition that the *Great Commission includes unripe populations* also. Missionaries need faithfully to sow and weed till the harvest ripens.

b. Observe which *nations have friendly relations* with South Korea and will grant Koreans permits to enter the country. Other things being equal, Korean missionaries should go to receptive populations in *those* nations.

c. The *amount of money* for missionary support is also an important factor. It is very expensive to travel to some distant fields and to maintain an adequate missionary force there.

d. The *degree of the dedication* of the missionaries and their supporting churches is also important. Churches willing to continue support of missionaries who labor faithfully in spite of little fruit, qualify for difficult assignments. Others should go where the response is easier.

5. Missionaries should have the *goal of propagating the gospel* with the intention of baptizing new believers and incorporating them into the church. With 98% of Asia still unreached, fraternal delegates to already established churches, or the introduction of more just political systems must not become a *substitute* for evangelism.

6. Korean missionary societies ought to *survey populations* they hear are responsive and make recommendation to their churches. Feasibility studies are necessary, especially for new missionary societies. Earlier missions learned by trial and error. A few thousand dollars spent in survey will save tens of thousands in false starts (1975:440).

Missiological geography is a new field introduced by Ralph Winter to the Fuller Seminary School of World Mission. This study informs us not only where countries are located, the climate, the total population, natural resources, etc., but we learn about people. The missionary needs to know more than the national population or the average number of people per square kilometer. He *needs to know who lives where*.

A map showing population centers is an invaluable aid for the missionary. Rural evangelism is difficult in areas where most people live in the cities, just as industrial evangelism would be impractical in rural areas.

Population shifts are also significant. Frequently people who have just moved to a new area are more responsive to the gospel. Family ties and earlier religious traditions no longer have rigid control of people in new areas. Often these people are more progressive, seeking new things. Awareness of such principles are helpful to evangelists, missionaries and church planters.

Many people think of missions only in terms of geographical areas. Leaders of new missions think that they must send 10 or 20 new missionaries to different countries. This is poor mission strategy. A *team* of two or more couples is usually more effective than people working alone. This is one reason for the effective ministry of missionaries sent by the Burning Bush Mission in Taiwan to work among the Dyaks in Indonesia.

A nation or country may have a score or more of different social and language groups consisting of homogeneous units. The Chinese and Japanese living in Korea cannot expect to be evangelized by the Koreans. The ethnic, racial, linguistic and prejudice barriers make this difficult. Chinese or Japanese pastors could more readily establish a church among their own people, even in Korea.

David Liao studied the Hakka people living in Taiwan to learn why so few of them are Christians. He concluded that they are not necessarily unresponsive, but simply have not been effectively contacted in their own language and culture (1972:7).

"Status of Christianity Country Profile" is a project of Missions Advanced Research and Communication Center (MARC) for the International Congress on World Evangelization which met in Lausanne, July 1974. This information is the result of hours of research and is essential for every mission's library and should be carefully studied by directors of Asian mission agencies and their missionaries. A sample of these valuable profiles for Asian countries is included in the Appendix (MARC 1974b).

"An Unreached Peoples Survey" is also being conducted by M.A.R.C. The importance of this research was emphasized when the

Lausanne Committee For World Evangelization requested Dayton to
expand the operation of the system for collecting data.

The most obvious question related to a survey of "unreached"
people concerns how to determine when a nation or a group within
a country have been "reached." The idea that any group with less
than 20% Christians is "unreached," would put Korea with an estimated 15% Christians in the same category as Japan with an estimated 1% Christians. Also unclear is whether people are "reached"
according to the extent of the witness given, or if it depends
upon the response.

There is increasing acceptance of the definition that a perso
is "reached" when he has clearly understood the gospel in his own
linguistic and cultural setting, and is able to make an intel-
ligent decision either for or against faith in Jesus Christ. Some
say this can be done only when a person lives within the influence
of a gospel proclaiming national church.

Recognizing the limitations to any form of research, the emph
sis of focusing upon *segments within society* that have not yet
responded to the gospel, is a worthy effort. People who do horse
racing in Santa Anita may be as unreached as the Hakka tribe in
Taiwan.

Dayton has prepared computer print outs with information
received concerning several groups of people living in Asia. This
data includes information as the population, primary languages,
main religion, other religions, churches and missions present,
response, trends and attitude toward the gospel, literacy, etc.
Any new Asian missionary should be aware of this research as he
prayerfully considers the choice of country and work within that
nation. A sample of groups in Thailand is included in the Appendix (MARC 1974b).

Winter emphasizes the necessity of this type of research in
his article "The Demographic Imperative." Referring to the work
of early pioneers as William Carey and those that followed him,
he says that we can be grateful to God that there are over ten
million Christians in India. But the perplexing and distressing
fact is that there are at least 500 subcultures, and "that in at
least 480 of these entire subcultures there are no Christians at
all. Very bluntly, normal evangelistic outreach from existing
Christian churches in India is utterly inadequate to face this
challenge" (1972:213).

Recognizing the need for cross-cultural evangelism as our
ideal, we must emphasize continued research and training of worke
for this ministry. Though we do not endorse the doctrines of the
Church of Jesus Christ of Latter-day Saints (Mormon), we should
be aware of their valuable research for cross-cultural communications. The Language Research Center in the Brigham Young

University, Provo, Utah is producing four *Culturgrams* with information about Asian countries which are especially helpful to new missionaries.

The *Culturgram* has information on:

1. Customs and courtesies (greetings, visiting, gifts, eating, meetings, gestures)

2. The people: (attitudes, population, language, religion, holidays)

3. Lifestyle (the family, dating and marriage, customs, income and possessions, work and business hours, diet, recreation and sports)

4. The nation (history, government, economy, education, health, transportation, land and climate) (*Culturgram:* n.d.)

A sample of the Korea culturgram is included in the Appendix. More extensive culture-specific packets with over 30 pages of research material is also available to orient new missionaries eager to cross the cultural barriers in order to preach the gospel and to establish churches.

Asian missionaries are gaining importance in world evangelization. Recent Fuller Seminary School of World Mission research of 53 agencies in Asia indicates that 631 or 49% of the 1,293 responses were foreign missionaries (FM-1- 2 - 3) with 455 or 72.1% of these being diaspora missionaries (FM-1) and only 176 or 27.9% cross-cultural missionaries (FM-2 or FM-3). It is important that leaders of Asian missionary societies recognize their need to *train more cross-cultural foreign missionaries.*

An encouraging fact is that 91% of the missionaries responding are involved in evangelism. Even the 6.5% in Christian nurture are primarily pastoring diaspora churches, and this requires a strong evangelistic emphasis. Fortunately, most Asian missionaries have not yet succumbed to the "syndrome of church development" as experienced by many missionaries from the West (Wagner 1974:92).

While realizing the need for more cross-cultural missions, both home and foreign, let us recognize the Asian pattern of missions and evangelism following lines of migration, especially for the Koreans and Chinese. They have the primary responsibility and opportunity for evangelism and church planting among their own ethnic group in other countries.

Koreans are literally scattered around the world with embassies in 44 countries and consulates in 9 other countries. Many of these places have Korean communities active in trade, industry, business, etc. Less than 10 of these countries have established Korean churches.

As Korean Christians pray about world evangelism, they should pray not only for those in North Korea, temporarily closed to the gospel except via radio, but mission agencies, churches and mission committees need a world map showing the location and approximate size of every Korean community. These areas are open to the gospel. Pastors with a burden for evangelism should be sent to these strategic areas. Korean Christians are loyal to their churc and give sacrificially. It is highly possible that Korean churche could be established in 50 different nations during the next decad

The Korean church needs continually to emphasize missions and evangelism. Obedience to the Great Commission may be a factor in God's continued protection of this divided peninsula with a population of 33 million in the South. There are plans to establish a new Korean church in Iran. This is good. The momentum of diaspora missions must continue and increase while the cross-cultural missionary candidates receive further training.

The Chinese are more scattered than the Koreans. There is a new awareness of their responsibility to evangelize their own group. Western Christians are surprised to learn that 10 Philippine Chinese churches are sending out 173 missionaries, with 47 of these being supported by the Grace Gospel Church in Manila.

However, the Chinese also have travel limitations, especially those entering or leaving Taiwan, the Republic of China. Even the Chinese missionaries sent by the Christian and Missionary Alliance of Hong Kong to work in Indonesia experience problems. As these missionaries were originally from Communist China, the Indonesian government recently refused to renew their residence permit (Lam 1976).

Overseas Chinese are becoming more aware of their responsibility to their own people in mainland China. Many of these Chinese Christians are successful businessmen, able to travel to the mainland, and often take money and Bibles to their friends and relatives. Communist China leaders apparently approve this, at least for the moment, eager to receive more dollars and good-will from the free world.

"Love China '75" was a study conference that met in Manila, September 7-11, 1975. Since the Chinese Communists came to power this was the first international conference scheduled to discuss how to speak to the people on the Chinese mainland most effective about the gospel and how to hear from and about the church.

"Love China '75" was convened by Open Doors with Brother Andrew, *Decision* magazine (Chinese edition), Chinese Committee of Underground Evangelism, Christian Communications Ltd., China Graduate School of Theology, Overseas Radio & Television Inc. of Taiwan, The New Chinese Bible Commission, Living Bible International, Hong Kong, Far East Broadcasting Company and many others.

"Love China '75" set itself the task of bringing to life a massive effort of prayer and action on behalf of the Body of Christ in China; of planning the educational and spiritual training of a new generation of Christian workers for China; and of arousing millions of overseas Chinese and other Christians throughout the world to take up the spiritual burden for China.

Topics discussed included Christian churches in China, learning the lessons of the past; Chinese communist attitudes towards the church; the new China; new Bibles for the new China; radio evangelism; and personal evangelism inside the new China. Each speaker was carefully selected for his wide experience and knowledge (Love China '75, 1975).

Though large Western style churches no longer exist in Communist China, there are increasing reports of Christians meeting secretly in small groups for prayer, Bible reading and worship. *Time* magazine printed a report by two missionaries that an underground Chinese Christian community numbering more than 1,200 has grown up in Foochow over the past five years. If the story of the Foochow revival is indeed basically true, it signals that the Christian faith can still spark enthusiasm in a land where Mao's revolution has tried to snuff it out (1974:55).

In addition to reports from Foochow, other travelers speak of finding groups of underground Christians in many villages and cities. In Shanghai, according to one account, the prayer groups are nurtured by "Bible women"--lay ministers who took over pastoral leadership after the male leaders were arrested. How many Christians are there in China now? Generous estimates range from 1 million to 2 million (*Time* 1974:55).

The faith of these Christians has been tested and has become more meaningful than life itself. If this country ever again freely opens the door for missionaries to re-enter, one could seriously wonder who would be qualified to preach and teach these Christians who have suffered so much. W. Stanley Mooneyham said, "When China is evangelized it will almost certainly not be by non-Asians" (*Asia Pulse* 1972:3).

Though missionaries cannot enter Communist China, there are still opportunities to contact those who have come out, either temporarily or permanently. Numerous efforts have been made

to distribute Bibles to 20,000 Chinese working on projects in
Zambia and Tanzania (*Asian Report* 1974:2).

There are now hundreds of Communist Chinese "technicians and
experts" on the tiny, strategic island of Malta--a N.A.T.O. base.
"They are like visitors from outer space," a Maltese said wonder-
ingly. "They walk around in groups of never less than four.
They don't talk. They don't smile. They all wear blue Mao suits
with Mao badges" (Harris 1976:A-13).

Western diplomats view the Chinese presence on Malta, estimated to number 400 or 500 men and women, with curiosity. Though
a direct Christian witness to these "hard core Communists" may be
impossible, yet concerned Christians can seek various ways to give
them the gospel. Who could have imagined that a Christian Maltese
technician or government official might have such an opportunity
to witness cross-culturally to people who deny the very existence
of God.

Chinese Communists are not all in China, Africa, or on the
island of Malta. Many are on ships that dock temporarily at sea-
ports where Christians could give a witness *if such a team were
mobilized*. Churches in port cities should organize evangelistic
bands to secure Scriptures and Christian literature in various
languages and prayerfully distribute these to crew members of
foreign ships.

Many Communist students are studying in universities in Canad
and the United States. Geraldine Nelson, a former missionary to
Ethiopia and now a staff member of International Students Inc.
working on the campus of Iowa State University wrote, "Two weeks
ago it was my privilege to discuss the Christian faith with a
newcomer from Hong Kong, a young man who's a Communist. I
couldn't help but think--I could have been a missionary there
for 20 years without ever coming across him, and here is is at
the I.S.U!" (1976). Many opportunities await those who have a
vision for communicating the gospel cross-culturally.

As we think of potential areas of missionary work, we must
concentrate upon various *groups of people* to be reached. Some
may be across the street, in another part of the country or in
a distant nation separated by an ocean. Some countries closed
to Western missionaries are still open to Asians and vice versa.

With the threatening spread of Communism, prayerful thought
must be given to ways to prepare Christians to resist this political power, as in Korea, or how to live under it, as in Poland,
etc. Christians need to consider the importance of Scripture
memory and ways to protect copies of the Bible in case of severe
persecution. Pastors may be forced to become laborers, but they

will still need to learn how to encourage believers to remain
faithful. Laymen need to develop small cells for Bible study
and prayer in anticipation of the time when large churches may
be closed.

All Christians cannot be airlifted to free nations when Communist governments take over. Neither will all Christians escape
martyrdom. Surely an important subject for consultations by missiologists is how to prepare Christians to live under various
types of Communist governments.

Communism is one of the greatest hindrances today to the
spread of Christianity. And yet it is breaking down religious,
social and cultural barriers that have hindered the growth of
Christianity in free nations. In God's sovereignty, we may be
seeing economic, social and political changes that will soon make
possible a large response to the gospel. Laborers for the harvest
are needed, and they are also now being recruited through scores
of new Third World mission agencies. As groups of unreached people
are identified, we can anticipate a turning to the gospel as Asian
missions expand into new areas.

12
Conclusion

Out of the Berlin Congress on Evangelism in 1966 came the statement voiced by Ted W. Engstrom: "The great challenge confronting the Church today is to identify and to locate every person in the world by the end of this century. There is no individual, no people, who cannot be reached with the Gospel if we set ourselves to this supreme task of the Church. We can truly go to *every* creature" (Henry and Mooneyham 1966:315).

Significant progress is being achieved through World Vision' M.A.R.C. project to identify the unreached. This will help us to *see* more clearly those needing an opportunity to hear the gospel. This research is essential for mission leaders and missionaries from the East and the West.

Even with our present knowledge, we recognize the shortage of qualified, trained, cross-cultural workers. The task of world evangelization requires involvement of all who belong to Jesus Christ. A Filipino wrote, "If we got a hundred thousand more Western missionaries tomorrow, we Asians must still obey the Great Commission written in our own language" (Pentecost 1973:11

Just as many non-Western nations are making rapid progress in their economic and technological development, many younger churches are also growing. Concentrated efforts are being made to disciple the unreached and to incorporate these new believers

into local churches. New mission organizations are being established. Church-mission structural relationships are being recon-
sidered. New patterns of financial support are being tried.

   *Missions From the Third World: A World Survey of Non-Western
Missions in Asia, Africa and Latin America* by Wong, Larson and
Pentecost (1973) caused mission leaders to realize that a new
movement is underway. Building upon this survey, a research
project conducted in the School of World Mission in 1976 received
responses from 53 societies in 8 countries. These questionnaires
reported 1,293 Asian missionaries now on the field. Of these,
631 or 49% are foreign missionaries (FM 1-2-3) working in another
country. The vast majority of 455 or 72.1% are working as diaspora
missionaries, seeking to reach their own ethnic group living in
other countries. Though this is important evangelism, it should
not be confused with cross-cultural evangelism.

   Only 176 or 27.9% are doing cross-cultural evangelism in other
countries, as FM-2 or FM-3. It is interesting to note that the
highest percentage (83%) of these missionaries come from Japan,
with 39 of their 47 workers involved in *foreign* missions. As
the total number of Christians is comparatively small in Japan,
they may not yet see the need to evangelize and establish churches
among Christians who have emigrated to other countries as do the
Korean and Chinese diaspora missionaries.

   Another fact revealed was the large number of cross-cultural
missionaries being sent by mission agencies *within* countries as
India, the Philippines and Indonesia. The 1976 research revealed
that 662 or 51% are doing evangelism among people of a similar
but significantly *different* culture (HM-2). Only 3 were considered
as HM-3, but this interpretation may be different for people living
in countries having so many different languages, cultures and
religions.

   It is important to recognize that this is the type of missions
being done by many non-Western missionaries. Many of these workers
are *laymen* who have received various amounts of theological education and cross-cultural training. They are zealous, sacrificial
and dedicated people, usually supported by the prayers and finances
of Christians in their own nation. - While emphasizing the importance of cross-cultural foreign missions, we must not neglect
the *urgency of cross-cultural home missions*. This must be recognized as a valid mission work, and a type that can be done with
a *minimum of logistical problems* experienced by those going to
another country.

However, these workers need thorough training. Some go as representatives of established churches with no intention of planting new churches. Others see their responsibility as witnesses, with workers evenly spread over large areas instead of concentrating on responsive people. Policies and practices of missions need constant review and evaluation.

Using the elevation grid, the results of the research on 1,293 missionaries in 53 countries would be as follows:

Cultural Difference	Location		Primary Activity				
	HM	FM	E	N	S	W	Total
M-1		455	361	36	2		
M-2	659	104	589	24	19		
M-3	3	72	31	10	6		
Total	662	631	981	70	27	215	1,293
	51%	49%	91%	6.5%	2.5%		

Diagram 12:1. Primary activity and cultural difference of missionaries from 53 agencies in 8 countries, 1976.

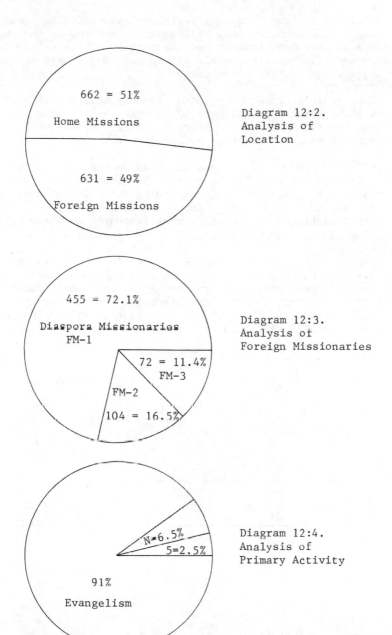

Diagram 12:2.
Analysis of
Location

Diagram 12:3.
Analysis of
Foreign Missionaries

Diagram 12:4.
Analysis of
Primary Activity

While it is true that many Western missionaries have become
channels for interchurch aid, falling into the trap of the church
development syndrome, this is not the pattern of the Asian missionary societies studied. This can be one of the most encouraging discoveries of this research.

Many Western missions need new strategy and priorities. Some
become their own doctor and seek to analyse their problems in orde:
to "heal thyself." Perhaps Western missions need an outside catalyst and synthesizer for world evangelization.

Edinburgh 1980 could become an occasion for such a synthesis,
if the Western "elite" will be humble and quiet long enough to
learn what the Spirit of God is saying to Asian Christians. The
"muscle" of the West is important, but secondary to the "spirit"
of Asian Christians. Together we must listen to what the Spirit
is saying to the church today.

George Paik, referring to the 1907 revival in Korea said,
"The Koreans who were at the original meetings have gone forth,
like Wesley's converts, their preaching has been wonderfully
successful--so much so that there are not a few who say that it
is through Korea that the light of Christianity will shine to the
Far Eastern world" (1929:360).

"Even so, come, Lord Jesus."

Appendix

APPENDIX A
QUESTIONNAIRE OF ASIAN MISSION SOCIETIES

Dear Christian Friends,

This is the important questionnaire about Asian Mission Societies I wrote about in my recent letter. I want you to be included in the report that will be published as a result of this seminar. In appreciation for your help <u>we will send you a FREE COPY of the completed report on "Asian Missionary Societies."</u> Please complete both sides and return before January 20, 1976 in the enclosed AIR MAIL envelope with any literature available about your mission.

Sincerely in Christ,

(Miss) Chaeok Chun

A. Name and address of the MISSION
   1. Name: _____
   2. Address: _____
   3. Name of Leader: _____

B. History of the MISSION
   1. What year was the Mission organized? 19___
   2. What is the name of the person or the group who began the Mission?
      _____
   3. Is the Mission part of a church denomination? Yes ( ) No ( )
   4. Does the Mission receive money from Western countries? Yes ( ) No ( )

C. Information about MISSIONARIES
   1. How many missionaries do you NOW have? Total _____
      a. Number of single women? _____   c. Number of married women? _____
      b. Number of single men? _____   d. Number of married men? _____

D. The primary ACTIVITIES of your missionaries
   1. Missionaries do many things. For each activity listed below please give the appropriate number of missionaries who have this work as their <u>primary</u> activity.

   _____ Doctor   _____ Translation   _____ Film Evangelism
   _____ Nurse   _____ Radio and TV   _____ Literacy
   _____ Social Worker   _____ Literature   _____ Student Evangelism
   _____ Mission Administrator   _____ Pastor of Local Church
   _____ Teacher in Seminary   _____ Church Planting
   _____ Teacher in Bible School   _____ Housewife
   _____ Teacher in Christian College   _____ Evangelist
   _____ Teacher in Secular School   _____ Other: _____

   2. From which of the following do your missionaries receive financial support?
      a. A church denomination?   Yes ( ) No ( )
      b. Several church denominations?   Yes ( ) No ( )
      c. A non-Asian mission society?   Yes ( ) No ( )
      d. A single church or congregation? Yes ( ) No ( )
      e. Individuals?   Yes ( ) No ( )
      f. Other _____ Yes ( ) No ( )
               (please describe)

Please turn over

3. If you plan to send out more missionaries in 1976-77, please give the approximate number:

4. If you plan to send out more missionaries in 1976-77, please list the countries or areas within the country where they plan to go.

a. _____ c. _____ e. _____

b. _____ d. _____ f. _____

E. Information about your MISSION

1. Do you have a printed Constitution or literature about your mission? Yes ( ) No ( )

2. If you have any literature we would appreciate your sending it to us AIR MAIL. The literature does not need to be in English. THANKS.

COUNTRIES WHERE YOUR MISSIONARIES ARE WORKING

Name of Country	Province or State	People Among Whom Missionaries Are Working	Language Spoken by These People	Is There An Established Church?	Number of Missionaries	Language Used by Missionaries
_____	_____	_____	_____	_____	_____	_____
_____	_____	_____	_____	_____	_____	_____
_____	_____	_____	_____	_____	_____	_____
_____	_____	_____	_____	_____	_____	_____
_____	_____	_____	_____	_____	_____	_____
_____	_____	_____	_____	_____	_____	_____
_____	_____	_____	_____	_____	_____	_____
_____	_____	_____	_____	_____	_____	_____
_____	_____	_____	_____	_____	_____	_____
_____	_____	_____	_____	_____	_____	_____

Please return to Miss Chaeok Chun, 135 N. Oakland Ave., Pasadena, California 91101, U.S.A.

	HM		FM			E			N			S			W	Tot.
	2	3	1	2	3	1	2	3	1	2	3	1	2	3	W	Tot.
HONG KONG																
Baptist Convention of Hong Kong				4					2						2	4
Foreign Missionary Society of the Christian & Missionary Alliance of H.K.				10			7		1						2	10
Sub-total (2 agencies)				14			7		3						4	14
INDIA																
All India Prayer Fellowship	163			8			161			4			6			171
Ambassadors for Christ India	16						8								8	16
Bharosa Ghar Mission	38						5			15			4		14	38
Friends' Missionary Prayer Band	75						75									75
Hindustan Bible Institute	107		1	6		95		3	1		3				12	114
Indian Evangelical Mission	38		2	1		20	1								20	41
Indian Missionary Society	9	3					2	3	1				2		4	12
Makedonia	5						4								1	5
National Missionary Society of India	49			2			42								9	51
Pakal Mission																
Servants of the Cross	12						12									12
Sub-total (11 agencies)	512	3	0	13	7	0	424	7	0	21	3	0	12	0	68	535
INDONESIA																
Indonesia Missionary Fellowship	72		1	2	2	1	56	1							19	77
Sub-total (1 agency)	72		1	2	2	1	56	1							19	77

Agency	HM		FM			E			N			S			W	Tot.
	2	3	1	2	3	1	2	3	1	2	3	1	2	3	W	Tot.
JAPAN																
Committee for Ecumenical Ministries – United Church of Christ in Japan – Kyodan			2	2	4		1	1	1		1				4	8
Immanuel General Mission					8			1			3				4	8
Indonesia Senkyo Kyoryo-kukai (Indonesia Mission Cooperative Ass'n.)					6			1			2				3	6
Japan Baptist Convention, Foreign Mission Cttee.			2			1									1	2
Japan Committee–Wycliffe Bible Translators					8		6								2	8
Japan Evangelical Free Church				3				2							1	3
Japanese Evangelical Missionary Society	8		2					4	1						5	10
Japan Overseas Christian Medical Cooperative Service			8											5	3	8
Kakudai Senkyo Kai (World Mission Expansion)																
Kinki Evangelical Lutheran	1				1											1
Life Ministries, Inc. (formerly Bible Institute Mission)			1									1				1
Sub-total (11 agencies)	8	0	8	5	34	2	7	9	2	0	6	1	0	5	23	55
KOREA																
Daegu Presbyterian Foreign Mission				2		1									1	2
Daegu Sam Duck Presbyterian Church					2		1								1	2
Ewha Womans' University					1		1									1
Foreign Missions Committee, The Presbyterian Church of Korea (Koryo)			6	4			2		3						5	10

	HM		FM			E			N			S			W	Tot.
	2	3	1	2	3	1	2	3	1	2	3	1	2	3	W.	Tot.
Korea (Cont)																
Full Gospel Central Church			14		2			1	7						8	16
Independent				2	2		1	1							2	4
Korea Christian Mission Society																
Korea Evangelical Church (Holiness)			10	2				1		5					6	12
Korea International Mission, Inc.					6			3							3	6
Korean International Mission for Christ			2						1						1	2
Methodist			6		2			1	3						4	8
Mission for Vietnam			2						1						1	2
National Organization of the Presby. Women of Korea (Tong-Hap)			2	2	2	1	1	1							3	6
Presbyterian Church of Korea (Tong-Hap) plus Women's organization and Daegu Missions)			6							3					3	6
Presbyterian Church of Korea (Hap-Dong)			12		2	1			1	5					7	14
Salvation Army					2							1			1	2
World Omega's Revival Missionary Society			5		1				1	3					2	6
University Bible Fellowship			157	1	2	157	1	1							1	160
Sub-total (18 agencies)	0	0	224	11	24	160	6	12	31	0	1	0	0	0	49	259
PHILIPPINES																
CAMACOP Foreign Mission in Indonesia (Christian and Missionary Alliance Church of the Philippines)				4			2								2	4
Convention of Philippine Baptist Churches 13	13						2			3			2		6	13
Missionary Diocese of the Philippines (Episcopal Church)																

	HM		FM			E			N			S			W	Tot.
	2	3	1	2	3	1	2	3	1	2	3	1	2	3	W	Tot.
Philippines (Cont)																
Overseas Missionary Fellowship, Philippine Branch.				5			2							1	2	5
Philippine Chinese Church			173			173										173
Philippine Missionary Fellowship	54						27							5	22	54
Sub-total (6 agencies)	67	0	173	4	5	173	31	2	0	3	0	0	7	1	32	249
SINGAPORE																
Asia Evangelistic Fellowship				45			45									45
Overseas Missionary Fellowship				16			16									16
Sub-total (2 agencies)				61			61									61
TAIWAN – Republic of China																
Burning Bush (Mustard Seed Inc.)				8			4								4	8
Overseas Missions Cttee of the Presbyterian Church in Taiwan			35			18						1			16	35
Sub-total (2 agencies)			35	8		18	4					1			20	43
Grand total	659	3	455	104	72	361	589	31	36	24	10	2	19	6	215	1,293

Category totals						
662	631	981	70	27	215	
51%	49%	91%	6.5%	2.5%		
1,298			1,078	+	215	=	1,293

DIRECTORY OF ASIAN MISSION SOCIETIES

HONG KONG

*Baptist Convention of Hong Kong
1st Floor, 73 Waterloo Road
Kowloon
Chrm. Rev. Do-Shang Wong

Christian Nationals' Evangelism
Commission, Inc.
P. O. Box 5307
Kowloon

*Foreign Missionary Society of
the Christian and Missionary
Alliance of Hong Kong
216 Nathan Road, 3/F
Kowloon
Dir. Rev. Philip Teng

Hong Kong Swatow Baptist Churches
c/o 191 Prince Edward Road
Room 305
Kowloon

Ling Liang World-Wide Evangel-
istic Mission
No. 1, Grampian Road
Kowloon

INDIA

*All Indian Prayer Fellowship
Green Park Extenstion
New Delhi 16
Dir. P.N. Kurien

*Ambassadors For Christ India
No. 18, 6th Cross
Hutchins Road
St. Thomas Town
Civil Station
Bangalore
Dir. Augustine Salins

Bharat Evangelical Mission
41 Main Road
Saint Thomas Mount
Madras 16

INDIA continued:

Bharosa Ghar Mission
Bhagalpur
P. O. Deoria Dist. U.P.
Dir. Rev. James S. Morar

Board of Missions of the Methodist
Church in Southern Asia
15, Nehru Road
Dilkusha
Lucknew 2 U.P.

Chompatta Agricultrual and
Industrial Mission
P. O. Berenag, District
Pithoragarh
Kumaon U.P.

Christian and Missionary Alliance
of India
P. O. Box 5
Marashta

Church of North India
Bishop's House
51 Chowringhee Road
Calcutta 16

Church of South India
Cathedral
P. O. Madras 6

Dipti Mission
Sahighunj
Bihar

Evangelize India Fellowship
P. O. Box 16
Tiruvalla
Kerala

Fellowship of Evangelical Friends
Jehova Jireh, Isaac St.
Nagercoil 629001
Dir. Mr. D.T. Rajah

*Indicates organizations included in this research project.

INDIA continued:

*Friends' Missionary Prayer Band
P. O. Box 2
Palayankottai
Tamilnadu 627002
Pres. Dr. Samuel Kamaleson

Full Gospel Young Men's Ass'n
P. O. Box 188
No. 6 Old Town
Vellore 632001
Tamilnadu
Dir. Mr. R. Stanley

*Hindustan Bible Institute
2 Madavakkam Tank Road
Kilpauk
Madras City
Dir. Dr. Paul V. Gupta

India Evangelical Lutheran Ch.
Ambur
N.A. District
Madras State

*Indian Evangelical Mission
4 Kingston Road
Bangalore 25
Dir. Rev. Theodore Williams

*Indian Missionary Movement
5 Waddell Road
Madras 600010
Dir. Rev. M. Ezra Saravnam

*Indian Missionary Society
11-A, Trivandrum Road
Tirunelvili 2, 627002
Dir. Rev. E.P. Gnanasigamoni

*Makedonia
P. O. Lunglei 796106
Mizoram
Dir. Pachuau Muanthanga

Mulug Mission
C.S.I., Mulug via Kazipet
Warangal District
Andhra Pradesh

INDIA continued:

*National Missionary Society
of India
102 Peter's Road
Royapettah
Madras 600014
Dir. Bishop R.D. Joshi

*Pakal Mission, now named
Nekonda & Narsampet Pastorates
Church of So. India Mission
Compound
Nekonda, Warangal District
Andhra Pradesh
Dir. Bishop P. Solomon

Samayesam of Telugu Baptist Ch.
C.A.M. High School Compound
Nellore-3
A.P.

*"Servants of the Cross"
Karmel Daira
P. O. Kandanad
via Thiruvankulam
Kerala State
Dir. Phillipos Kor Episcopa

INDONESIA

*Christian and Missionary Church
of Philippines Foreign Mission
in Indonesia
20 Ilir, Jln. Kapt
Marjuki 2611
Palembang
Sumsol
Dir. Rev. Leo Madrigal

*Yayasan Persekutuwan Pekabaran
Injil Indonesia
Indonesian Missionary Fellowship
Jalan Trunojoyo 2
Batu - Malang
East Java, Timur
Dir. Rev. Petros Octavianus

JAPAN

Angelican Episcopal Ch. in Japan
1-4-21 Higashi
Shibuya-ku
Tokyo

Association for the Relief of
Leprosy in Asia
No. 7, Yuraka-cho
1 Chone, Chiyoda-Ku
Tokyo

Church of the Nazarene
237 Oyama-cho
Tamagawa
Setagaya-Ku
Tokyo

*Committee for Ecumenical Minis-
tries,
United Church of Christ in Japan
(Kyodan)
Room 31, Japan Christian Center
2-3-18 Nishi Waseda
Shinjuku-Ku
Tokyo 160
Chrm. Rev. Gosaku Okada

Gospel of Jesus Church
1548 Semohoya
Tanashi P. O.
Tokyo

*Immanuel General Mission
Foreign Missions Department
3-1-4 Marunouchi
Chiyodaku
Tokyo 100
Dir. Rev. John Y. Fukuda

Indonesian Missionary Fellowship
33-2, Higashi one-cho
Keyama, Kita-Ku
Kyoto

*Indonesia Senkyo Kyoryokukai
Indonesia Mission Cooperative
Association
1-38-1 Kamihamuro
Takatsuki, Osaka
Dir. Rev. Yosuke (Andrew) Furuyama

JAPAN continued:

Irian Barat Missionary Society
c/o Koiwa Kyokai 732-6
Koiwa Machi
Edogawa Ku
Tokyo

Japan Alliance Church
255 Itsukaichi-Machi
Saiki Gun
Hiroshima Ken

Japan Assemblies of God
20-15-3 San Chome
Komagone, Toshima Ku
Tokyo

*Japan Baptist Convention
350, 2-chome
Nishi Okubo
Shinjuku-Ku
Tokyo 160
Dir. Rev. Sueo Kitahara

*Japan Committee - Wycliffe
Bible Translators
4-24-23, Soshigaya
Setagayaku
Tokyo
Dir. Rev. Shin Funaki

*Japan Evangelical Free Church
Mission
33-4 Higashi Ouo cho
Koyama, Kita Ku
Kyoto
Supt. Lea N. Little

*Japanese Evangelical Missionary
Society
CPO 1000
Tokyo
Dir. Dr. Akira Hatori
Exec. Dir. Rev. Sam Tonomura
112 No. San Pedro St.
Los Angeles, Calif. 90012

JAPAN Continued:

Japanese Evangelical Overseas
Mission
6-4136, Shiina-machi
Toshima-Ku
Tokyo

Japan Evangelical Free Church
Overseas Missions Department
33-2 Higashiono-cho
Koyama
Kita-Ku
Kyoto

Japan Gospel Church
5-2209 Komigawa-cho
Chiba-shi

Japan Holiness Church
Megurit
Higashimurayama-shi
Tokyo

*Japan Overseas Christian Medical
Cooperative Service
2-3-18 Nishi-Waseda
Shinjuku-Ku
Tokyo
Dir. Tsunegoro Nara

Kirisuto No Kyokai (Christian
Churches)
Shimo-ochiai Church of Christ
1-5-12 Naku-ochiai
Shinjuku-Ku
Tokyo

*Kakudai Senkyo Kai
(World Mission Expansion)
1817-33 Mizumachi
Hanagashima-Cho
Miyazaki City
Dir. Rev. A. Nagai

*Kinki Evangelical Lutheran Church
Isoji 2-2-18
Mianto-Ku
Osaka City
Pres. Tomio Ueno

JAPAN Continued:

Koganei Free Methodist Church
1714-5
Chome Honcho
Koganei Shi
Tokyo

Kyoto Overseas Missionary Inter-
cessory Prayer Fellowship
c/o CLC Termachi Imadogawa
Sagaru, Kamigyoku
Kyoto-shi

*Life Ministries, Inc.
(formerly Bible Institute Mis.)
Box 311
Franklin, Pa. 16323
Dir. Earl F. Tygert

c/o S.A.M.
74 Shimomukai Yama
Gamagori Shi
Aichi Ken

Sekai Fukuin Senkyo Kai (NTC)
CPO Box 5
Ibaragi Shi
Osaka

Tohok Kirisuto Kyokai
c/o 16, Hachiyaura
Yamoto Machi
Miyagi Ken

Union of Holy Christ Convention
5 39-1 Tsubakirori-cho
Chiba-shi

World Gospel Missionary Society
c/o Box 5, Ibaraki
Osaka

KOREA

*Chung Kyo Methodist Church
Mission
Kwangwhamoon
P. O. Box 740
Seoul 110

KOREA Continued:

Daegu, Presbyterian Foreign
Mission
50 Nam Sung-ro
Kyung Sang Buk Do 630-10
Dir. Dr. Sang Kun Lee

*Daegu Sam Duck Presbyterian Ch.
153 Bong San Dong
Daegu
Kyung Sang Buk Do 630-10
Dir. Rev. Sang Koo Kim

*Ewha Womans University
Department of Mission
San 1, Tai Hyun Dong
Sudaemun Ku
Seoul

*Foreign Missions Committee,
Presbyterian Church of Korea
(Koryo)
P. O. Box 190
Busan 600
Dir. Rev. Myung Dong Han

*Full Gospel Central Church
CPO Box 385
Seoul 100
Pastor Rev. Yong Gi Cho

*Korea Christian Mission Society
136 Yun Ji Dong
Jongno Gu
#604 Christian Building
Seoul 110
Dir. Rev. Simeon C. Kang

*Korea Evangelical Church
12, Moo Kyo Dong
Chung Ku
Seoul

*Korea International Mission Inc.
IPO Box 3476
Seoul
Dir. Rev. David J. Cho

*Korean International Mission For
Christ
P. O. Box 5381
Mission Hills, Calif. 91345
Dir. Rev. Won Yong Koh

KOREA Continued:

*Korea Methodist Mission Department
194-8 Insadong
Chongro-Ku
Seoul

*National Organization of the
Presbyterian Women of Korea
(Tong-Hap)
P. O. Box 335
307 Yunji-Dong
Chong no-ku
Seoul 110
Dir. Mrs. Youn Ok Lee

*Presbyterian Church of Korea
(Tong-Hap)
136-46 Yunji-Dong
Chong no-ku
Seoul 110
Gen'l. Sec'y. Rev. Yoon Shik Kim

*Salvation Army
CPO Box 1192
Seoul 100

*University Bible Fellowship
37 Hoi Je Dong
Chong no-ku
Seoul 110
Dir. Mr. Chang Woo Lee

*World Omega's Revival
Missionary Society
CPO Box 93
Seoul
Dir. Rev. Hong Suck Choi

PHILIPPINES

^Christian & Missionary Alliance
Church of the Philippines
P. O. Box 290
Zamboanga City N-329
Dir. Rev. Carlos Cristobal

*Convention of Phil. Baptist Ch.
P. O. Box 263
Jajardo St., Jaro
Iliolo City K-421
Dirs. Dr. Eric Lund &
Braulio Manikaa

PHILIPPINES Continued:

General Council of the Assemblies
of God in the Philippines
P. O. Box 3549
Manila

*Missionary Diocese of the Phil.
(Episcopal Church)
P. O. Box 2217
Manila D-406

North Philippine Union Mission
of Seventh-Day Adventists
P. O. Box 401
Manila

*Overseas Missionary Fellowship
Philippine Branch
P. O. Box 2217
Manila 2800

Philippine Independent Church
1320 V. Concepcion
Santa Cruz
Manila

*Philippine Chinese Church
c/o Grace Evangelical Association
419 Pina Avenue
Manila

*Philippine Missionary Fellowship
P. O. Box 3349
32-A Karuhatan, Valenzuela
Bulacan
Manila
Dir. Rev. Immanuel C. Pascua

United Church of Christ in the
Philippines
P. O. Box 718
Quezon City

United Methodist Church
640 Menalosa
Tondo
Manila

SINGAPORE

*Asia Evangelistic Fellowship
GPO Box 579
Singapore
Dir. Dr. G.D. James

Bible Presbyterian Missions
9 A Gilstead Road
Singapore 11

Board of Missions of the Methodist Church
23-B, Coleman Street
Singapore 6

*Overseas Missionary Fellowship
2 Cluny Road
Singapore 10
Dir. Dr. M.C. Griffiths

TAIWAN

*Burning Bush (Mustard Seed)
P. O. Box 17-131
Taipei 104
Dir. Lillian R. Dickson

*Presbyterian Church in Taiwan
89-5 Chang-Chun Road
Taipei 104
Dir. Rev. Tien Ming Su

Taiwan Baptist Convention
P. O. Box 427
Taipei

*Indicates organizations included in this research project.

STATUS OF CHRISTIANITY COUNTRY PROFILE

KOREA

Many unreached peoples are classified in socio-economic groups, and include prisoners, students in various levels of school, apartment residents, etc.

CHRISTIAN POPULATION BY ETHNIC GROUPS

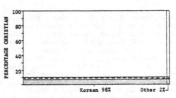

(NOTE: These figures are representative approximations. They should be seen as indications of magnitude, not precise.)

INTRODUCTION

This publication is a summary of available information on the status of Christianity in one part of the world. Its purpose is to provide an introduction for those not familiar with Korea, and to increase the overall awareness of Korean Christians of what God is doing in this country. The emphasis of the material is on Protestant Christianity but relevant information on other Christian traditions is included where available.

As the Church sees herself and the world which surrounds her more clearly, we hope that improved communication will result that will encourage Christians toward the common goal of proclaiming Christ to all men. There are millions upon millions of people in the world who have had little or no contact with the Gospel of Jesus Christ. Within each country there may be unique groups of such unreached peoples. This publication tries to identify unreached peoples within their national setting. Such a setting includes not only the national and social environment, but also the activity of churches and missions.

This is just a beginning, an introduction to the total task of proclaiming Christ to those who have not heard. Hopefully, it will encourage those who are concerned with evangelism to identify unreached peoples and to discover effective means of reaching them with the Gospel.

UNREACHED PEOPLES

The Christian community of South Korea comprises about 10% of the country's total population. Protestants number about 7.5% and Roman Catholics about 2.5%. The great majority of the Korean people practice the traditional religion of shamanism, which is a form of animism. Buddhists themselves claim as much as 15% of the population.

Ethnically, Korea is a relatively homogeneous country. The non-Korean population numbers only about 50,000, most of whom are Chinese.

CURRENT STATUS OF CHRISTIANITY

Though Christians are only 10% of the 34.5 million population, their influence extends far beyond their numbers. Many Protestant Christians especially are educated and influential.

Despite wars and persecutions, Christianity in Korea, and Protestantism in particular, has emerged growing and dynamic. From 1940 through 1970, the Protestant community has had an average annual growth rate of about 10%, compared to a total annual population increase of about 2.5%. The Catholic population in recent years appears to be slowing its growth. In certain parts of the society, notably the military, conversions to Christianity have been increasing rapidly.

Churches and missions have little or no interference in their ministries from non-Christian groups or from the government. This is a welcome relief to Korean Christians after years of suffering inflicted by the Japanese and later by Communist forces. Christian ministries in Korea have been varied, but have been notable in education, medicine, relief and rehabilitation, and literature, as well as evangelism and church planting.

NATIONAL CHURCHES

Wars, persecution, and divisions have afflicted the churches in Korea. For many, the suffering seems to have been an encouragement to spiritual

Prepared for the **INTERNATIONAL CONGRESS ON WORLD EVANGELIZATION**, Lausanne, July 1974

TO PREACH THE GOSPEL TO THE POOR
TO HEAL THE BROKENHEARTED   TO PREACH DELIVERANCE TO THE CAPTIVES
AND RECOVERING OF SIGHT TO THE BLIND   TO SET AT LIBERTY THEM THAT ARE BRUISED

LAUSANNE

and numerical growth, rather than a deterrent.
The relative peace and economic recovery of more
recent years perhaps, has had a lulling influence which may slow the growth of the Church.
Most churches, however, still have daily early
morning prayer meetings.

PROTESTANTS

The total Protestant community numbers an estimated 2,250,000 persons, about two-thirds of them
belonging to one of several Presbyterian church
bodies.

The Presbyterian Church is the oldest Protestant
church body in Korea, the first missionaries having arrived in 1884. Divisions within the church
have resulted in four major Presbyterian bodies,
plus about a dozen other smaller groups. The
largest Presbyterian churches include: Koryu
Presbyterian Church; Presbyterian Church (ROK);
Presbyterian Church (Hapdong); and the Presbyterian Church of Korea. This last is an outgrowth
of the ministries of the Australian Presbyterian
Board, the Presbyterian Church in the US, and the
United Presbyterian Church USA. Since 1907 leadership of this church has been in the hands of
Koreans, and in 1971, Korean workers and ordained
ministers totalled almost 2,700. (There were almost 6,400 Presbyterian ministers and workers for
all of the Presbyterian bodies combined.) Korean
Presbyterians have placed emphasis on evangelism
and church planting both in Korea and elsewhere,
and have sent a number of missionaries to other
countries.

The Methodist Church is the second largest Protestant church body and one which has also experienced divisions. However, the largest segment of
the denomination had a total membership in 1967 of
about 60,000, and a community of almost 302,000 of
1971. This denomination, like the Presbyterians
and others, has had substantial ministries in social and educational services. It has an extensive list of Methodist-affiliated community centers, hospitals, clinics, literature centers,
colleges, and seminaries.

Another large church is the Korea Holiness Church,
an outgrowth of the ministries of the Oriental
Missionary Society (OMS). In 1971 it had a reported community of about 177,000. A second and
smaller Holiness Church (Yeisu) has a community
of about 77,000.

The 1972 Prayer Calendar of Christian Missions in
Korea lists 29 Protestant church bodies. Other
groups with more than 10,000 persons in their com-
munities include the Baptist Church, Seventh-day
Adventists, Salvation Army, Assemblies of God,
Church of the Nazarene, and the Episcopal Church.

In addition to evangelistic, educational, and social concern activities, Korean churches have also
shown interest in foreign missionary outreach. In
the 1930's Korean missionaries were serving in
parts of China. Today there are Korean mission-

aries overseas in 13 countries from Presbyterian
churches, the Methodist Church, and the Korea
Holiness Church.

ROMAN CATHOLICS

The Roman Catholic Church in Korea claims a Catholic population of 788,700 (1970), or about 2.5%
of the entire population. This percentage has increased over the past ten years, but appears to
be leveling off. The Catholic population is
somewhat more urban than the general population,
and 17% of Korean Catholics are found in four out
of the ten dioceses: Inchon, Suwon, Chongju, and
Wonju. In 1970 there were 520 Korean priests and
363 foreign priests. The Catholic Church operates
over 100 charitable institutions plus over 200
schools, ranging from nursery to college.

EASTERN ORTHODOX

There is a small Russian Orthodox community in
Korea, numbering several hundred people.

INDIGENOUS CHURCHES

Indigenous religious movements have flourished in
Korea since at least the mid-19th century, and
there are about 70 some "new religions" that are
presently known. A number of these have grown out
of traditional Christian churches. Two large
Christian-based groups, with about one million
followers total, are the Olive Tree Church, which
emphasizes faith healing, and the Holy Spirit Association for the Unification of World Christianity,
which claims to have a Korean Jesus, and which is
seeking converts in other countries.

COUNCILS AND ASSOCIATIONS

Korea's National Council of Churches (NCC) began
as the Federal Council of Churches in 1919. The
name was changed to the National Christian Council
in 1924 and then in 1969 both name and structure
were changed to form the present NCC. Membership
is now denominational and six denominations belong.

FOREIGN MISSIONS TO KOREA

Korea's first knowledge of Christianity came in
1631, when a book written by a Jesuit missionary
was taken from China to Korea. A hundred years
later a group of Korean scholars organized themselves to study Christianity from this book and
others, and they began to practice its teachings.
A Chinese Catholic priest, the first to come to
Korea, came in 1794 to minister to a Catholic
community that already numbered 4,000 baptized
members and which had been undergoing persecution
for several years. Persecutions continued inter-
mittently throughout much of the 19th century.

PROTESTANTS

As early as 1832 an itinerant Protestant missionary from Germany visited Korea leaving behind

copies of Scriptures. Thirty-three years later an agent from the National Bible Society of Scotland also distributed Scriptures. When the first Protestant missionaries arrived in 1882, they found small communities of Christians waiting for further teaching.

The Protestant missionary community in South Korea is largely from North America. In 1971 there were 53 foreign mission agencies in Korea, 43 of which were North American. The total number of Protestant missionaries was 600 - 700.

The largest Protestant mission agency is also one of the oldest. The American Presbyterians (North) first sent missionaries to Korea in 1884. In 1973 Presbyterian Church in the United States reported 73 missionaries in Korea and the United Presbyterian Church had an additional 36 people.

Other large mission agencies include the Southern Baptist convention with 70 missionaries reported in 1973, and the United Methodist Church with 42 people in that same year. The Methodists first sent missionaries in 1885, while the Southern Baptists are relatively new, having come in 1950.

The Evangelical Alliance Mission (TEAM), with a staff of 30 (1970) is the fifth largest Protestant mission agency. In addition to evangelism, literature and correspondence courses, the mission has had a specialized ministry through its radio station HLKX, which broadcasts to all of Korea and parts of Mongolia, China and the Soviet Union.

ROMAN CATHOLIC

Though there are indications of some Roman Catholic influence having reached Korea earlier, the formal introduction began through lay converts in the latter part of the 18th century. By 1857 there were 15,000 Catholics reported. The 19th century was one of persecution and thousands died as a result. In 1962 a hierarchy was established, and progress of the Catholic Church reported. At present there are 12 parishes, with 850 priests, and 588 seminarians. There are 175 U.S. personnel working with the church at present in various capacities.

FOREIGN MISSIONS FROM KOREA

The early missionary endeavors by the Korean Church to her neighboring countries are not widely known. As a result of the great revival movement of 1907, churches in Korea began sending out missionaries to Northern Asia. By 1908, missionaries had gone to Cheju Island and to Japan. In 1912, the Presbyterian Church in Korea organized its foreign mission board and sent three missionary families to China in 1913.

After the Korean War, the churches in Korea were looking for new mission fields. In 1956, two couples were sent to Thailand and to other parts of the world. It was the signal for the missionary advance of the Korean Church for new fields and a new era. Even before they were restored

from the destruction of the war and from poverty, churches sent many full-time missionaries to places such as Thailand, Taiwan, Japan, Vietnam, Hong Kong, Indonesia, Pakistan, Nepal, Ethiopia, Okinawa, Brazil, Mexico, Argentina, Brunei, and the USA. The total number of Korean Protestant missionaries overseas is now over 230.

Some of these missionaries are supported by denominations or by independent societies (such as the Korea International Mission). Most missionaries are self-supporting or are supported by local churches.

MAJOR CHRISTIAN PROGRAMS AND ACTIVITIES

The following descriptions are intended to make readers aware of the potential for various types of ministries. Not all church agencies are specifically mentioned.

EVANGELISM

The period following the Korean War was a time of opportunity for evangelistic activities. Both Korean and missionary evangelists worked in prisoner-of-war camps where over 160,000 Koreans were held. Some 60,000 prisoners professed Christ during this time. Another evangelistic program, this one to reach children, was the Bible Club Movement which reported 60,000 children enrolled in its ministry in 1969. Clubs were also started by many of the denominations. Evangelistic crusades were held by men such as Billy Graham and Bob Pierce, founder of World Vision, Inc. In 1965 a nationwide evangelistic campaign was held by 17 denominations, celebrating the 80th anniversary of Protestant ministry in Korea. Twenty thousand conversions were reported. In 1969 a Korea Congress on Evangelism was held, supported by most of the denominations. Student work, urban and industrial evangelism, and military evangelism have proved themselves to be fruitful ministries, with many thousands of military men being baptized in recent years. In 1973, American evangelist Billy Graham spoke to the largest known evangelistic meeting in history, with over one million persons attending.

BROADCASTING

Korea is one of the few nations in Asia with a network of Christian radio stations. Station HLKY in Seoul, which is sponsored by evangelical churches and missions, began broadcasting in 1956 and reaches most of central Korea and into North Korea. Four other stations have since been added to this network, and surveys have shown that the vast majority of listeners are non-Christians. Station HLKX, located in Inchon and operated by The Evangelical Alliance Mission, broadcasts not only to both Koreas, but into China, Mongolia, and parts of the Soviet Union. Far East Broadcasting Company operates a transmitter on Cheju Island, broadcasting to China and the Soviet Union. The Lutheran Church - Missouri Synod has also been active in producing both radio and television programs.

LITERATURE

In 1969 there were 34 active Christian publishers, compared to 139 in 1962. In the past, much of the literature has been produced for church leadership rather than the laity and the non-Christians. Literature observers state that Korean writers need to be trained and encouraged. In 1971 an evangelical literature fellowship was formed, representing 22 different groups, to try to raise publishing standards and increase readership.

BIBLE TRANSLATION AND DISTRIBUTION

The Korean Bible Society became independent in 1940. Distribution figures, excluding commercial publishers, for 1972 were reported as follows:

Bibles	181,559
New Testaments	1,879,791
Portions	2,211,016
Selections	7,139,538
TOTAL	11,404,899

An interconfessional translation of the Bible is in progress. The New Testament was completed in 1971, and the Old Testament is about half finished. The translation is geared to those 30 years of age and under, which is about 70% of the population.

EDUCATION

Theological. There are almost 50 Protestant Bible schools and seminaries in Korea, most of them having been started since 1953. As a consequence, most of them are small. Presbyterians maintain five seminaries, the largest one being operated by the Presbyterian Church (Hapdong). This seminary is not only the largest one in Korea, but is also one of the largest in Asia. Other large seminaries are operated by the Presbyterian Church (Tong Hap), Oriental Missionary Society, and the Methodist Church. In 1966 the United Graduate School of Theology was opened at Yonsei University, offering the highest level of theological education to students from several supporting denominations. Other graduate schools of theology are found at the Presbyterian Theological Seminary, Hankuk Theological Seminary, and Seoul Seminary. The Catholic Church has two major seminaries and one minor one. The number of seminarians has declined in recent years.

Christian. Both Protestants and Roman Catholics are active in various aspects of education. These include kindergartens, elementary and secondary schools, college, vocational schools, literacy classes, libraries, and scholarships. In higher education, there are 17 Protestant-related colleges and universities, all headed by Koreans. The Presbyterians operate three colleges; four Korean denominations and five overseas churches cooperatively support Yonsei University. Ewha Women's University is considered to be the largest of its kind in the world. The Catholic Church operates a medical school, two women's colleges, and a university.

SOCIAL CONCERN

The Methodists and Presbyterians have the largest hospitals, which provide nursing, residency and internship training. There are at least 13 church-related hospitals, scores of clinics and dispensaries, mobile clinics, boat clinics, TB clinics and a sanitarium, eye clinic, visiting nurse centers, and leprosy care centers.

Only about 23% of Korea's land is arable, and food production is not adequate to care for the population. Consequently a number of Protestant and Roman Catholic missions sponsor or operate experimental farms to teach improved methods of crop productions, soil cultivation, and animal husbandry. Irrigation projects have been started to increase crop yield; and animal banks to improve livestock strains.

Mission-related organizations have sponsored or aided in the reclamation of more than 30,000 acres of land from the sea. Grants have been given for rural development. Spinning and weaving are taught to increase cottage industries. There are training programs for civic and social leaders. Cooperatives and credit unions have been started to grant financial assistance. Funds have been provided to build roads, bridges, drainage canals, and family homes which were destroyed by war and floods. Finances have been arranged to create small businesses.

Many Korean churches and missions have an extensive ministry of distributing food, clothing, vitamins and medicine to refugees and needy families. Some of the groups involved in this work include World Vision International, Church World Service, World Relief Commission, Christian Children's Fund, Compassion, and Holt Adoption Agency. In 1970, 120 relief and voluntary agencies were operating in Korea as members of the Korea Association of Voluntary Agencies, although some of these agencies are now phasing out their ministries.

Other church-related welfare programs include orphanages and child care centers, homes for convalescent children, youth hostels, rehabilitation centers for delinquent youth, nurseries and homes for non-infected children of lepers, schools and homes for deaf, dumb, and blind children, resettlement projects for lepers, school lunch programs for refugee children, homes for widows and aged, rehabilitation centers for amputees, subsidies to needy families, milk and feeding stations, training centers for social workers, servicemen's centers, and recreational centers.

THE NATION AND ITS PEOPLE

POPULATION

The estimated population of South Korea is 34.5 million with an annual growth rate of 2.0%. The 1985 population is projected to be about 46 million. The current population density averages about 328 persons per square kilometer (850 per square mile). However, in some urban centers the density is as much as 3,090 per square kilometer (8,000 per square mile).

After the Korean War industrialization was intensively stressed by the Government and, as the industrial facilities and factories were sprouting near the cities and towns, the rural population started to move into the urban areas.

The greatest concentration of people is in the Seoul-Inchon area and the fertile plains in the south. Seoul has now passed the six million mark, making it the seventh largest city in the world. In 1966 approximately 30% of the population lives in cities of 100,000 or more inhabitants, and this percentage has been steadily increasing. Farm population had fallen to 46% of the total population by the end of 1970. Population is sparse in mountain and hill regions.

COMPOSITION

Korea is one of the most ethnically homogeneous countries in the world. The primary ethnic origin is thought to be Tungusic, which is basically Mongol. Apart from a small group of Chinese immigrants there is relatively little immigrant population or influence. There are more than 500,000 Koreans living in other countries, especially Japan, Manchuria and the Soviet Union.

More than 40% of the population is under 15 years of age.

LITERACY AND LANGUAGES

Approximately 85% of the population is literate, and that figure is rising. About 97% of the school-age children are in elementary schools throughout the entire country

Korean is the official language, although English is spoken as a second language by many of the educated. Many Koreans who lived through the 35 years of Japanese occupation also speak Japanese.

RELIGION

According to the latest census, 90% of the population claims to hold to the traditional Korean religion (shamanism). 15% are claimed by the Buddhists, though only about 5% profess themselves to be Buddhist. Church statistics show Protestants to have about 7.5% and Roman Catholics about 2.5% of the population.

ESTIMATED RELIGIOUS AFFILIATION

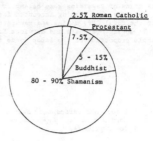

2.5% Roman Catholic

Protestant

7.5%

5 - 15% Buddhist

80 - 90% Shamanism

GEOGRAPHY AND CLIMATE

The Republic of Korea is a mountainous peninsula projecting out of the northeastern border of China. It is approximately 965 kilometers (600 miles) long and 217 kilometers (135 miles) wide. Winters are cold and dry; summers are hot and wet. There is usually a rainy season in June and July.

HISTORY

Korea was a semi-independent state affiliated to China, when Japan annexed Korea in 1910. At the conclusion of World War II in 1945, the USSR occupied the northern portion and the United States the southern portion. The Soviet Union was not agreeable to unification, and in 1948 the south had its own elections under the sponsorship of the United Nations, establishing the Republic of Korea. In 1950 North Korean armed forces invaded South Korea and war was declared. Sixteen countries of the United Nations sent troops to resist the aggression. Hostilities were ended in 1953 through an armistice signed at Panmunjom, in which the 38th parallel was designated as the dividing line. Dissatisfaction with 1960 election procedures resulted in a change of the political party in power. Unrest continued and there was a military coup in 1961. In 1962 extensive amendments were made to the constitution, and a year later another election was held returning civilian leaders to head the government.

GOVERNMENT

The constitutional powers allotted to Korea's head of state allows for a strong presidential form of government. Both the president and members of the unicameral National Assembly are to be elected every four years. The Chief Justice of the Supreme Court is appointed by the President with approval by the Assembly.

ECONOMY

In 1969 the economy grew at the rate of 16% and
showed signs of regaining some balance. Agriculture, forestry, and fishing accounted for about
29% of the total GNP; mining and manufacturing
for 21%; social overheads and services for 50%.
A sizable proportion of the labor force remains

unemployed or underemployed. Lack of natural re
sources, proficient technicians and managers,
dense population, and a large military budget
limit the country's economic development, but h
rates of economic growth have been achieved sin
the early 1960's.

Per capita GNP is about 100,000 won (U.S. $250)

CHURCH MEMBERSHIP STATISTICS

*Note: Statistics have been taken from different sources and are the most current
data available. Definitions of "membership" vary among churches and may not always
be comparable.*

Church or Mission Name	Communicants (Full Members)	Estimated Community*
Assemblies of God	11,254	38,840
Baptist Bible Fellowship	NA	6,214
Baptist Church	NA	31,771
Bible Presbyterian	NA	7,728
Chosun Church	NA	2,591
Church of Christ (CC)	NA	2,523
Church of Christ (KCM)	NA	6,842
Church of God	NA	3,866
Church of the Nazarene	2,416	12,255
Episcopal	NA	20,000
Far East Apostolic Mission (FEAM)	1,420	3,000
Free Methodist	5,000	3,045
Gospel Church	NA	4,140
Holiness (Yeisu)	NA	77,000
Korea Holiness Church	28,856 (1970)	177,305
Korea Lutheran Mission	314	700
Korean Evangelical Movement	NA	1,000
Korean Methodist Church	144,000	301,810
Methodist (Yeisu)	NA	10,041
Presbyterian (Hapdong)	NA	590,870
Presbyterian (Koryu)	NA	105,798
Presbyterian, Reconstructed	NA	2,300
Presbyterian Reformed (Kae Hyuk)	NA	19,278
Presbyterian (ROK)	112,000	194,793
Presbyterian (Tong Hap)	NA	532,020
Presbyterian Unaffiliated (Moo Wee)	NA	12,500
Salvation Army	18,982 (1970)	50,000
Seventh-day Adventists	28,435 (1966)	29,462
True Church of Jesus	NA	1.812
United Pentecostal Church Mission	NA	3,000
TOTAL PROTESTANTS (approximate)		2,252,500
Roman Catholics (c. 1970)		788,100

Notes:
* From Prayer Calendar of Christian Missions in Korea, 1972.

NA   Information not available.

SELECTED BIBLIOGRAPHY AND INFORMATION SOURCES

The sources listed below are to help the reader find additional information on this country and Christian ministries there. This list does not try to be comprehensive or complete.

DOCUMENTS

General

Chung, Kyung Cho, New Korea: New Land of the Morning Calm, New York: Macmillan, 1962.

Henderson, Gregory, Korea: The Politics of the Vortex, Cambridge: Harvard University Press, 1968.

McCone, Shannon, Korea: Land of Broken Calm, Princeton: D. Van Nostrand Co., 1966.

Sohn Pow-key, Kim Chol-choon, Hong Yi-sop, The History of Korea, Seoul: Korean National Commission for UNESCO, 1970.

Yi, Kyu-tai, Modern Transformation of Korea, Seoul: Sejong Publishing Company, 1970.

Christian

Breidenstein, Gerhard, Christians and Social Justice: A Study Handbook on Modern Theology, Socio-Political Problems in Korea, and Community Organization, Seoul: Korean Student Christian Federation, 1971. (Available in English from Rev. Fred Bayliss, 190-10 2Ka Choong Jung Ho, Sudaimoon Ku, Seoul.)

Clark, Allen D., A History of the Church in Korea, Seoul: The Christian Literature Society of Korea, 1971.

Clark, Allen D., ed., Prayer Calendar of Christian Missions in Korea, Seoul: The Christian Literature Society of Korea, 1972.

Kane, J. Herbert, A Global View of Christian Missions, from Pentecost to the Present, Grand Rapids: Baker Book House, 1971.

Moffett, Samuel Hugh, The Christians of Korea, New York: Friendship Press, 1962.

Shearer, Roy E., Wildfire: Church Growth in Korea, Grand Rapids: Wm. B. Eerdmans, 1962.

ORGANIZATIONS

Korean Bible Society, P. O. Box 1030, Seoul, South Korea.

National Council of Churches (formerly National Christian Council), #136-46.

ACKNOWLEDGMENTS

The information in this profile was taken from many sources
which were the best available to the editors at the time of
preparation. However, the accuracy of the information cannot
be guaranteed. Views expressed or implied in this publication
are not necessarily those of the ICOWE convenors or staff. The
editors have tried to present the ministries of various organizations in an objective manner, whithout undue bias or emphasis.
Where we have failed, we apologize for erroneous impressions
that may result and request that comments and corrections be
sent to MARC, 919 W. Huntington Drive, Monrovia, California,
USA 91016. We appreciate and acknowledge the comments and contributions of various organizations and individuals in the preparation of this publication, with special recognition to Rev.
Samuel I. Kim.

APPENDIX D
MARC UNREACHED PEOPLES DATA FILE: THAILAND

05/20/74

MARC UNREACHED PEOPLES DATA FILE

GROUP NAME: MOSLEMS   COUNTRY: THAILAND

OTHER NAMES: PATTANI MALAY   GROUP TYPE: ETHNO-LING

GROUP POPULATION: 600,000 DATE:C1973 % OF NATION: -1 GROUP TREND:GROWING
                                                    MARC ID: 39S

PRIMARY LANGUAGES: MALAY

                              LITERACY: GENERAL-60%. CHRISTIAN-95%

MAIN RELIGION: ISLAM   % OF GROUP: 99 TREND: STABLE

OTHER RELIGIONS	% OF GROUP	GROWTH TREND	CHRISTIAN COMMUNITY	% OF GROUP
CHRISTIANITY	-1	GROWING	PROTESTANT	-1
ISLAM	99	STABLE		
ANIMISM	95	STABLE		

CHURCHES & MISSIONS(LARGER)	TRAD	YEAR BEGUN	ADHERENTS FROM GROUP	GROWTH TREND	TOTAL ADHERENTS IN COUNTRY
INDEPENDENT CHURCH (OMF)	PRO	1956		GROWING	100

FIRST CHRISTIAN WITNESS: 1953 OMF MISSIONARIES

OPEN TO CHANGE: NO   % HEARING GOSPEL: -10 ATTITUDE: OPPOSED

COMMENT: THAI MOSLEMS ARE LINGUISTICALLY & RELIGIOUSLY DISTINCT; INCLUDES
STUDENTS & AGRICULTURAL WORKERS OF LOWER CLASS. THEY ARE SEMI-ISOLATED
WITH POSTAL & RADIO MEDIA. ISLAM COMBINED WITH ANIMISM PREDOMINATES. NO
CHURCHES EXIST FOR THAI MOSLEM CHRISTIANS. EFFECTIVE EVANGELISTS ARE
FOREIGN MISSIONARIES. CASSETTAPHONES, CHRISTIAN WITNESS & PERSONNEL TO
TRANSLATE WOULD ENCOURAGE CHRISTIANITY. HINDRANCES ARE LACK OF MATERIAL,
CONTINUED POLITICAL & RELIGIOUS INTOLERANCE.   0000000

INFORMATION SOURCES: I.MURRAY, OMF, BOX 1, YALA, THAILAND; DR.D.SIMPKIN,
CHRISTIAN HOSPITAL, SAIBURI, S. THAILAND

TOTAL ORIGINAL SOURCES: 1   ORIGIN DATE: 10/73 LATEST ENTRY DATE: 10/73

This chart shows total numbers and composition of Church membership in Korea according to be used to conveniently determine trends and relationships, such as the following:

In Korea the number of adult females is three-fourths of the number of adult males.

Three-fourths of adult males are prospective elders.

About two-thirds of the males age 12-19 hold the Aaronic Priesthood.

There are almost three times as many adults (19 and over) as youth (0-19 years of age).

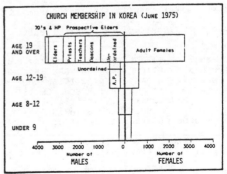

KOREA

CUSTOMS AND COURTESIES

<u>Greetings</u>: While bowing slightly, shake hands with friends, either by taking the other's hand in both of yours or shaking with your right hand while holding your right forearm (usually from beneath) with your left hand. Women usually do not shake hands, and young children bow or nod their heads unless invited to shake hands (which invitation is a great honor). Complete attention is always paid to the person one is greeting.

<u>Visiting</u>: One should be urged two or three times before actually entering a Korean style house, and then shoes are always removed, even if one's host insists that it is not necessary. Talking or laughing loudly is often offensive. After a visit or interview, the host sees his guest to the door or even outside before saying goodbye.

<u>Gifts</u>: Gifts are not usually opened at the time they are received unless the giver insists repeatedly. If money is given as a gift, it must be enclosed in an envelope.

<u>Eating</u>: Eating in the streets is avoided. A person covers his mouth when yawning or when using a toothpick. People usually eat quietly and converse after the meal is finished. Guests never joke about food. Food or other items should be passed with the right hand while the left hand is supporting the right forearm. It is common to take turns singing a solo for entertainment after the meal.

<u>Meetings</u>: Proper posture while standing or sitting is emphasized. Especially during song and prayer, legs are not crossed; at other times they should be crossed cautiously, with knee over knee and soles and toes pointed downward. Yawns are smothered in meetings. Dark glasses (and often regular glasses) should be removed while talking to someone.

<u>Gestures</u>: Although Korean men often hold hands in public, putting an arm around the shoulders or slapping on the back are considered excessive unless between very close friends. Feet should never be put on a desk or chair. Both hands should be used when giving or handing something to another person and when giving or receiving gifts.

THE PEOPLE

<u>Attitudes</u>: Social stratification has been the rule for many centuries, making proper social relationships all-important. Converts in every class are accepted in the Church but a slight feeling of higher social status might still accompany Church callings. Rituals of courtesy, formality in behavior and dress, and extreme modesty in speaking of one's own status, wife, family, and accomplishments are the social tradition. Reluctance to accept high honors is the mark of a true Korean gentleman. Compliments are graciously denied.

Success depends greatly on social contacts. Traditionally, gifts were given before requesting a favor from a person, but this practice is now strongly discouraged. To avoid an obligation, large gifts were often returned to the giver with the comment, "This is too large; I can never repay you. Please send a smaller remembrance."

Harmony in social interaction is prized. Open criticism, abruptness, and public disagreement are avoided because Koreans feel that no one has the right to corner, upset the feelings of, or tarnish the self-esteem of another. Friendships are highly valued and it is usually considered much better to quietly accept an injustice to preserve harmony than to assert one's individual rights.

A historically strong anti-Japanese feeling is not generally felt between Japanese and Korean Latter-day Saints. Koreans are justly proud of their country's cultural and economic acnievements (such as the world's first moveable metal type printing, and the first iron-clad warship).

Population: The population of Korea is 34.5 million, with fifteen times the density per square mile of the United States.

Language: The official language is Korean, which is written with phonetic characters (Hangul).

Religion: Korea is mostly Buddhist, with strong Confucian tradition and some Shamanist influences. The four million Christians are mostly Protestant. Christianity is growing at four times the population growth rate, and many government officials are Christian. Mass publicity is usually favorable to the Church, often because of association with America.

Holidays: New Year, solar and lunar; Arbor Day (April 5); Buddha's birthday (April 8 on the lunar calendar); Children's Day (May 5); Memorial Day (June 6); Constitution Day (July 17); Independence Day (August 15); Harvest Day; National Foundation Day (Oct. 3); Korean Language Day (Oct. 9); United Nations Day (Oct. 24); Christmas (Dec.25

LIFESTYLE

The Family: The family is the foundation of society and is bound together by a strong sense of duty and obligation among its members. The love and regard of family members in many ways exemplifies Church ideals. Although the modern trend is toward smaller family units, many generations may live in the same household. Society is group-oriented; individuality is subordinate to one's group, such as family, school class, or business associations. Church members, however, may be more open and individualisti than other Koreans in their Church relationships.

Dating and Marriage Customs:Dating between young people is often in groups of two or three couples or two of one sex and one of the other. Marriages are still sometimes arranged by the families involved. Men marry around thirty years of age. Movies are the biggest entertainment but youth also like hiking, taking small trips, and socializing at bakeries.

Income and Possessions: The average income is just enough to buy necessities for the family. Many Church members have television sets, but few have telephones.

Work and Business Hours: Sixty percent of the people are farmers, living mainly in rural villages and cultivating small irrigated plots. Small family stores are usually open seven days a week, from sunup to 10 or 12 p.m., but the larger department stores close earlier.

Diet: The most common foods are kim-chee (a highly spiced, pickled cabbage), boiled rice, and fresh fruits for dessert.

Sports: Popular sports are baseball, soccer, basketball, judo, taekwondo (karate), volley-ball, hiking, tennis, and swimming.

THE NATION

History and Government: Until it was annexed by Japan in 1910, Korea was an independent dynastic kingdom paying tribute to China. The Yi dynasty was one of the longest in history (1392-1910). The end of World War II brought freedom from Japan, but left Korea divided in half geographically and politically, the North under Communist control, and the South strongly anti-Communist. The war of 1950-53, beginning with an attack from the North, further devastated Korea. North Korea continues to pose a Communist threat to the South, and incidents of violence still occur along the 1953 truce line. Peaceful reunification of the country is a fervent desire of most people.

General Park Chung Hee has been president since 1963. In 1974 an assassination attempt was made on him in which his wife was killed. Avoid talking about politics.

Economy: Food production is becoming adequate to feed the population. The prize crop is rice. Economic development and industrial growth are strongly emphasized by the government. Although unemployment has been a problem, economic growth rates have been ten to sixteen percent annually.

Education: Education is the most highly valued aspect of Korean culture. An education brings wealth and success. Technical education is gaining popularity although highly educated men have traditionally avoided manual labor. Education is compulsory between ages six and twelve. In secondary schools, lack of facilities and teachers sometimes limits enrollment; selection of students is based on stiff academic examinations. The public school system is financed by student fees. Korea's literacy rate is very high. Forty to sixty percent of Church members attend school until age eighteen; six to eight percent are university graduates. All males must serve in the armed forces, usually for three years.

Transportation: Transportation is mainly by bus or taxi; few Church members own cars.

Land and Climate: Humidity makes summer seem hotter and winter colder. The monsoon season occurs in summer, mid-July to mid-August. Spring and fall are the most pleasant times of the year, with seasonal changes corresponding to the Northern Hemisphere. Korea is traditionally known as "the land of the morning calm."

SUGGESTIONS FOR VISITORS

Tipping is usually expected only in modern tourist hotels.

SUGGESTED READING

Area Handbook for the Republic of Korea. Washington, 1969.
Crane, Paul S. Korean Patterns. Seoul, Korea: Hollym Corporation, 1967.
O-young, Lee. In This Earth and in That Wind. Seoul, Korea: Hollym Corporation, 1967.
Kyu-tae, Yi. The Modern Transformation of Korea. Seoul, Korea: Sejong Pub. Co., 1970.
For further information contact Internal Communications Department, 531-2834.

Bibliography

ADENEY, David
    1966 "Student Evangelism;" *One Race One Gospel One Task*
          Vol. II, Henry and Mooneyham, eds.

ALL-ASIA MISSION CONSULTATION
    1973 "The Statement of the All-Asia Mission Consultation
          Seoul '73," *The All-Asia Mission Consultation Seoul
          '73.* Chaeok Chun, ed., pp. 349-350.

ASIA MISSIONS ASSOCIATION
    1975 "The Seoul Declaration on Christian Mission,"
          Seoul, Korea. East-West Center for Missionary
          Research and Development.

ASIA PULSE
    1972 "Korean Missionary Agency Opens Office in Wheaton,
          Illinois," *Asia Pulse,* Vol. III, No. 3, April 1972.

ASIA PULSE
    1972 "Overseas Missionary Association Formed," *Asia Pulse,*
          Vol. III, No. 3, April 1972.

ASIA PULSE
    1972 "Some Opinions on China Opening to the Gospel,"
          Asia Pulse, Vol. III, No. 3, April 1972, p. 3.

ASIAN OUTREACH
    1974 "Grace Gospel Church Missionary Program," *Asian
          Outreach.* March 1974.

ASIAN OUTREACH
    1974 "First Asian Student Missionary Convention," *Asian
          Outreach,* April 1974 (*Excerpts from The New Way*).

    1974 "Red Chinese in Black Africa," *Asian Outreach,* November
          1974 (Reprint from *Asian Report,* August 1974).

ASSOCIATION OF CHURCH MISSIONS COMMITTEES
    n.d   Brochure, *Association of Church Missions Committees.*

ASSOCIATION OF CHURCH MISSIONS COMMITTEES
    1975 "Report of the Ad Hoc Committee on Relations with Third
          World Mission," Pasadena, California, ACMC. Mimeo-
          graphed.

BEYERHAUS, Peter and LEFEVER, Henry
    1964 *The Responsible Church and the Foreign Mission.*   Grand
          Rapids, William B. Eerdmans Publishing Company.

BEAVER, R. Pierce
    1970 *The Warp and the Woof.* pp. 43-51 (reprint)
    1971 "A Plea For A New Voluntarism," *Concordia Theological
          Monthly,* June 1971

BROWN, G. Thompson
    1975a A Letter to author, March 6, 1975.

    1975b Letter to the author, December 4, 1975.

BUTLER, Bill
    1974 "Four Questions," *Decision,* Vol. 15, No. 8, August
          1974, p. 7.

CAREY, William
    1792 *An Enquiry Into The Obligation Of Christians To Use
          Means For The Conversion Of The Heathen.* London, The
          Carey Kingsgate Press Ltd.

CHANG, Joseph
    1976 Interview with author, March 29, 1976.

CHENG, Kor
    1974a "The Church And Missions." (delivered at the First
          Asian Student Missionary Convention, Dec. 26-31,1973,
          Baguio City, Philippines, *Grace Monthly.*

    1974b "Missionary Vision," *Asian Outreach,* April 1974.

CHO, David J.
    1973 "Severance, Succession, Solidarity, and Sodality,"
          The All-Asia Mission Consultation Seoul '73,
          Chaeok Chun, ed.

    1975 Interview with author, March 1974.

CHO, Yong Gi
    1975 Interview with author, March 26, 1975.

CHOYE, In Won
    1976 Interview with author, March 29, 1976.

CHUA, Wee Hian
    1968 "Missionaries Must Change, "*Eternity,* Vol. 19, No. 5,
          May 1968.

    1969a "Encouraging Missionary Movement in Asian Churches,"
          Christianity Today, Vol. XIII, No. 19, June 20, 1969.
          p. 11.

    1969b "Campus Evangelism Korean Style," *World Vision Maga-
          zine.* Vol. 13, No. 10, November 1969, pp. 20-23.

CHUN, Chaeok
    1973 "Asia's Turn For Missionary Outreach," *The All-Asia
          Mission Consultation Seoul '73,* Chaeok Chun, ed.,
          pp. 15-28.

CHUN, Chaeok, ed.
    1975 *The All-Asia Mission Consultation Seoul '73,* an un-
          published Thesis for Master of Theology (In Missiology
          The School of World Mission and Institute of Church
          Growth, Fuller Theological Seminary, Pasadena, Cali-
          fornia.

CHUN, Chaeok and NELSON, Marlin L.
    1976 "Asian Mission Societies," M.A.R.C. World Vision
          International, Monrovia, California.

CHUN, Paul
    1975 "Korean Church and World Mission," Term project (type-
          script), School of World Mission, Fuller Theological
          Seminary, Pasadena, California.

CLARK, Dennis E.
    1971 *The Third World and Mission,* Waco, Texas, Word Books.

COOK, Harold R.
1975 "Who Really Sent The First Missionaries?" *Evangelical Missions Quarterly*, Vol. 11, No. 4, October 1975, pp. 233-239.

CRANE, Paul S.
1967 *Korean Patterns*. Seoul, Korea, Hollym Corporation Publishers.

CULTURGRAM
n.d "Hong Kong, Japan, Korea, The Philippines, Taiwan, Indonesia," Language Research Center, Brigham Young University, Provo, Utah.

DAYTON, Edward R., ed.
1973a "A Survey of Predicted Trends In North American Based Missions in the '70s," *Mission Handbook: North American Protestant Ministries Overseas, 10th Edition*, Monrovia, California, MARC.

1973b *Mission Handbook: North American Protestant Ministries Overseas, 10th Edition*. Monrovia, California, MARC.

DAYTON, Edward R. and NEEDHAM, William L.
1973 "Changes and Trends in Missions Today," *Mission Handbook: North American Protestant Ministries Overseas, 10th Edition*, Edward R. Dayton, ed.

DOUGLAS, J.D., ed.
1975 *Let the Earth Hear His Voice: International Congress on World Evangelization, Lausanne, Switzerland*. Minneapolis, Minnesota, World Wide Publication.

DYE, Wayne T.
1974 "Stress-Producing Factors In Cultural Adjustment," *Missiology: An International Review*, Vol. 2, No. 1, January 1974, pp. 61-77.

EASTMAN, Addison J.
1967 "Burma: Mission Without Missionaries," *World Vision Magazine*, Vol. 11, No. 10, November 1967.

ENGEL, Frank
1969 "Missionary Activity in Asia," *International Review of Mission*, Vol. LVIII, No. 231, July 1969, pp. 308-316.

ENGSTROM, Ted W.
1971 "Airing of Mission Tensions," *World Vision Magazine*, Vol. 15, No. 10, November 1971.

ENGSTROM, Ted W.

    1972 "Some Positive Thinking on Missions," *World Vision
            Magazine,* Vol. 16, No. 11, December 1972.

ESPINOZA, Hector
    1972 "Grim Facts About Green Lake '71," *Church Growth
            Bulletin,* Vol. 7, No. 4, March 1972, pp.205-207.

FARREN, Edward, J.
    1970 "Focus on Korea. The Church That Laymen Built,"
            Worldmission, Vol. 21, No. 4, Winter, 1970.

FORMAN, Charles W.
    1970 "Missionary Force of the Pacific Island Churches,"
            International Review of Mission, Vol. LIX, pp. 215-
            226.

FURUYAMA, Andrew
    1973 "Japan Report to the First All-Asia Mission Consul-
            tation," *The All-Asia Mission Consultation Seoul '73,*
            Chaeok Chun, ed., pp.244-247.

    1974 "Japan Overseas Missions Association," *Asian Outreach,*
            March 1974.

GATU, John
    1974 "Missionary, Go Home," *In Search of Mission,* Joel
            Underwood, ed.

GLASSER, Arthur F.
    1973 "Timeless Lessons From the Western Missionary Pene-
            tration of China," *The All-Asia Mission Consulta-
            tion Seoul '73,* Chaeok Chun, ed.

GLOBAL REPORT
    1976 "Bangalore," *Global Report,* Waldron Scott, ed., Vol.
            6, No. 1, January 1976, Colorado Springs, Colorado,
            World Evangelical Fellowship.

GOLDSCHMIDT, W.
    1966 *Comparative Functionalism.* Berkeley, University of
            California Press.

GORDON, Robert C.
    1973 "The Silent Language Every Missionary Must Learn,"
            Evangelical Missions Quarterly, Vol. 9, No. 4,
            Summer 1973, pp. 216-222.

GRAHAM, D. Bruce
    1975 "Everything You Need to Know to Become a World Chris-
          tian," Pasadena, California, Fellowship of World
          Christians, printed booklet, 13 pp.

GRAHAM, Billy
    1966 "Opening Greetings," *One Race, One Gospel, One Task,*
          Henry and Mooneyham, eds.

    1974 "Let The Earth Hear His Voice," *Let The Earth Hear
          His Voice,* J.D. Douglas, ed.

HALL, Edward T.
    1959 *The Silent Language.* Garden City, New York, Doubleday.

HAMILTON, Keith E.
    1963 *Church Growth in the High Andes.* Lucknow, Lucknow
          Publishing House.

HAN, Kyung Chik
    1973a "Opening Address," *The All-Asia Mission Consultation
          Seoul '73,* Chacok Chun, ed., pp.34-37.

    1973b "Details of the Seoul '73 Consultation," *The All-
          Asia Mission Consultation Seoul '73,* Chaeok Chun,
          ed., p. 80.

    1973c "A Korean Pastor Evaluates Seoul '73," *The All-Asia
          Mission Consultation Seoul '73,* Chaeok Chun, ed.,
          pp. 376-378.

HARNACK, Adolf von
    1904-05 *The Mission and Expansion of Christianity in the
          First Three Centuries,* Vol. 1, London, U.K., G.P.
          Putnam's Sons, p. 486.

HARRIS, John
    1976 "Chinese on Malta a Curiosity to West," *Los Angeles
          Herald-Examiner,* Sunday, March 21, 1976, A-13.

HARRIS, Thomas A.
    1967 *I'M O.K.--You're O.K.* New York, Harper and Row.

HATORI, Akira
    1966 "The Far East" (Japan, Korea, Taiwan, Hong Kong), *One
          Race, One Gospel, One Task,* Vol. I, Henry and Mooney-
          ham, eds.

    1968 "Christ Seeks Asia," *Christ Seeks Asia,* W.S. Mooneyham,
          ed., pp.259-267.

HENRY, Carl F.H. and MOONEYHAM, W. Stanley, eds.
1967   *One Race, One Gospel, One Task,* Vol. I and II.
       Minneapolis, Minnesota, World Wide Publications.

1968   "An Assessment," -- *Christ Seeks Asia,* Mooneyham, ed.

HILLIS, Dick
1972   "Be a Better Missionary Because You Check on Yourself,"
       Evangelical Missions Quarterly, Vol. 8, No. 2, Winter
       1972, pp. 84-87.

HOGG, William Richey
1952   *Ecumenical Foundations.*   New York, Harper and Brothers.

HORNER, George R.
1953-4 "The Need for Anthropologically Trained Missionaries,"
       Practical Anthropology, Vol. 1, No. 5, 93-97.

HUNT, Jr., Everett, N. (Sec'y.).
1974   "Korean National Strategy Group Report," *Let the Earth
       Hear His Voice,* J.D. Douglas, ed., pp. 1398-1399.

INTERNATIONAL CONGRESS ON WORLD EVANGELIZATION (ICOWE)
1974   "The Lausanne Covenant," *Let the Earth Hear His Voice,*
       J.D. Douglas, ed.

INTERNATIONAL REVIEW OF MISSION
1967   "Survey-Asia," -- *International Review of Mission,*
       Vol. LVI, January 1967.

JAMES, G.D.
1968   "Asia's Future and Our Response (Part 2)," *Christ
       Seeks Asia,* W.S. Mooneyham, ed., pp. 151-157.

JOSEPH, Kenneth R.
1961   "Asians Evangelizing Asians," Sending out National
       Foreign Missionaries A Wave of The Future," unpublished
       typescript.

KAMALESON, Samuel
1975   "The Friends' Missionary Prayer Band," *Church Growth
       Bulletin,* Vol. XI, No. 4, March 1975, pp. 433-435.

KANE, J. Herbert
1974   *Understanding Christian Missions.*   Grand Rapids,
       Michigan, Baker Book House.

KAUFFMAN, Paul E.
1975   "Love China '75," *Asian Report,* No. 69, October 1975.

KIM, John
1976   Interview with author, March 29, 1976

KIM, Samuel I. (Soon-Il)
1973   "Problems of Third World Missionaries," *The All-Asia
        Mission Consultation Seoul '73*, Chaeok Chun, ed.,
        pp. 113-123.

1976   Interview with author, March 29, 1976

KING, Louis L.
1971   "A Definitive Statement On Church-Mission Relationships,"
        Church Growth Bulletin, Vol. 8, No. 2, November 1971,
        pp. 175-190.

KOH, Won Yong
1972   "The Missionary Vision of the Korean Church,"
        Church Growth Bulletin, Vol. VII, No. 4, March 1972.

1976   Interview with author, March 29, 1976

KRAFT, Charles H.
1971   "Younger Churches - Missionaries and Indigenity,"
        Church Growth Bulletin, Vol. VIII, No. 6, July 1971.
        pp. 159-161.

KWAK, Sunhee
1976   Interview with author, March 29, 1976.

LAM, Cyrus
1976   Interview with author, March 30, 1976.

LARSON, Donald N.
1973   "Linguistic and Sociolinguistic Factors in Mission-
        ary Allocation," *Evangelical Missions Quarterly*,
        Vol. 9, No. 2, Winter, 1973, pp. 74-84.

LARSON, Peter
1974   "Ambassadors From The Third World," *The Standard*,
        October 15, 1974, p. 15.

LARSON, Robert and GRIFFITHS, Michael C.
1975   "The New International Missionary," *World Vision
        Magazine*, Vol. 19, No. 5, May 1975.

LATOURETT, Kenneth Scott
1943   *A History of the Expansion of Christianity, Vol. V.
        The Great Century: The Americas, Australia and
        Africa.*   Grand Rapids, Zondervan (edition) 1970.

LATOURETTE, Kenneth Scott
    1944 *A History of the Expansion of Christianity, Vol. VI,
          The Great Century: North Africa and Asia.* Grand
          Rapids, Zondervan (edition) 1970.

    1953 *A History of Christianity.* New York, Harper & Row,
          Publishers.

LEE, Chang Woo
    1975 Interview with author, April 26, 1975

LEE, Hae Suk
    1975 Interview with author, January 30, 1975

LEE, Min Woo
    1975 Letter to author, February 5, 1975

LIAO, David C.E.
    1972 *The Unresponsive: Resistant or Neglected?* Chicago,
          Moody Press.

LOFFLER, Paul
    1964 "Laymen in World Mission," *International Review of
          Mission,* Vol. LIII, July 1964, p. 297.

LOVE CHINA '75
    1975 "Mainland China Evangelism Study Seminary," *Love
          China '75.* Bulletin No. 1, Manila, Philippines.

LOW, Helen C. and HOWE, James W.
    1975 "Focus on the Fourth World," *The U.S. and World
          Development Agenda For Action 1975.* New York,
          Praeger Publishers, Inc.

MARC
    1974a Unreached Peoples Data File, May 20, 1974, Monrovia,
          California, MARC.

    1974b "Status of Christianity Country Profile," July 1974,
          Monrovia, California, MARC.

McGAVRAN, Donald
    1966 "Logistics and Mission," *Church Growth Bulletin,*
          Vol. II, No. 6, July 1966, pp. 6,7.

    1970 *Understanding Church Growth,* Grand Rapids, Eerdmans.

    1973a "Seoul, Lausanne, And Africasian Missionary Societies,"
          Church Growth Bulletin, Vol. IX, No. 5, May 1973,
          pp. 327-329.

McGAVRAN, Donald
    1973b "Asian Missionary Societies Advance," *Church Growth
        Bulletin,* Vol. X, No. 2, November 1973, pp.327-329.

    1975 "Basics of Effective Missions Anywhere," *Church Growth
        Bulletin,* Vol. XI, No. 4, March 1975, pp. 430-432.

McGAVRAN, Donald A. and ARN, Win
    1973 *How To Grow a Church.* Glendale, California, Regal,
        p. 38.

MILLER, J. Melvin
    1972 "Mission Priorities and Personnel Placement,"
        Evangelical Missions Quarterly, Vol. 7, No. 2,
        Winter, 1972, pp. 78-83.

MISSIONARY NEWS SERVICE
    1974 "Mission Societies Meet," *Missionary News Service,*
        May 15, 1974.

MOFFETT, Samuel
    1968 Report in *The Presbyterian Journal,* Vol. XXVII, No. 31,
        November 27, 1968, p. 4.

MOFFETT, Sam and Eileen
    1971 "Newsletter," December 2, 1971.

MONSMA, Timothy M.
    1975 "The Advantage of Carrying Coals To Newcastle,"
        Missionary Monthly (Part I, June; Part II, July-
        August).

MOONEYHAM, W. Stanley, ed.
    1969 *Christ Seeks Asia* (Asia-South Pacific Congress on Evan-
        gelism, Singapore, 1968), Minneapolis, Minn., World
        Wide Publications, Asia Edition, Kowloon, Hong Kong,
        The Rock House, Publishers.

MOTT, John R.
    1900 *The Evangelization of the World in This Generation.*
        N.Y., Student Volunteer Movement for Foreign Missions.

MUIR, James and REYBURN, William D.
    1958 "The Missionary and Human Relations," *Practical
        Anthropology,* Vol. 5, No. 4, pp.87-89.

NACPIL, Emerito, P.
    1974 "Mission But Not Missionaries," *In Search of Mission,*
        Joel Underwood, ed.

NELSON, Geraldine V.
    1976 Letter to the author, January 24, 1976.

NIDA, Eugene A.
    1960 "The Ugly Missionary," Practical Antrhropology, Vol. 7
          No. 2, March-April, 1960.

ORCHARD, Ronald K., ed.
    1964 Witness in Six Continents, London, Edinburgh House
          Press.

PAIK, L. George (Nak Joon)
    1929 The History of Protestant Missions in Korea 1832-1910.
          Pyeng Yang, Korea, Union College Press.

PARK, Chang Hwan
    1975 Interview with author, January 22, 1975

PARK, Dal Jin
    1976 Interview with author, March 29, 1976

PENTECOST, Edward C.
    1973 "The Mission Outreach of the Third World," World
          Vision Magazine, March 1973, pp. 10,11.

PENTECOST, Edward, WONG, James and LARSON, Peter
    1972 "Third World Missionary Agencies," Research Project
          For M.A. in School of World Mission, Fuller Theolo-
          gical Seminary, Pasadena, California, 367 pp. (mimeo-
          graphed, bound).

PETERS, George W.
    1972 A Biblical Theology Of Missions. Chicago, Moody Press.

    1974 "Contemporary Practices of Evangelism;" Let the Earth
          Hear His Voice, J.D. Douglas, ed., pp. 199-2-4.

PHILLIPS, Godfrey E.
    1942 The Old Testament in the World Church.
          London, Lutterworth Press.

PRESBYTERIAN CHURCH IN THE U.S.
    1971 "Internationalization of Personnel," Handbook for
          Missionary Service, Presbyterian Church in the U.S.,
          April 1971.

PU, Philip
    1973 ...let's go on! Taipei, Taiwan, The Mustard Seed, Inc.

RADER, Paul
    1975 Interview with author, January 30, 1975.

RAY, Chandu
    1971 Newsletter, *Coordinating Office for Asian Evangelism*,
          Vol. 3, No. 4, p. 2.

    1973a "An Asian Director of Evangelism Evaluates Seoul '73,"
           The All-Asia Mission Consultation Seoul '73, Chaeok
           Chun, ed., pp. 371-375

    1973b Newsletter, *Coordinating Office for Asian Evangelism*.
           Vol. 5 No. 9, October 1973.

    1974 Newsletter, *Coordinating Office for Asian Evangelism*,
          Vol. 6, No. 1, January 1974.

REYBURN, William D.
    1958a "The Missionary and Human Relations." Muir and Reyburn
           Practical Anthropology, Vol. 5, No. 4, pp. 87-89.

    1958b "Don't Learn That Language!" *Practical Anthropology*,
           Vol. 5, No. 4, pp. 151-178.

    1960 "Identification in the Missionary Task," *Practical
          Anthropology*, Vol. 7, No. 1, pp.1-15.

RHODES, Harry A., ed.
    1934 *History of the Korea Mission Presbyterian Church
          U.S.A. 1884-1934*, Seoul, Chosen, Chosen Mission
          Presbyterian Church U.S.A.

SAHU, Sabodh
    1973 "The Biblical Principle of Missions and Missionaries,"
          The All-Asia Mission Consultation, Chaeok Chun, ed.,
          p. 56.

SANSOM, Donald
    1976 Interview with author, March 9, 1976

SCOTT, William Henry
    1973 "The Missionary As A Good Foreigner," *Missiology:
          An International Review*, Vol. I, No. 3, July 1973,
          pp. 383-388.

SHEARER, Roy E.
    1966 *Wildfire: Church Growth in Korea*, Grand Rapids, Michi-
          gan, Eerdmans.

SHENK, Wilbert R.
    1971 "Missions Under Divine Scrutiny," *World Vision Magazine*,
          Vol. 15, No. 10, November 1971.

SHEPHERD, Jack F.
    1973 "Continuity and Change In Christian Mission,"
          God, Man and Church Growth, Alan R. Tippett, ed.,
          pp. 70-93.

SPRADLEY, James P. and PHILLIPS, Mark
    1972 "Culture and Stress: A Quantity Analysis," *American
          Anthropologist 74,* Vol. 3, pp. 518-529.

STOTT, John R.W.
    1975 *Christian Mission in the Modern World.*
          London, Falcon.

STRONG, Robbins
    1972 "Practical Partnership with Churches Overseas," an
          address to the KKKMI, *International Review of Mission,*
          Vol. LXI, July 1972, pp. 281-287.

TABER, Charles R.
    1967 "The Training Of Missionaries," *Practical Anthropology,*
          Vol. 14, No. 6, pp. 267-274.

    1974 "Unevangelized Peoples: Whose Responsibility?
          Church Growth: Canada, Vol. 1, No. 3, November 1974,
          pp. 7-9.

TEGENFELDT, Herman G.
    1972 "The Karens of Burma: Early Asian Missionaries."
          an unpublished typescript, School of World Mission,
          Fuller Theological Seminary, Pasadena, California.

TIME
    1974 "China's Secret Christians," December 16, 1974, p. 55.

TINGSON, Gregorio
    1966 "Group Evangelism in Asia," *One Race, One Gospel,
          One Task,* Vol. II, Henry and Mooneyham, eds.

TIPPETT, Alan R.
    1962 *The Dynamics of Church Planting in Fiji.* Eugene,
          Oregon, an unpublished typescript.

    1967 *Solomon Islands Christianity: A Study in Growth and
          Obstruction.* London, Lutterworth Press.

    1968 "Anthropology: Luxury or Necessity for Missions?"
          Evangelical Missions Quarterly, Fall 1968, pp. 7-19.

    1969 *Verdict Theology.* Lincoln, Illinois, Lincoln Christian
          College Press.

TIPPETT, Alan R.
    1973a "The Suggested Moratorium on Missionary Funds and
          Personnel," *Missiology: An International Review*,
          Vol. I, No. 3, July 1973.

    1973b "Mission(s)," *Dictionary of Christian Ethics*, Carl
          F. H. Henry, ed., Grand Rapids, Baker Book House.

    1974 "Report of the Curriculum Committee On The Training
          of Missionaries," *Milligan Missiogram*, Tetsunao
          Yamamori, ed., Vol. I, No. 3, Spring 1974, pp.1-3.

    1975 "Fourth World," *Missiology, An International Review*,
          Vol. III, No. 2, April 1975.

TIPPETT, Alan R., ed.
    1973 *God, Man and Church Growth*. Grand Rapids, Eerdmans.

U KYAW, Than
    1971 "Partnership of the Churches In World Missions."
          Lutheran World, Vol. XVIII, No. 4, 1971, p.364.

UNDERWOOD, H.G.
    1908 *The Call of Korea*. N.Y., 3rd Edition, Fleming H.
          Revell Co.

UNDERWOOD, Joel, ed.
    1974 *In Search of Mission, The Future of the Missionary
          Enterprise*, N.Y. International Documentation on the
          Contemporary Church, Dossier No. 9, 1974.

UNITED PRESBYTERIAN ORDER FOR WORLD EVANGLIZATION
    1975 "Newsletter," *United Presbyterian Order for World
          Evangelization*, November 1975, Pasadena, California.

WAGNER, C. Peter
    1972a *Church/Mission Tensions Today*. Chicago, Moody Press.

    1972b "The Goal is the Fourth World," *Church Growth Bulletin*,
          Vol. VII, No. 4, March 1972.

    1973 "The Danger of a Truncated Missionary Goal," *Evangeli-
          cal Missions Quarterly*, Winter, 1973, p. 96.

    1974 *Stop the World I Want to Get On*. Glendale, California,
          Regal.

    1975a "Colour The Moratorium Grey," *International Review
          of Mission*, Vol. LXIV, April 1975, pp. 165-176.

WAGNER, C. Peter
    1975b "Missionaries and Missions Can "Salt The Soup"
          Too Much," *Evangelical Missions Quarterly*, Vol. 2,
          No. 2, April 1975, pp. 90-98.

    1976 "A Bicentennial View: Missions In America's Third
          Century," *Today's Christian*, February 1976, p. 3.

WILLIAMS, Theodore
    1975 "The Indian Evangelical Mission," *Church Growth
          Bulletin*, Vol. XI, No. 4, March 1975, p. 435.

WINTER, Ralph D.
    1969 "The Anatomy of the Christian Mission," *Evangelical
          Missions Quarterly*, Vol. 5, No. 2, November 1969, re-
          printed in *The Warp and the Woof*, Ralph D. Winter
          and R. Pierce Beaver, eds., South Pasadena, California,
          William Carey Library, pp. 10-25.

    1970a *The Twenty-five Unbelievable Years, 1945-1969*, South
          Pasadena, California, William Carey Library.

    1970b *Say Yes To Mission*, South Pasadena, California,
          William Carey Library. (Reprinted by IVCF in 1973).

    1971a "The New Missions and the Mission of the Church," *In-
          ternational Review of Mission*, Vol. LX, January 1971,
          pp. 89-100.

    1971b "Churches Need Missions Because Modalities Need
          Sodalities," *Evangelical Missions Quarterly*, Vol. 7,
          No. 4, Summer 1971, pp. 193-200.

    1972a "The Planting of Younger Missions," *Church/Mission
          Tensions Today*, C. Peter Wagner, ed., pp. 129-145.

    1972b "The Demographic Imperative," *Church Growth Bulletin*,
          Vol. XVII, No. 8, January 19, 1973, pp. 10-13.

    1973a "Existing Churches: Ends or Means?" *Christianity Today*
          Vol. XVII, No. 8, January 19, 1973, pp. 10-13.

    1973b "The Two Structures of God's Redemptive Mission,"
          The All-Asia Mission Consultation, Chaeok Chun, ed.,
          pp. 313-333.

    1974a "The Two Structures of God's Redemptive Mission,"
          Missiology, An International Review, Vol. II, No. 1,
          January 1974, pp. 121-139 (reprint available from the
          William Carey Library).

WINTER, Ralph D.
1974b "Seeing The Task Graphically," *Evangelical Missions Quarterly*, Vol. 10, No. 1, January 1974, pp. 11-24.

1974c "The Highest Priority: Cross-Cultural Evangelism," *Let the Earth Hear His Voice*, J.D. Douglas, ed., pp. 213-241.

1974d *The New Macedonia: A Revolutionary New Era in Mission Begins*. South Pasadena, California, William Carey Library. This is 1974c plus a long introduction by McGavran.

1976 "1980 and That Certain Elite." *Missiology: An International Review*, Vol. IV, No. 2, April 1976, pp. 145-160.

WINTER, Ralph D. and BEAVER, R. Pierce
1970 *The Warp and the Woof*. South Pasadena, California, William Carey Library.

WOMACK, David A.
1973 *Breaking the Stained-Class Barrier*. New York, Harper and Row Publishers.

WONG, James, LARSON, Peter, and PENTECOST, Edward
1973 *Missions from the Third World: A World survey of non-Western missions in Asia, Africa and Latin America*. Singapore, Church Growth Study Center.

WONG, James
1974 "Regional Strategy Report on East Asia," *Let the Earth Hear His Voice*, J.D. Douglas, ed., pp. 1322-1323.

YANG, Synn Suk
1976 Interview with author, March 29, 1976.

Index

DATE DUE

JUL 15 '77			
JU 29 '77			
JAN 23 '78			
12-14-83			